SIX CAMPAIGNS

SIX CAMPAIGNS

National Servicemen on
Active Service 1948-1960

by
Adrian Walker

LEO COOPER

LONDON

First published in Great Britain in 1993 by
LEO COOPER
190 Shaftesbury Avenue, London WC2H 8JL
an imprint of
Pen & Sword Books Ltd
47 Church Street, Barnsley, South Yorkshire S70 2AS

A CIP catalogue record for this book is available from the British Library

ISBN 085052 320 6

Typeset by Yorkshire Web, Barnsley, South Yorkshire in Plantin 10 point.

Printed by
Redwood Books
Trowbridge, Wiltshire

This book is dedicated to all National Servicemen,
especially those who died on active service,
1948-1960.

CONTENTS

ACKNOWLEDGEMENTS

This book has been very much a team effort and I am particularly grateful to all those ex-National Servicemen who so willingly contributed their experiences. I am also indebted to the following who put me in touch with the contributors or who gave advice and practical help during the book's long gestation; these are - John Barnes, Jayne Clementson, Christopher Dowling, John Dunn and his Radio 4 team, Silvia Edwards, Alan Foote, Mike George, David Gray, Roger and Margaret Head, Samantha Jackson, David Lewisohn, Liz Maclean, Ros Marsh, Nicola Meakin, Maggie Percival, Ken and Phillipa Saunders, Carol Varlaam, Andrew Walker, David Walker and Anne West.

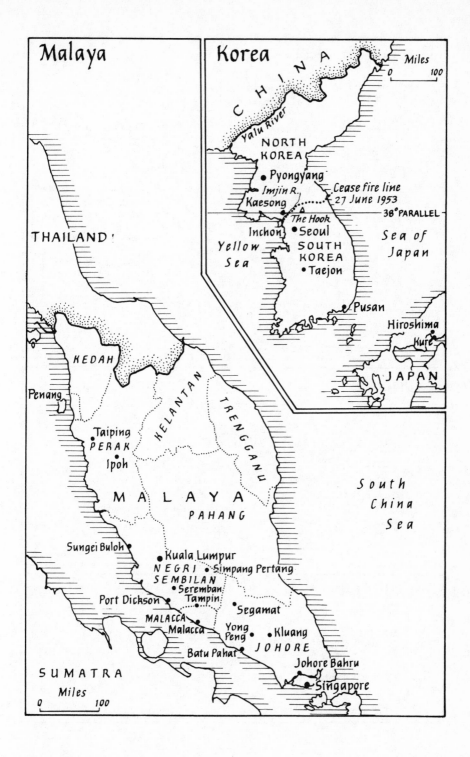

Malaya

Korea

CHINA

Yalu River

NORTH KOREA

● Pyongyang

Imjin R.

Kaesong

Cease fire line
27 June 1953

38° PARALLEL

THAILAND

The Hook

Inchon ● Seoul

Yellow Sea

SOUTH KOREA

● Taejon

Sea of Japan

KEDAH

● Pusan

Penang

Hiroshima

Kure

JAPAN

Taiping
PERAK

Ipoh

KELANTAN

TRENGGANU

MALAYA

PAHANG

South China Sea

Sungei Buloh

Kuala Lumpur

NEGRI SEMBILAN

Simpang Pertang

Seremban

Port Dickson

Tampin

Segamat

MALACCA

Malacca

Yong Peng

Kluang

JOHORE

Batu Pahat

Johore Bahru

SUMATRA

Miles

0   100

Singapore

Miles

0   100

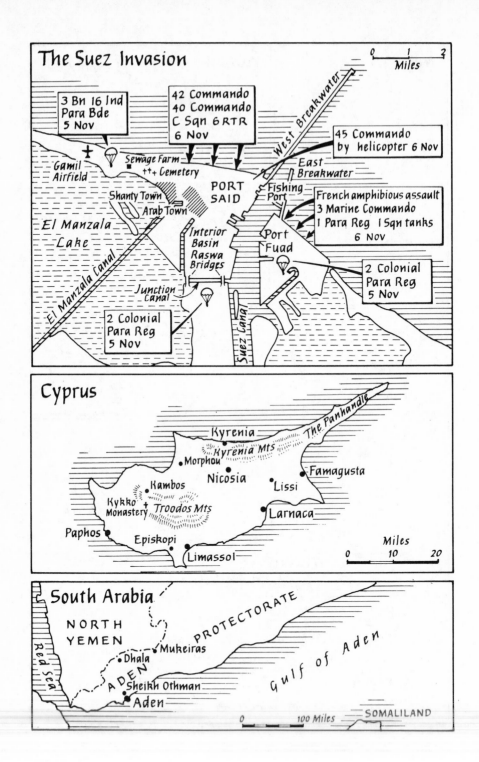

The Suez Invasion

3 Bn 16 Ind
Para Bde
5 Nov

42 Commando
40 Commando
C Sqn 6 RTR
6 Nov

45 Commando
by helicopter 6 Nov

West Breakwater

Gamil
Airfield

Sewage Farm
+ + + Cemetery

East
Breakwater

PORT
SAID

Fishing
Port

Shanty Town

Arab Town

French amphibious assault
3 Marine Commando
1 Para Reg 1 Sqn tanks
6 Nov

El Manzala
Lake

Interior
Basin
Raswa
Bridges

Port
Fuad

2 Colonial
Para Reg
5 Nov

El Manzala Canal

Junction
Canal

Suez Canal

2 Colonial
Para Reg
5 Nov

0   1   2
Miles

Cyprus

Kyrenia

The Panhandle

Kyrenia Mts

Morphou

Nicosia

Famagusta

Kambos

Lissi

Kykko
Monastery

Troodos Mts

Larnaca

Paphos

Episkopi

Limassol

Miles
0   10   20

South Arabia

NORTH
YEMEN

PROTECTORATE

Red Sea

Mukeiras

Dhala

Gulf of Aden

ADEN

Sheikh Othman

Aden

SOMALILAND

0   100 Miles

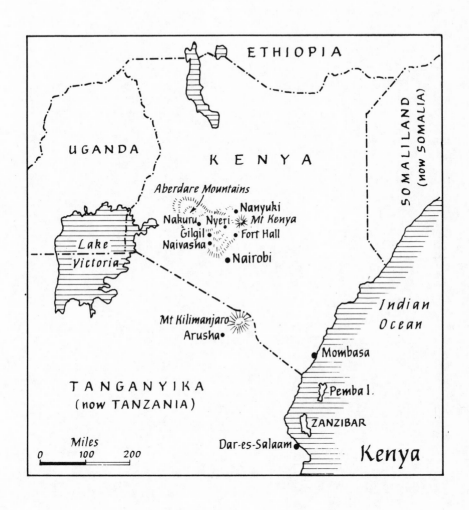

ETHIOPIA

UGANDA

SOMALILAND (now SOMALIA)

K E N Y A

Aberdare Mountains
Nanyuki
Nakuru Nyeri Mt Kenya
Gilgil Fort Hall
Naivasha
Nairobi

Lake
Victoria

Mt Kilimanjaro
Arusha

Indian
Ocean

Mombasa

TANGANYIKA
(now TANZANIA)

Pemba I.

ZANZIBAR

Dar-es-Salaam

Kenya

Miles
0   100   200

INTRODUCTION

This book tells the story of the half-forgotten colonial wars of thirty or more years ago, as seen through the eyes of the young men who were conscripted to fight in them. Six campaigns were undertaken by the British armed forces in the years 1948-1960, which coincides almost exactly with the period during which universal male fixed-term *peacetime* conscription (National Service) was in force in Britain, for the only time in its history. Apart from providing the men to stand eyeball to eyeball with the Red Army across the Iron Curtain, the main reason for the existence of National Service seems therefore to have been to guarantee a continual flow of trained manpower for these six campaigns. During these years, approximately a million and a half young men were called to the colours, and perhaps one in twelve served in an active theatre of operations.

The system was operated as follows: at eighteen, every male in the country was required by law to register for National Service, set initially in 1949 at eighteen months, but almost immediately—in 1950—increased to two years. Exemption, or an indefinite deferment equivalent to exemption, was granted to certain groups such as mental defectives, clergymen, coalminers, deep-sea fishermen and merchant seamen. In addition, call-up could be deferred, for a fixed period, if one was an apprentice or at a college or university. It was possible to declare oneself to be a conscientious objector, but very few did this—perhaps a few hundred out of the more than a quarter of a million registering each year. Every young man who had registered was subjected to a medical examination traditionally viewed as cursory in the extreme, but which, nonetheless, rejected one in six. Call-up day was heralded by the arrival, through the post, of a standard buff official envelope emblazoned with the letters OHMS—popularly supposed in this instance to stand for 'O Help Me, Saviour'. This envelope would contain an enlistment notice telling the National Serviceman when and where to report for basic training, a railway warrant to enable him to get there and various information leaflets.

For a great number of young men, their first few weeks of service life was a traumatic experience. For some, it was their first time away from home, with all the attendant problems of adjustment; others, including myself, were perhaps more fortunate, the incessant bullying and senseless brutality making it not unlike the daily life at the public schools from which we had come. Nonetheless, it was in some ways more frightening than the active service which succeeded it. It would be pleasant to suppose that the NCOs in charge of training were simply adhering to the famous dictum of Frederick the Great: 'Train hard, fight easy'; it seems more likely that in many cases it was a manifestation of the hostility felt by long-service junior NCOs (lance-corporals and corporals) towards civilians temporarily in their power.

Once basic training – which took about three months – was completed, the National Serviceman was sent (unless he was going forward for a commission, or specialized training of some sort) to the unit where he would normally spend the remainder of his service. Given the worldwide commitment of British forces at the time, there was a wide range of possible postings, although the National Serviceman was not usually the one to make the choice. One could go to Hong Kong, Kenya, Easter Island or somewhere in the United Kingdom or to the British Army of the Rhine (BAOR) in what was then West Germany. It was here that the National Serviceman was most likely to encounter the conscript's eternal enemy: long-term, mind-crushing boredom. Many a man has spent eighteen months of the springtime of his youth doing nothing but counting left boots and crossing the days off his demob chart. Nevertheless, even these cushy postings could be dangerous. There is a wealth of anecdotal evidence of fatal casualties, usually ascribed to accidents with heavy vehicles or firearms in the hands of inexperienced youths – one artillery unit in BAOR lost seven men in this way over an eighteen-month period.

Those who were posted to one of the trouble spots overseas would normally receive two or three weeks' embarkation leave before departing for active service. During the 1950s, British forces were engaged in six campaigns: Malaya (1948-60); Korea (1950-53); Kenya (1952-55); Cyprus (1955-59); Suez (1956) and South Arabia (1957-60). As well as being very different in terms of the characteristics of the enemy, the environments in which they were fought and the way in which they were conducted, they also varied greatly in length. Malaya at twelve years was the longest campaign involving British forces, while Suez – which effectively lasted only a matter of hours as far as the ground forces were concerned – must be one of the shortest. Thus, because each campaign displays its own distinctive characteristics, it is worth studying each in some detail, in the order in which they occurred.

The first action where National Servicemen were involved was in Malaya, where the emergency began during the summer of 1948. The Communist Terrorists (CTs) – almost exclusively Chinese who constituted about 40% of the whole population – attempted to wreck the country's infrastructure by destroying its two main economic bases – the rubber plantations and the tin mines – in a series of attacks on their management, buildings and equipment. Although they had some initial successes, including the assassination of the British High Commissioner in 1951, the CTs were defeated after a protracted jungle campaign. This victory was achieved by means of a three-pronged strategy. First, the security forces gathered all Chinese workers in rural areas into protected villages in order to deprive the CTs lurking in the surrounding jungle of popular support, as well as sources of food and other essential supplies. Second, small foot patrols of not more than twenty men, who were mostly conscripts, roamed the jungle seeking the enemy; this was known as jungle-bashing and was effective but very time-consuming – it has been calculated that one thousand man-hours of patrolling were required to achieve one contact with the enemy, and almost double that figure for a 'kill'. Third, the country was divided into a number of different zones, and one by one these were cleared of the enemy. Thus, in conjunction with Malayan police, soldiers and home guards, as well as Dyak trackers imported from Borneo, the security forces cleared each area; the CTs were gradually overwhelmed and, by the time Malaya achieved its independence in 1957, the 500 or so remaining CTs had been forced to flee across the border into Thailand. This was a striking victory by an Army fighting a ruthless and well-organized enemy on its own terms and on its own ground – particularly when one considers the fact that at least half the British troops were conscripts and that in the patrols that were so instrumental in winning the war, this proportion may have been as high as three-quarters.

At the height of the emergency there were more than 30,000 British troops involved, backed by about ten times that number of Malayan regular soldiers, police and home guards. In the course of the campaign, almost 7,000 CTs and about 2,400 members of the security forces were killed.

In 1950, while still heavily involved in Malaya, the British found themselves involved, willy-nilly, in another Far Eastern war, this time in Korea. At the end of the Second World War, Korea had been partitioned by the two superpowers into a Communist North and a 'Democratic' South. The North Koreans, with Soviet acquiescence, resolved to reunite the country by force and in June 1950 invaded South Korea, quickly occupying the entire country except for a small pocket in the far south known as the Pusan Perimeter, which was held by South Korean and United States troops. The United Nations accused the North Koreans of unwarrantable aggression and UN forces – mainly American in composition and led by the American General MacArthur, were dispatched to Korea. They quickly drove the enemy back across both South and North Korea to the Chinese frontier. Alarmed by MacArthur's sabre-rattling and particularly by his threat to cross the Yalu River into their territory, the Chinese got their retaliation in first.

The PLA (People's Liberation Army) crossed the Yalu in great numbers and the UN forces, taken by surprise, were sent reeling back in disorder. However, they eventually advanced again to establish a defence line roughly on the original frontier between North and South. There they dug in and for two years resisted human wave attacks by the Chinese, until a ceasefire was signed in July, 1953.

From start to finish, about 40,000 British troops were deployed in Korea, of whom some 700 were killed in action—compared with a total of more than a million civilians. Although few in number compared to their American colleagues, the British contingent acquitted itself well, particularly at the Imjin River in 1951 where, after a desperate defence, the Gloucesters were overrun, and again at the Hook in May, 1953, where the Duke of Wellington's Regiment fought off vastly stronger forces at a cost of twenty-nine of their own men being killed and five times that number wounded. Max Hastings wrote of this action: 'The Dukes had mounted a fine defence for a battalion three-quarters composed of National Service conscripts, rewarded by a grateful country with the princely sum of £1.62 a week.'

While British forces were still engaged in both Korea and Malaya, trouble erupted in East Africa. In October, 1952, the Mau Mau rebellion began in Kenya, still at that time a British colony. This was an uprising mainly by the Kikuyu tribe, aimed at achieving independence from Britain. The Mau Mau (the meaning of the name is unknown) was a political secret society which used terrorist tactics against both European settlers and indigenous Africans—particularly the latter—in pursuit of its aims. The campaign, conducted with great savagery by both sides, was fought by the British mostly with locally recruited troops, police and auxiliaries, although five British regular battalions were also used. About 10,500 suspected terrorists and 320 African and Asian civilians were killed; thirty-two white soldiers and settlers died at the hands of the Mau Mau.

Although the Mau Mau was defeated in the field, Jomo Kenyatta, who as one of its leaders had been imprisoned, was released in 1961 and two years later led his country to independence.

While British troops were still flushing out CTs in the jungles of Johore and hunting Mau Mau in the Aberdare Mountains, further trouble flared up in Cyprus, a British possession inhabited by 400,000 Greeks and about a quarter as many Turks. An underground organization, known by the Greek acronym EOKA (National Organization of Cypriot Freedom Fighters) and led by Colonel George Grivas, a retired Greek Army officer, conducted a skilful campaign of sabotage and murder against the British and their Turkish-Cypriot allies. Their objective was to drive the British out and attain *enosis*—union with the Greek motherland. The rebellion dragged on until

February, 1959; subsequently, a fragile sort of independence — although not *enosis*—was achieved.

At the peak of the troubles (as they were known) the British had 40,000 troops and police on the island, all searching for Grivas. This represents approximately one member of the security forces for every tenth Greek Cypriot man, woman and child. But they never caught Uncle George — as the British troops half-affectionately called him. The security forces lost fifty police and just over a hundred soldiers, most of the latter in accidents. For example, the Norfolks suffered eighteen fatalities — mostly National Servicemen — of whom only two were killed by EOKA. Rather more than 200 guerrillas were killed, while in an appalling outburst of what was euphemistically called inter-communal strife (which I witnessed) during the summer of 1958, some 120 Greeks and Turks were murdered in a variety of imaginative ways. This aside, the British troops—who, it must be admitted, treated the civilian population with some brutality—managed to keep the situation under control for most of the three and a half years of the emergency.

It is worth recording that this 'last hurrah of British imperialism', as Patrick Brogan calls it, occurred because Britain acquired the island in 1878 as a useful naval base on the sea lanes to India, as Malta and Gibraltar. Unfortunately, there are no deep-water harbours in Cyprus able to take large warships.

While still blundering about in the Cypriot labyrinth, Britain allowed itself to become entangled in what became known as the Suez Affair. In the summer of 1956, Israel and France began to plot the overthrow of Colonel Nasser, the Egyptian leader. Israel wished to force Egypt to the conference table, and France was anxious to eliminate Egyptian support for the FLN guerrillas who were fighting to free Algeria from French rule. Both countries were later joined in their machinations by Britain, for reasons which to this day remain unclear.

At the end of October, 1956, a well-planned and executed blitzkrieg took the Israelis to the banks of the Suez Canal. On the last day of that month, Britain and France issued an ultimatum demanding that both sides withdraw from the Suez Canal. Understandably, since the canal lies within her territory, Egypt rejected this out of hand. RAF bombers from Cyprus then destroyed the Egyptian Air Force on the ground and a hastily-assembled Franco-British invasion fleet set sail from Malta, which is more than a thousand miles from Suez. On 5 November, British paratroops dropped into the Canal Zone and, on the following day, allied troops landed at Port Said. The United States and the Soviet Union promptly threatened reprisals against Britain and France, forcing them to agree to withdraw, and, at midnight on 6 November, a ceasefire came into effect.

About 22,000 allied troops took part in this farce, many of the British being demobilized National Servicemen recalled for the occasion. Only thirty-three Allied servicemen were killed and one hundred and twenty-nine wounded, but the Israelis reported that 3,000 Egyptians were killed, and it is not known how many civilians died in the bombing that preceded the landings. Colonel Nasser remained in power, his popularity among his fellow countrymen if anything enhanced.

Barely had the British armed forces drawn breath after this debacle than they were caught up in yet another Middle Eastern war. The southern part of Yemen – the territory lying inland from the port of Aden with its naval base at the entrance to the Red Sea which guarded the sea route to India (lost in 1947) – had been designated a British protectorate. In 1958, the ruler of North Yemen allied his fiefdom with Nasser's United Arab Republic, consisting of Egypt and Syria. Guerrillas from the north had already been infiltrating into the south (mostly in search of booty, one suspects). They were opposed by the Aden Protectorate Levies (APL), a locally recruited force led by British officers, by several units of the RAF and by one British infantry battalion. At any one time, therefore, some 2,000 British military personnel may have been deployed in South Arabia. It is not known how many casualties they suffered – or inflicted on the enemy – in this semi-covert operation. In 1967, the last servicemen vacated Aden, thus ending 128 years of British rule.

The men who served in these campaigns and who contributed to this book represent all three armed services. Most National Servicemen joined the Army: out of one hundred conscripts, seventy-two would be soldiers, twenty-six RAF men and two sailors. For this reason, and because the Army bore the brunt in all theatres of operation – apart from South Arabia, where the RAF was heavily committed – the great majority of contributors are ex-soldiers. The number of contributors from each campaign is very roughly proportional to the estimated total of National Servicemen involved. No exact statistics are available; since throughout the 1950s approximately half of all soldiers were conscripts, I have assumed that this proportion would be maintained in active service. However, given that regular soldiers would be more likely to hold positions in the B echelons – administration, logistics etc – the proportion of National Servicemen at the sharp end may in many instances be as high as three-quarters or even more – for example, the Dukes in Korea. Neither the Army Medals Office nor the Historical Branch of the Ministry of Defence was able to give exact figures for the numbers of National Servicemen who served in these campaigns, but, from the fragmentary evidence available, it appears that about 50,000 National Servicemen served in Malaya; 20,000 in Korea; 3,000 in Kenya; 45,000 in Cyprus and a few hundred at Suez and in South Arabia. This book deals only with operations for which a campaign medal was awarded; thus, service in the Canal Zone in the early 1950s – probably as stressful as being in Cyprus later in the decade – is not included because no medal was awarded. Neither does Palestine qualify; although a General Service Medal was awarded, the operations (1947-48) took place before the institution of fixed-term conscription.

Three hundred and ninety-five National Servicemen were killed in action, and it is to them that this book is dedicated.

Neil Ascherson

Neil Ascherson served with the Royal Marines in Malaya in 1951-52. He is now Senior Assistant Editor of *The Independent on Sunday* and lives in London.

In the summer of 1951 I went on a troopship to Malaya. I was very young – eighteen – and a National Service officer in the Royal Marines: 42 Commando. The troopship was the *Empire Pride*. The whole thing was amazing; I'd never travelled very far before. To set out from Liverpool, then go to Gibraltar, through the Mediterranean, then through the Suez Canal; to see all this, as well as the people on the troopship, was very interesting. There were all the usual kinds of idiocies – tensions, fights and feuds; there was also the spectacle of people swelling with self-importance as they got East of Suez – there was a fair number of that sort of colonial civil servant aboard. We experienced the customary near-riot, which is traditional: Marine drafts attack Army drafts on the troopdecks and attempt to scrub them with scrubbing-brushes.

We called at Port Said, Aden and Colombo; when we reached Malaya, we were just unloaded straight from the ship and on to a train. Of course, the whole thing was completely dazzling, as you may imagine – the sights, the sounds, the smells and all the rest of it. We were on an amazing little train; the train commander was a captain in the Gordons. In fact, he was killed; not that night, but a week later – it was a very strange sort of ambush. Somebody just fired a rifle at the train and hit him in the head as he lay asleep, and killed him. Anyway, we went up country, and got out of the train at Ipoh.

We arrived wearing khaki drill; we received scornful looks from all the others, who were in jungle greens. When we arrived at Ipoh we were taken straight to Command Headquarters; our uniforms were taken away then, and we were issued with jungle greens. We were given the strangest guns; some of us had not even heard of them. We had been told, 'You're going to use a rifle, or a Bren gun,' and all that sort of thing. Instead – though some people had rifles, and some had to carry Bren guns, poor things *[a rifle*

1

weighs about 10lb, and a Bren gun more than twice as much] — we were given some Sten guns, which were quite useless, really; also a wonderful weapon called the Owen gun. It was an Australian machine carbine. It had a vertical feed and almost never jammed — unlike the Sten; altogether, a wonderful weapon. Then, some of us — including myself — received M2 carbines, an American weapon, which could fire bursts or single shots. We wore our equipment hung round our waists rather than over our backs, and we had jungle boots and all the rest of it.

Almost at once we were sent on our operations. All the troops of the commando were posted out to different stations; my troop — B Troop — was at the bottom of an extremely high, jungle-covered mountain range. *[A troop is the equivalent of an infantry company and a commando is roughly equivalent to a battalion of 500-600 men.]* There were some rubber plantations where B Troop was posted, but principally it was a very rich tin-mining area — flood-bottom valley covered with tin mines and then these very steep mountains rising all the way round — in which there were a lot of guerrillas operating. I was taken out on operations almost immediately; I went out with a patrol to familiarize myself and see how things were done. Then I took patrols out into the jungle for perhaps a day or two at a time. A lot of it was going out in the evening and doing night ambushes and coming back in the morning; some of it was going out patrolling — just exploring areas to see what was there, that kind of thing — and sometimes we'd be involved in major operations. When we were out, we carried with us all we needed; we weren't ever supplied by air, but there were occasions when we'd go down and meet a truck to take on supplies.

I was at a number of ambushes when something happened — what we called a contact; none of them were very large affairs. On one occasion when I was in charge, some shadowy figure who was playing both sides had given us some information. We were positioned where some rubber trees had been chopped down to make a clearing; guerrillas were supposed to be coming out of the jungle to pick up supplies — or to meet somebody — at such-and-such a time. We hid ourselves among the dead rubber trees and watched the edge of the jungle. Sure enough (for once!) they came and we let them get very close, until they nearly walked into us; and then we opened fire. They were all killed; I think there were four or five. In terms of the numbers involved in the campaign, it was a major contact. Of course, you got an unbelievably violent emotional release — this tremendous explosion. People have said that there is a kind of sexual comparison, and there is; but you've been trained to do this for nearly two years. Then there's the endless frustration; you wait and they don't come — or somebody comes quite near and then runs away before you can fire. But sometimes the whole thing suddenly comes together, like then; it was a moment of discharge, in every sense. There were some strange things about it, which at the time I registered very strongly. I saw a man give his life for another; he was one of theirs, which made it all the more significant for me. Some of them were running back as the first people went down under the bullets; one of them got into the edge of the jungle, which of course made him completely safe. However, the man behind him fell, about two yards short of the jungle's edge, so the first man came out again, seized him under the armpits and tried to drag him to safety. This was utterly hopeless, because the range was so short; he was at the furthest edge of the range of our shooting – I don't suppose this was more than thirty yards – but nevertheless, he did this, and he died. It leaves a great impression on you when you see somebody do that; in any case, I'd never seen anybody dead by gunshot, blown to pieces, torn to bits by bullets in that way. It was, so to speak, the summit of my career in Malaya.

I'd previously been regarded with great doubt and suspicion by the other Marine officers; the Royal Marines tried to avoid taking National Servicemen as far as possible. They were extremely professional – probably the most professional of all units – and they hated the idea of being diluted by part-timers, which is how they regarded National Servicemen. But they were obliged to take a few; I only got there because I had consented to do Royal Marine Volunteer Reserve training for two years before I was actually called up. I started this when I was sixteen; my father was in the Navy, and I wanted to do my National Service in the Navy, but for reasons I've never quite understood he said, 'I think it would be more interesting if you went into the Royal Marines.'

Overall, our casualties were extremely light. Whilst I was with the commando in Malaya, I don't think more than three or four people were killed by the enemy. A number of people died – jeep accidents, and that kind of thing. Quite a lot of men became ill, though I don't remember anyone dying of illness. A lot of people got malaria and, despite the drugs and all the rest of it, were extremely ill. I remember having to go and pick up someone from the hospital, and I didn't recognize the boy; he was absolutely skeletal. Of course the roads were bad, made of red mud. If you drove fast in heavy rain, you just skidded straight off. You could come round a corner and meet a Chinese timber lorry, a huge thing travelling at sixty miles an hour – you didn't have an earthly chance. There was a lot of folklore about road accidents in Malaya – I was surrounded by extraordinary stories that I was never able to verify; one was of some officer in a jeep who had been killed by a durian (a large fruit with a very hard skin) which fell on his head. It might well have been true.

Obviously I felt – as did most National Service officers – that I was really in an extremely false position. Almost half the men were regulars; all

3

of the NCOs were, many of them with immensely long histories, and very interesting ones, too, because the Marines had done things like fighting with the Greek partisans in the Second World War. The ones I met had mostly been in the Balkans, on all kinds of silent, curious missions. I was a greenhorn; I was uncoordinated and very young for my age: a very inexperienced virgin soldier. So meeting these working-class boys, who had lived – which I certainly hadn't yet – was important to me. I must say, they were very affectionate towards me, and helpful. They were also ironic, and very entertained by my ignorance. I think one good thing about the Marines was that we all did basic training together; there was no segregation. So, in a sense, this was a hurdle I had passed. They knew I could do what they could do, which made them respect me.

It turned out that, for some reason, I had a marvellous sense of direction, so I was a very good jungle navigator, for which of course they were grateful. We all used to get drunk quite frequently; they'd say, 'Sir, say what you like, you may be a complete and utter cunt, but at least you can find your way,' and things like that, so I know they were grateful.

I'd never been a terribly political person, but within ten days of arriving in Malaya it seemed to me that something was quite wrong. Very broadly, the situation was this: I don't know what the exact populations were, but something like 45% of the population was Malay, and they monopolized the government and administration of the country in so far as it was not British. The majority were Chinese immigrants and they were mostly working class, employed in the tin mines and rubber plantations, also running shops to some extent and 'squatting' – in other words, on smallholdings which they had carved out for themselves on the edge of the jungle. The Chinese had no rights whatsoever; they had no citizenship at that time and of course the guerrillas were 95% Chinese. There was another group: the Tamils. Their community was regarded as completely null by everyone. They were quite difficult to communicate with – timid, friendly and frightened of everybody. They were the lowest of the low, and condemned to do all the really dirty jobs at the bottom of society. But when it came to the Chinese, I felt increasingly distressed by what I was being asked to defend; it seemed to be a system based on political injustice. I had occasion to talk about this with my fellow officers, who regarded me with a sort of incredulous contempt. They didn't even think I was a dangerous subversive or anything. They were very professional, but they didn't go in for large, wide conversations about the rights and wrongs of the world. But one of the nice things about them was that they weren't just blindly obedient. All ranks were trained to think for themselves and never, ever to take an order just like that. The idea of a Commando soldier was to be self-reliant and so, when an NCO gave an order, he would explain why – if there was time.

A Marine officer wasn't one of those bone-headed upper-class boobies which you find in English regiments. I never met a Marine like that, but as soon as you went into an Army mess you met such people. The Marines were looked down on socially by some of the very smart regiments, like the 60th Rifles and the Brigade of Guards, but they — the Marines — had in return bottomless contempt for people like that. Occasionally we met other regiments — we had some contact with the Suffolks, although I didn't get to know them well. The people we did get to know were the Gurkhas. We saw a lot of them, because when we were in Selangor there was a Gurkha unit quite close by. Sometimes we did things together. We had a couple of catastrophic cocktail parties — as they were called — in the open air. The drinks consisted of equal measures of Navy rum and Tiger beer. I've never seen anything like the devastation. My last memory is of those Gurkhas sitting there like good little schoolboys, singing their songs, wearing their little shorts and their little round hats, while their white officer conducted them. Meanwhile, the Marines were all upside down in monsoon drains. But apparently even the Gurkhas collapsed a bit later on.

Each troop of the Commando had attached to it two Iban trackers, as they were called, who came from North Burma. They were extremely engaging human beings. They were covered in tattoos from head to foot and wore their hair in long black ponytails. They had a number of superstitions, which fortunately I never saw put into practice. Like, if you woke them by shaking their feet, they thought a devil was taking them away to some dark place and they would hit you, before even waking up, with their iron swords. I was warned not to do this, and indeed I never did. They were members of what you might call head-hunting tribes. Their appearance was very strange, they looked just like little old ladies, really. They were admirable — very interesting. One could talk Malay to them a little; they spoke their own sort of Malay. They used to tattoo British soldiers and marines. I have a tattoo on my left leg, which they did with a mixture of lamp-black, gun oil and spit, using pins tied together with a bundle of straw. This was, naturally, completely forbidden.

Each unit would also have two Chinese interpreters, whom I now realize were in a very anomalous position — they could have been assassinated at any time, or something unpleasant could have happened to their families. We had one called Mr Lim and one called Mr Ng, which baffled everybody, because you can't shout for someone whose name is spelt Ng. We had a sergeant-major who was always exasperated by this, and would end up screaming, 'Fucking Mister Ong!'

The food we had was varied, to say the least. They used to issue us with tins of mixed fruit pudding — it was inconceivable. The only creatures who liked that stuff were the giant centipedes. I can remember hearing a loud clattering from a rubbish heap which contained a lot of empty cans, as these three-foot centipedes rushed about gobbling up the contents of the fruit-pudding tins. Apart from that, we got K rations in rectangular cans. Sometimes, if you were cunning, you could get hold of Gurkha K ration tins, which were much more interesting and, if you were a real pro — which some people were — you didn't bother with anything like that; you just took a bag of rice and a few dried chillis as a bit of flavouring, a piece of dried meat or dried fish and that was it, that's what you lived on. One of the interesting things was that some people — we were all very young, remember — began to sink into the environment in the most impressive way. That's the whole attraction of the jungle; you sink into it, become part of it. There was one lad, who was what they call in the Navy a 'tiffy' — sick-berth attendant — and he became heavily 'Malayanized'; his Malay became bilingual, and this can only have happened over a period of about a year. He wore sarongs and so on, and by the end of the time he was moving away from us perceptibly. He was fascinated by Malaya — he'd probably seen nothing in his life except run-down areas of Liverpool, and he wanted to be part of this environment.

Part of our work involved co-operating with the administration. At that time, all the District Officers were British, and there was said to be one somewhere in the Malay Peninsular who had mastered a Chinese language. So you never met one who spoke one bloody word of Chinese; they all addressed the Chinese in a sort of kitchen Malay. This was an outrageous situation; in part, the insurgency arose out of the Chinese campaign to build their own schools. You see, nobody would pay for their schools — the Chinese didn't exist as far as the government was concerned, and so they had to build schools for themselves. I felt that was wrong.

The guerrillas we were fighting regarded themselves as part of the mainland Chinese Eighth Route Army. They were deeply romantic. Occasionally we would capture documents, which in fact were pages of squared exercise-book paper, which were closely covered in Chinese characters and folded dozens of times. They would say things like, 'Today our advance storm units captured Ap Hong Hill,' or something like that. It was extremely difficult to associate that with what really happened. Their perception of what we were all doing was utterly unlike ours; they didn't see themselves as guerrillas — they thought of themselves as preparing the second Maoist stage of liberated zones. They lived to see themselves as a regular army and, as I've said, I'm sure their fantasy was very much that they were the Eighth Route Army. In fact, they did wear a uniform, with a kind of rubber-soled canvas ankle boot which left a very distinctive zigzag track, so you could always see where they'd been. Our jungle-boot track was quite different. They tended to wear long khaki trousers and puttees, to protect them against leeches. They also wore bandoliers and stuff, and little five-pointed hats with a red star in them, usually made of green canvas. There were very few occasions that I can remember when there was any real confusion about who was who. Almost everything in Malaya was conducted on the basis of anyone who is here at this place at this time of night could be shot, because there was only one sort of person they could be.

My feelings now about Malaya are ambiguous. There's a sense in which I wouldn't have missed it for anything. It taught me an enormous number of things, like how to look after myself, and how little a human being needs to stay alive and healthy. It showed me another world; it taught me all about Empire in a very rapid way. It taught me things which I'm still learning. Thinking over those times, some things still strike me which I hadn't really thought of before. In a small way, it showed me what war was like — rather like an immunization — but nothing like World War Two or Korea, though.

I hated coming home. We had to go first to Malta and we had to pull ourselves together. We had a new Commanding Officer, and we got new troop commanders, who said, 'You've got to wear khaki drill and stand up straight and carry all these old-fashioned weapons again.' Everything that one had learnt which was useful and practical, and which one had really paid to learn, too, was being battered out of us. I really hated and resented that, and I was very depressed coming home on the troopship.

When I got back, I didn't talk to my father about Malaya, but I did tell my mother some of the more horrific things which weighed on my conscience. There was an occasion on a night operation when I suggested we use a flame-thrower, and of course the bloody thing went wrong and two civilians in a tent were burnt alive. I saw them the next day, too — I'll never forget that. I felt that, if I hadn't been such a prick by trying to show how keen I was by impressing more senior officers with bright ideas, it would never have happened.

As for the Malayan campaign in general, it's difficult for me to say I would do it all again. I would feel differently about so many things, but the other cliché is true: I wouldn't have missed it for worlds. It was a very judicious, gentle introduction to the reality of the world which we live in.

Pat Baker

Pat Baker was in Cyprus in 1958 with the East Surreys during the EOKA campaign. He is married, works as a self-employed butcher and lives in Tilbury.

I had to register during February, 1957; I had the medical in March and was whipped in during April. I served my twelve weeks' basic training down at Canterbury with the Buffs. But, having got down there frightened to death because I'd never been away from home before, we were then rushed around like a load of sheep, given our equipment and sent to the various barrack rooms. One interesting thing happened when we arrived at Canterbury; this sergeant was there, shouting and bawling and making us all jump into this lorry. When we got to the barracks, this same sergeant read out all our names, and he said, 'Is there anyone's name I haven't called?' and this poor chap put up his hand and said, 'I haven't been called.' So the sergeant said, 'Who are you? Where were you meant to be going?' and the chap said, 'I was going to work.' He'd somehow got on the truck willy-nilly when this sergeant was dragging everybody about, and got hold of him as well.

I think one of the worst things about National Service generally is that you are taken from an environment you're used to. In my case, and that of dozens of other boys, you'd never been away from home, and then you're thrown into an army. That first night I went in, I'll always remember it because there were all these lads of eighteen years of age, snivelling like babies in their beds. You could hear them crying, and you'd think to yourself: My God, what is all this about?

Anyway, we did our training with the Buffs and, when we finished basic training, we were due to come home on leave – instead of which, we were sent direct to Bury St Edmunds, which was the home of the East Surreys because, although we were trained by Buffs NCOs, we were really part of the East Surrey Regiment. We arrived there to find the place in absolute chaos. No one seemed to know what we were doing, or where we were meant to go, or anything. The next thing that happened was that we were issued with weapons and ammunition and put aboard these lorries; the rumours that were flying about were incredible – we were going to Malaya, to Korea, to Singapore – you name it, we were going there. They ended up taking us down to Heathrow and we boarded a plane, still not having the faintest idea of where we were going, or what we were meant to be doing. Once on the plane, we landed for refuelling at Nice and again at Malta, and it was only then that we had an inkling of what our destination was to be, because people were saying, 'We're over the Mediterranean; we must be going to Cyprus'...and so we landed at Cyprus.

It was dark when the plane landed, and there were these sergeants, shouting here, there and everywhere: 'Get your heads down and run!' and of course we did this, and ran to these tents, so we spent the night at Nicosia Airport. The following morning, we were herded on to these lorries, and I was told by the sergeant, 'You're escort.' So I said, 'What's an escort? What does he do?' He said, 'You sit in the last place on the lorry and protect the back of it.' I then had to load my weapon, the old .303; we hadn't got the SLRs, or anything like that in those days. We were taken to the 1st Paras' camp, just outside Nicosia. Again, this was all tents; there were no buildings whatsoever. We settled in there in four-man tents with duckboards on the floor. It was a base camp, so we were whipped away to almost anywhere as needed – patrol duties into the mountains and what have you.

On about the third day there, I was put on guard duty. In our battalion, you had to make sure you could see the man to the right of you and the man to the left of you at all times, and you sort of walked around in a half circle, guarding the perimeter of the camp. We were told the words of warning to give any intruder, which were: 'Halt, *Stomata, Dur*' [English, Greek and Turkish respectively], and you had to say this three times. We were round by the ammunition dump, and we saw this flickering light inside a tent. I waved to my colleague to come nearer, while I approached this tent. I approached the tent and shouted, 'Halt, *Stomata, Dur*' – I didn't know any other words to say. I repeated the warning and, on the third occasion, I put one up the spout. Of course, as I did this, a head poked itself out and said, 'Do you mind? I happen to live here.' It was the second-in-command of our battalion.

Another incident that happened on the actual camp-site was that open lorries manned by Greeks used to come to the camp to empty the latrines, because all we had was a bucket with a seat fixed to it. Everyone dreaded getting escort duty on this lorry. Anyway, on this particular day, they came with the lorry and, as I said, nobody wanted to go on it and I assume nobody did, because about half an hour after it had gone there was a terrific explosion. They'd brought in pipe bombs and buried them in the sand by the latrines. But no one was hurt, which was rather fortunate.

Sometimes we used to go out on patrols and on cordon-and-search. The earliest memory I have is of a village called Lissi. It's out towards the panhandle – you go through the Kyrenia Pass. Now, I suppose, it's on the Turkish side of the island. Anyway, we put a cordon on this village; we were on cordon this particular night, and you had to be able to see the man on either side of you. It was a Turkish village, but we'd been tipped off that there were arms there. We'd got the place cordoned off while it was being searched by our battalion; also, we were trying to keep the Turks in and the Greeks out. But the first night we were there, these Turks went through our lines and murdered some Greeks from the next village down, and on the way back they themselves were murdered. The strangest thing was that we were there all night – and you never slept on those cordons – and, do you know? we never heard a damned thing. Of course, there were these wretched fat-tailed sheep wandering in and out, and this is the way they would have done it: crouched down alongside the sheep. The only reason we knew they'd got out was because the villagers were four short from the previous count. Eventually, the villagers did decide that they would show us where the arms were – rather than have us there indefinitely – and actually they had hidden them in a well. I personally didn't have to go and get them; somebody else did that. A Turkish Cypriot showed the troops exactly where they were.

Another time, I had to go as escort on a 3-ton lorry. They had a sort of hatch in the roof of the cab above the passenger seat, so that you could stand up on the seat and look out. We had to go up in the mountains, and the road was nothing but a goat track. We were coming back, and an officer decided that he would sit in the passenger seat of the lorry to which I was escort, so I had nowhere to put my feet or anything. So I'm perched on the rim of that silly little hole, weapon at the ready. Not that I could have done anything. I was being chucked about from here to nowhere and all of a sudden, as we've gone past this tree, a branch whipped my hat off. What do you do about a situation like that? You can't stop the lorry and say, 'I've got to go and get my hat'; you're not out in the street somewhere, you've got a great long convoy of lorries behind you. Do you know? I nearly got put on a charge for losing it!

While we were in Cyprus, my unit didn't get any casualties, but we did have an accident. A chap was cleaning a Bren gun at a guard post and inadvertently set the damned thing off and it was spraying bullets everywhere, but luckily nobody actually got hurt. He was court-martialled, but wasn't made to leave the Regiment; he served his time with us there in the glasshouse.

Our living conditions were always very primitive. As I've said, we were four to a tent. The washing arrangements were in the open air; you had jerrycans of water that you poured into a sort of sink affair, and you had to have your wash and shave like that, and we had no electricity at all. While we were there, the Pioneer Corps sent in a platoon of men to dig some latrines. But we did have a cinema which was safe to visit; it was only about fifty yards from the main gates of the camp. It was a military cinema, so it showed English films.

Because we were only a relief battalion, we didn't have any set routines; we would go anywhere at any time. You could be called out at six o'clock in the morning, you could be called out at three o'clock in the afternoon; but the officers obviously had more idea of what was going on than we did. The way it worked was that one company would stay in camp on emergency standby. If you were not in that company, then you were stood down. Then we were taken in a rota of A, B, C, D (Companies) to Six Mile Beach for an afternoon of swimming, which I suppose was part of the hygiene of the thing, because we hadn't got any facilities. I think the whole battalion had dysentery when we first arrived on the island. We lived on corned beef and tomatoes. Then we went up into the Troodos Mountains. I can't recall what we were doing there; it may only have been training. I think we were in a village putting a curfew on it as a form of training. We were also at Lissi almost a week doing cordon-and-search, and we were doing two hours on and four hours off continually for that week. You never got a break.

We were living on compo rations of corned beef and tomatoes, of course, but while we were in Troodos we were sent some fresh meat. One day when we got back to A Company, someone said, 'Are there any butchers here?' Well, I was a butcher in Civvy Street, and I'd never admitted to this fact because I didn't want to end up working in the cookhouse. When you have the experience of two years' National Service, you want to get the most out of it. Well, reluctantly I said, 'Yes, I'm a butcher,' and they said, 'Can you cut this piece of meat up?' So I got a knife and a big block of wood, and I cut this beef up and was throwing it straight into the boiling water there. Do you know? that damned stuff was off before it was cooked! It looked fresh when I was cutting it up, and I couldn't smell anything, but it was completely off. So we never had any fresh meat from the time we arrived to the time we left, and that was about five months or more.

When I was in training, I palled up with a bloke called Dave. We stayed together right through our two years, funnily enough. While we were in the Army, Dave and I became good friends, but when we were still in basic training he said to me, 'After we've done our two years, I don't want to know you.' I said, 'What do you mean, you don't want to know me?' and he said, 'You're a nice guy, Pat; I think the world of you, and I'd do anything for you, but when we leave this fucking Army, no way do I want to have anything to do with anyone who was in it.' That was very sad. Anyway, about two years after I came out, another couple of the chaps came and dragged me out of a picture house in Tunbridge Wells. They'd been to my house, and my mum said I was at the pictures with my girlfriend. They'd had a message flashed up on the screen: 'Will Pat Baker please go to the foyer.' So we arranged to go down and find this Dave, because I'd previously met his parents and everything; we go down to their house and his mother makes us very welcome and explains he's round at his girlfriend's. We go round there and Dave's there with his girlfriend and her mother provides us with tea and sandwiches, all very pleasant in Whitstable, and we walked along the beach. He and I were really, really close during that time in the Army, but on that Sunday in Whitstable he was so distant it was untrue. It was very sad.

Going back to Cyprus, I didn't really know what we were doing there. I suppose I thought we were in Cyprus to keep the peace; that's what I thought we were there for. But as it must be in Northern Ireland today, you just do not know who the enemy is, and this makes it so damned hard and stressful. It makes you so mistrustful of everybody and everything that moves. I think you live in a sort of void for that period you are out there. Because you try to become alert all of the time, you don't allow yourself to relax, and I think that's the hardest part.

I remember we did a bit of guard duty at Nicosia Prison, a civil prison. You've got these sort of turrets all around the outside. One man goes to each gun turret and in each one you've got smoke grenades, tear-gas grenades, Mills grenades, a Bren gun, a great case full of Bren-gun ammunition, a telephone, a searchlight and your own rifle. I was bored to death up in this damned thing. Shortly after arriving on duty there, I was fidgeting about and I picked up one of the Mills grenades, and I was playing around with it and I've taken the pin out, and I don't know what to do with the wretched thing now. I knew I was all right as long as I held down the little lever on the grenade itself. I tried to put the pin back in; fortunately, I was holding the grenade in my left hand, so I could use my right. But it's a split pin and it doesn't want to go back in, does it? I suppose that for about an hour and three-quarters I was sweating with this damned grenade. I didn't know whether to make up a story about something out in the desert and throw the damned thing out there, or that some prisoners had tried to break out and had thrown it in. I suppose about five minutes before I was due to be relieved, I managed to get this wretched pin started, and I pushed it back in and chucked the grenade back in the box. That was the longest two hours I've ever spent. It was absolute purgatory. I tried everything. If I'd dropped it, I'd have just kicked it out. It still gives me nightmares.

When we were assigned to the 1st Paras' camp, we were told it might be for a week; then we were told a month. Then two months passed and, in fact, we were there for five months before we were posted to North Africa. By that time you're not hardened to it – you're never that – but I think you're more aware. You're sharper, and I don't think the fear aspect is so great; you overcome that side of it.

One interesting thing happened as we were leaving Famagusta for North Africa. There was our whole battalion travelling together, you see, so they loaded us on to these LSTs (Landing Ships – Tank) to take us across the Med to Benghazi. There was an Army ambulance down in the hold and it only had one driver. Now, on Cyprus, all our vehicles had two men on them, so that if one wanted to go for a cup of tea, there'd always be someone to guard the vehicle. Of course, this ambulance had nobody. We don't know whether it was Greeks or Turks, but they put a load of bombs in the toolbox on the side of the ambulance. At midnight, just as we were sailing, there was this almighty explosion. We were all asleep, and of course it threw us out of our bunks, and we were all running around in a blind panic because we hadn't a clue what was going on. All of a sudden, Sergeant Hannigan, who was an Irishman, appeared: 'Don't panic, lads, don't panic; the bastards have only tried to blow the ship up, but don't panic.' If you could have seen us, as we were, nineteen-year-old lads with fear in their eyes. Don't know whether to sink or swim. When I went down into the hold to investigate, every single vehicle was damaged, every single one, and yet the hull of the vessel was untouched; it was completely untouched, yet every bloody vehicle was smashed to smithereens.

In North Africa, we did four months with the Sussex Regiment. There we could relax – although, having said that, it was more violent than Cyprus at times, that bloody place. But in camp you were safe.

Then we came back to England. When we got back to the depot, the new intakes seemed to respect us quite a lot, because we'd been abroad and we'd got our knees brown, if you like.

My family never really asked me what Cyprus was like. I didn't really talk about it, other than to some friends who'd been out there with the Royal West Kents, and a couple of younger friends who wanted to know all about 'was it as bad as the papers said?' and this, that and the other. I think the mental torment is the biggest pain you suffer with these things, as it must be with this Irish business. The mental scars have got to be worse than the physical, because you understand what happens to you physically. By luck, it didn't harm us, but to live through a situation like the bombing of the LST, with the ship rocking about all over the blooming place, it's very scary. But people in general, relatives and so on, didn't want to know. My own brother was a regular soldier and had served in Korea, Suez and Malaya, and he had obviously been through similar situations, but even so we never really talked about it. In any case, when I talk to people who were there with me, it's always the same funny things you tend to remember.

I never received my medal; never ever. After I came out, about a year or eighteen months later and I'd just got married, there was some trouble somewhere, so I got a letter through the post to say I was on emergency standby; there were rail tickets and everything. Frightened my wife to death, but nothing ever came of it.

But there again, having done National Service, I would recommend it for anybody. I think it would be wonderful for the youth of today. Forget the Cyprus, forget the Northern Ireland and the rest of it; actual military service and the discipline that goes with it is a marvellous thing to have.

Bill Billings

Bill Billings joined the Royal Signals as a National Serviceman and served with the Aden Protectorate Levies in South Arabia in 1958-60. He is a poet, painter and sculptor, and lives with his wife and son in Bletchley.

After doing my basic training in the Royal Signals, I passed out top of my class and became a corporal instructor at Catterick Camp. I didn't really sign on for the Levies *[Aden Protectorate Levies]*, a colonial army; I just saw a piece of paper asking for volunteers on a notice board in the camp. As I couldn't get out of Catterick and I was going mad with boredom, I was willing to try almost anything to avoid spending the rest of my National Service there. I'd applied for a lot of different things, even Christmas Island, and had been turned down because they wanted to keep me at Catterick, but the Levies accepted me to go out to the Aden Protectorate (as it then was), to instruct Arab soldiers in the use of signals equipment.

I was in the Levies, rather than just going out as a member of the Royal Signals, because there were areas where the presence of a British soldier would be seen as an act of war against Russia, which was backing the Communist guerrillas from North Yemen, who we were fighting against. So a group of us flew out from Hendon in civvies in a civilian aircraft with passports that said we were government officials. We went first to a British base in Libya and then on to Arabia in a military aircraft. It was a sort of covert operation —we were like very second-rate spies. But perhaps the British Army isn't clever enough to be covert?

The main camp at Aden was a few rooms of wooden billets constantly filling up with blowing sand. Some days were so unbearable that the word prickly-heat sums it all up. The food was normal Army cookhouse supplies —your usual choice of breakfast of warm milk and cereal, a rubber egg and a minute piece of bacon. Gallons of tainted tea in the magic tin mug, which I can taste the rim of to this day. Field rations —the tough dog-biscuits, melted wine-gums in those funny tins, tinned milk and tinned pom and tinned egg —all, I believe, reminded me of the war supplies of the '40s. This fast food put me ahead of McDonalds by twenty years.

15

The only luxury food to keep up morale was normally the sea mail packages from families in which we all shared. Fruit cake from Scotland was my favourite —from the Pollack family in Greenock. They posted it continually by the ship load. This was our main morale booster next to letters —God bless food parcels. The bits and pieces we were unable to eat we let the shitehawks or wild dogs share with us. Mind you, while on active service I found consistently the cooks in high spirits and great characters —no one can understand field cooking at 100 degrees in the shade but them....

I was stationed up country in an area where the enemy was infiltrating across the border. Their main objective when they came across was to kill a BOR [British Other Rank], get his weapon and take it back. Apparently —so I've heard —their government would pay them money for doing this. Most of the action was not long-range artillery stuff, long-range shots here and there; although that did happen, it was mainly sniping and small-scale skirmishes, really.

The terrain had baked sandy surfaces, and was very boring. The smell is a constant factor that stays with me, and that camel smell was something else. We had to cross a lot of dried-up *wadis*; this always gave you the feeling you were being watched, and made you feel very vulnerable to attack.

A working day in Saudi was generally very stressful. We were always up early, as most soldiers are, especially on active service —and every day seems as important as the previous one. Signals responsibility can be a heavy load. You feel that many men out there are relying on you. My responsibilities included Slidex coding, watching over the Arab operators' efficiency, constant frequency changes, logging each message and making temporary field links for page copy through the old 24-volt battery-operated teleprinters —which would relay details of any action going on.

The most pressure came when you were on convoy and you would be the only link with the Air Liaison Officer, who would give you cover for the whole journey. This is most tiring and puts a lot of strain on the signaller, especially if he is operating to some unknown RAF person. The aircraft covering us would usually be Venoms, with the Hunters just coming into service. I worked with a lot of interesting people — one Army officer who comes to mind is Major Balharrie, a gentleman who floated in and out while I was in charge of the signal centre. He was Intelligence and, I believe, had been an ADC to Royalty —a very impressive officer. Then there was Second Lieutenant Shapter, a happy-go-lucky signals officer that I was to meet years later in Hereford. Other names that come to mind are Mitchell, Hanson, Ankers and Dusty Bean. Good blokes, all of them.

The first time I was shot at, I was in a *sangar*, and I was getting pissed with a few of the other guys. We were drinking lukewarm to warm beer that made you sick, and some Chianti that had been parachuted in about two months earlier. We tried to keep it fresh, but it got like vinegar. We still drank it, because it was Christmas. The shots were just pinging away and we weren't giving a toss. We knew what the range was, you see, and we'd found from the experience of other guys that they'd taken potshots quite a few times. Sometimes you couldn't tell what sort of rifle they were firing; they were still using these old things like in an Errol Flynn movie − these long-barrelled guns and things like that. They didn't have a lot of sophisticated weapons at that time. I don't think the AK47 had come into its own then − I don't think so; my memory's blurred. All I can remember is my first time of being fired at, that Christmas in my *sangar*. Although we'd had a few drinks, we were still with it and we knew they'd have to cross open ground to get to us, and we had a few Bren guns and things like that. I won't say you didn't feel frightened; you knew you couldn't stick your head up over the parapet or go for a walk.

But in the night time I would say I did live on my nerves en route to some of the different places I had to visit. If you didn't make it in one day, you'd have to sleep in a *wadi*. I slept in a sleeping-bag − where the Army instructions were safety catch ON (the rifle). I can assure you I have slept with the safety catch off and the rifle outside the bag. Because no way was I having that rifle inside my sleeping-bag with the catch on. I wanted to be ready. Also, when I've been with my radio sets at an outpost, all my weapons have been near me, cocked and ready. No, I wouldn't say I wasn't nervous −I was.

As I say, it's funny when you think about it; when people are pinging away at you, you feel no fear, but you can go months and months without seeing the enemy, and gradually you realize that the biggest enemy is within yourselves. You feel you want to fall out and have a row with your mates; that can become an enemy. You became very minuscule over some things; it could be a bed space or something like that. I had a couple of scraps with a guy called Arthur Golding; he was junior to me, and he was really my maintenance man. We had visits from Sir Alan Lennox Boyd *[the then Colonial Secretary]* and people like that popping in, and Arthur and I had a row because I really wanted to make sure everything was tops, you know, for these VIP visits. Arthur was just slouching around and I picked on him because of tension −and there is tension, believe me. You don't realize it at the time; it's the waiting and the boredom and the waiting and the boredom. You know that there is an enemy, but you never really see him. Even when you're being fired at, and you know they're out there somewhere in the rocks, you never see them. I never ever at any time got to identify the enemy. Yet I knew he was armed and really, in a way as the years go by, you can realize why he wanted us out of there −it was his front room and we shouldn't have been there. He was saying something like, 'Go back to

17

Islington; this is our country.' The Communists said they were simply trying to get rid of the imperialists and the rich, and this fitted in with what he (the enemy) wanted. In fact, we did sneak out, didn't we, in the 1960s —in '66, wasn't it? —we crept out with our tails between our legs. It was ridiculous, after being in an area for 150 years, which I thought I was defending for my country, we left like that. Aden was supposed to be an important port, and then overnight it's no longer an important port. Our politicians actually seemed to have manipulated the world to suit themselves.

It was a wonderful experience for me, being in Arabia having just come from being a teddy boy in Islington, and having experienced the boredom of Catterick; the sunshine, the red rocks, the desert, the *camaraderie* and the small dangers —it came to be quite exciting. Now that I'm fifty-odd, it's some of the few days that I've actually lived in my life —it *was* life. I can understand sometimes why wars exist. They're not nice things, but some blokes say it was the best days of their life. And I can honestly say it was a good foundation for some strengths in myself. I think I learned a lot about myself, living with the Arabs. Living with them, working with them and sometimes fighting with them, I found them to be good people, and it's no good us putting Western values on them. When you find yourself living out there and you don't have a running tap and you don't have bloody nice soft toilet paper on a roll —you actually learn other humilities and other survival methods, which the Arabs had to learn —and you become a scavenger, which is a thing you may have thought they were and which you are now yourself. You've no right to be judging them through Western eyes at all. When I was there, they were still living feudally. I've been to market-places in a place called Sheikh Othman, and I have seen with my own eyes people actually having their hands cut off for thieving. I think maybe today in this country if we had the stocks back again.... For me, it was a mixture of colourful bandoliers, long-barrelled guns, fierce sunlight and sandstorms where you think you're choking to death. I remember all that and I think, Christ, I've lived —I've touched this earth. It's not the place especially; if you go to Malaya or go to battle in Saudi Arabia, it's the same. Active service is a perverse holiday; that's about the only way I can put it, really. Nowadays, there are a lot of rich people paying good money to go out on war games, and to be punished and tortured. Then there's these other rich people, who go to health farms on a spartan diet of bread and water —that seems partly like National Service to me.

The equipment we had was primitive, and the weapons were quite primitive. It seemed almost as though they were fighting a private kind of war. Apparently there was some Geneva Convention or some other rule that meant we couldn't have tanks or certain other types of equipment. The biggest thing we had was the armoured personnel carrier called Saracen or the Saladin — something like that. Nothing to what the Russians had on the other side of the border; they could have walked over us in minutes. They took it seriously. But we did have some Venom aircraft. I was out in the middle of nowhere and, being in signals, I had my ear to the ground; I heard that this Venom had been brought down, apparently by a single shot — which is funny when you think of these really sophisticated Tornados now being brought down in a similar sort of way in the Gulf *[this interview took place in April, 1991]*. Anyway, this Venom had come down and I went there with a small patrol. The aircraft was quite intact, but the pilot was chopped about quite a bit. The story, in fact (which I didn't know until I went back on leave about a year later) was that he had gone to the same school as me, Highbury County in Islington; that was really weird. Even stranger; I met his father on a railway station in North London — he was an old porter. As I was waiting for the train one Saturday morning, he was tidying up the platform. He noticed that I was very suntanned and asked me where I'd been, and I told him that I'd been in South Arabia. He said that his son had been out there and had been killed in action. The train was coming on the horizon and I didn't really have time to figure out what to say to him. He said his son was a pilot officer in the Royal Air Force. When he told me his son's name, my mind went back to fourteen months previously, and I remembered that I'd actually shovelled him up on to a piece of tarpaulin and picked up his dog-tags (identity discs). I bunged one on the tarpaulin and subsequently handed the other in.

When I came back to England, I went to a camp called Satan Camp (I think that's how you spell it) near Chester, and this was a very weird place, because all the eccentrics had come in from Malaya, Cyprus, South America — you name it — the North Pole, the South Pole. We all seemed to meet up at this camp — none of us came from the same regiment; there was just this odd little bunch of characters who were like in limbo. Some guys didn't even have proper uniforms. We'd come home to all these months of leave we were entitled to, or come to the end of a contract, or arriving there before being sent somewhere else; it was really weird. What I do remember mainly about this camp was the resentment from the regulars around the camp who'd never been anywhere or done anything; who were all pasty-faced and absolutely hated us.

I'm glad to have met people who I've still not seen in thirty years, who were with me out there (in Saudi Arabia). We were terrified together at times, frightened together and sometimes happy together. We came back and we puffed our little chests out because we thought we'd done something. They were good Englishmen. I'm sorry; I mean, good Brits — because there were Scotsmen, Welshmen and mad Irishmen, too. I was nineteen months in the Levies, and I think that experience gave me a kind of uniqueness.

19

The places I was at were just encampments really —like Foreign Legion outposts. These names are very rare; they don't exist any more except, maybe, on the map. There was Dhala, there was Beihan and Mukeiras. The guys I was out with were very lonely solitary signalmen, just managing to survive. Some of them were young men, married and missing their wives. It was really hard just to keep going. There was boredom and a lack of support; you'd get a newspaper from home in those days and it was twelve weeks old —you didn't get it next day, like you do now.

Coming home from the Aden Protectorate in the early 1960s, I felt completely out of step with everything I had known before, such as friends, family and local haunts. I went very introverted and felt at a loss for many years, and this distance from my family has stayed with me to this very day. The excitement out there added to the depression, of course, on coming home. Coming home, no one heralded anybody in those days. Soldiers get to be old hat, particularly when they are in their thousands, and I was one of the thousands. After you're demobbed and you talk to people about your experiences, you begin to realize after the first war story that you tell, nobody believes you. They think you must be bullshitting and you're adding that bit extra on. You begin to think that maybe it does seem a little bit like that, standing here in the middle of a sterile environment, where they've gone to work down the factory every day of their lives. They don't want to know that you haven't sat on a chair for a year, and had to drink stagnant water, and taken salt tablets as big as your fist...and all that rubbish. It doesn't mean anything to them, and they don't want to hear it. The places you can go for adventures —the African gold mines, the Khyber Passes and the deserts —are running out. Now you've got satellite television that pops it all down into your sitting-room. It would take a wiser man than me to explain it but, if someone said, 'Are you glad you did it, or would you rather have been without it?' —then I would have to say I'm glad I did it.

George Brown

George Brown served with the King's Liverpool Regiment in Korea in 1953 and was wounded just before the armistice. He is married with one son and one daughter, recently retired and lives in London.

I was called up in April, 1952, to the Inniskilling Fusiliers. Strange it may be, but my first night in the Army was spent on the Liverpool to Belfast ferry, because we had to go to Northern Ireland to join the Regiment. The Inniskillings were not exactly my first choice, because I really wanted to go into the REME (Royal Electrical & Mechanical Engineers); being a trainee mechanic at the time, I thought it was the most sensible thing to do. I remember meeting one chap who wanted to go into the Inniskillings because they had nice hats. When I met him again, he turned out to be in the REME and I'd taken his place in the Fusiliers. I did my basic training in Omagh, County Tyrone. At that time the Army was enlarging, and a lot of regiments were starting second battalions; the Inniskillings was one of these, so we went off to start the new battalion in Colchester. Then the Inniskillings were asked for replacements for the King's Liverpool Regiment, who were already in Korea or just going. They sent forty personnel, myself included, to a place just outside Liverpool. Then we went direct to Korea from Southampton on a ship called the *Asturia*. It had just been introduced into service. We were very lucky; we had cabins – six to each one.

We went to Kure in Japan and had a little battle training there. As a young guy of nineteen, I must admit I'd never seen foreigners living in their own country before and the Japanese came across to me as very nice people. I found it very hard to believe that, only a few years before, I was taught at school what a bad lot of people they were.

After our battle training we went on to Korea; I'm not sure of the date. It was just coming out of winter actually, but still very cold; chaps were still getting frostbite and that sort of thing. We landed at Pusan, went on to a transit camp and then they transferred us by train directly to the front line. Strange as it may seem, I wasn't frightened at all. I don't think any of us were. There's always a kind of strength in numbers, isn't there? There were

21

about forty of us in our draft, and also there were American personnel on the train, going to their line regiments. I went into B Company, 5 Platoon, and I suppose there were about four or five of us who stuck together all through this. The Regiment was mostly National Servicemen, but there seemed to be a lot of older chaps. I think it was because if a guy was in the Merchant Navy and left before he was twenty-six, he got pulled in for National Service. So we had National Servicemen who were twenty-six and who'd sailed around the world umpteen times. They were quite amusing – Liverpool people are, anyway, as you probably know.

Then the Regiment moved up into the line. I'm not sure of the date; it might have been early spring, but it was still very cold. Really that's when your soldiering started as such. Mostly you went out on these patrols at night. There were different types. There was what they called a fighting patrol, which I felt very comfortable in. That consisted of fifteen men plus one, the one being an officer or a sergeant. Then you had standing patrols which went forward of the line and held a position. Your job then was to report back on any activity – this was done by line phones (field telephones). Then you could have a one-and-one patrol, which would be one man and one officer, or perhaps four and one. All you did then was you went out and had a look round to see what you could find out – it has got a name but I can't remember it. On the fighting patrols you were heavily armed; about six or eight of you had rifles. A few of the blokes who had been out there a bit longer had these American carbines which fired very quickly. Then the Army introduced a sub-machine-gun to replace the Sten gun, because the Sten gun was very unreliable. This new gun was called the Patchett. Also on these patrols we carried two Bren guns, and sometimes they'd say to you, 'You're a bomber.' I'd never heard of this in all my training. You'd carry about sixteen grenades, all primed, in extra water-bottle holders. It was rather funny on those fighting patrols; it was like going back to the Boer War. The idea was if you did run into trouble you'd form a square.

It made you nervous going out at night, because you had to go over the top. You'd go down to the forward positions which the Regiment was holding. The chap would count you over: 'One!' and the first bloke would go; 'Two!' and the second would, and so on. But you know, you get brave people who do things. They counted to four and the first four went, but Five wouldn't go because he'd reached the end of his tether. But you can't stand waiting because the others have already gone, so the chap said 'Six!' and Six went, and I thought that was very, very brave. When we got back, Five had gone. He'd gone down with some sort of fatigue.

Sometimes bravery doesn't mean that a bloke gets up and fights whoever it is, but it's the action that they do. We were out on a patrol one night and, on the way back, we got caught up in an unmarked minefield in a valley.

It was coming up to dawn, and the officer says, 'We'll have to dig our way out.' *[Lift each mine individually to clear a path.]* I always remember that I said, 'We haven't got time' — if the light comes and they see you down there, that's it. Then this chap, I remember it was Johnnie Robertshaw — he got killed on my last patrol, actually — he said, 'This is no bloody good, we're better off if we try to run out. Those that get killed, get killed and those that don't, don't; but if we stay here, we're all going to get bloody killed,' and he jumped up and ran out and we all ran after him. It must have been a 'blind' minefield, because nothing went off. Whatever it was in there, the water had got to it, so it didn't explode. I thought that bloody brave; you get a medal for contact with the enemy or standing there shooting at them, but he'd actually risked his life — there are people like that there.

Another funny thing: when the Coronation took place, they marched us all up into these positions and fired red, white and blue shells and smoke-bombs at the Chinese — then we came back and got ice cream; the Americans supplied that. Actually, we all laughed at this. Who the bloody hell would think of that, marching up there to see red, white and blue shells being fired at the Chinese! What they made of it, I don't know; they must think we're a funny people. But the Americans did supply us with something tangible — ice cream.

They used to bring fresh water up to the front by porters, and one of the guys who was escorting them, somewhere along the line he'd picked up a piece of rope with a knot in the end. Like being on the old sailing-ships, he used to wallop these guys with it, and we used to sit and laugh at it, ever so funny. My thoughts about that now: I think to myself what my son would think of it if it was me who had to carry that water and someone was giving me a fourpenny one with a rope.

I have a fear of snakes. I was walking along the trench and there's a snake in the bloody way, so I climbed up the side and ran along the top, and there were bullets going Ping! ping! ping!; the Chinese were firing at me, but I couldn't go past that bloody snake. And I'm sure I would have done it on the way back as well; I wouldn't have gone past that bloody snake.

It's funny; you acquire certain abilities. I was very good at night and they used to use me a lot, because — it seems a silly thing to say — I could see at night. Some people can. But having that ability, sometimes you were overused. The night I was wounded, I went out on a standing patrol forward of what was called 355 on the map. The position we had to make for was called Victor, and the patrol was called Victor. There were four of us: a corporal and three kingsmen (privates) and we went forward to this position that night. When we got there, we *knew* it was wrong — it was about half a mile, or maybe more, in front of our lines. We got into position and someone said, 'It's not right.' You could feel it. We knew they were there somewhere.

We phoned back to the line and said, 'What shall we do? We know they're here.' They said, 'Well, hang on, because we have no notification that there's anything happening in the valley.' We hung on, and they were definitely around us; we could bloody hear them. So the corporal said, 'Whatever information I get back, we'll withdraw about 200 yards.' Well, anyway, they still said they couldn't get any information of known activity in that area, so we withdrew, and that's when it happened. When you withdraw, one of you goes and covers for the others, who come through. I went first and they came through me; then I went through them and I ran straight into it — a hell of a lot of gunshots and firing, a lot of noise. Then it went very quiet. I'd been shot fairly heavily in both legs. I had three bullet wounds in each leg, and one in my hand which didn't cause any problems. The next thing I knew, there was a Chinaman on me, so I did the proverbial act of playing dead. He pulled me about. We had scatter-jackets, an innovation for the British Army — flak jackets — and all he wanted then was to get my jacket, and of course he's pulling me about. Then a flare went up from our lines, and of course they went off. I tried to make my way to where the other guys would have been, but I couldn't; my leg was broken and I couldn't get up. I was in quite a lot of pain; not as much as you'd envisage when you see cowboys getting shot on the telly — I don't know any other way to kind of say that. So I went off in the other direction. All my mates had been killed, but I didn't find this out until later, of course. But I went away. It was a rice-growing area, a paddyfield. I crawled away and they (the Chinese) came back, and one chap — I was in this paddy row and he was in the next one — I could have touched him. I was a little bit scared that time, but I've been more frightened a few times since, rather than then, just thinking about it. There were two of them, actually, and I thought I haven't got a chance because there's two of them and I'm on the floor and I'm in bad shape. They came, and with that the flares go up again, and they went. But I could have actually stabbed him with my bayonet easy, because he was that near to me. Anyway, off they went and I lay down there for quite a time. Then one of our patrols came out and found me. One of them gave me morphine. I've seen one of the chaps that found me years after, at a reunion, and he was so surprised when I turned up because he thought I was dead. He said, 'How did you get on?' and I said, 'Bloody terrible; I'm sure you stuck that morphine in a bloody sandbag, not in me.' I was still in dreadful pain. Anyway, from there on was virtually the end of my service.

They carried me back on a stretcher. We had to start climbing to get out of the valley; that was a rough ride, very very painful. They took me to our MO, who cut my boots off. The strange things you get embarrassed about: I didn't have any socks on; I still remember that, and I apologized to him for having no socks. It was so damp at the time that it was easier to go without. Then a helicopter came and I was flown back to one of these MASH hospitals, and I was there for two or three days. Very sick I was; I didn't feel very well at all. I had the fear that they were going to take my leg off; it was just flapping about. That was my main fear, thinking they were going to take this leg off. Anyway, they didn't, and they were very kind to me. Then they moved me to Seoul, where there was a British hospital − or at least a ward − and they looked at my wounds again.

I had a visitation from the Regiment. Two chaps came and told me that the other three guys were dead. You get close in the line, and it was very sad. I don't think it did me any good. Also, I couldn't go to the toilet; there was something wrong with my waterworks. Then they shifted me to a big military hospital for Commonwealth forces at Kure. I was there for about eleven weeks; they couldn't transfer me, because my legs weren't mending properly.

I missed out rather; the Norwegians weren't involved on the ground, but they had a Red Cross boat and it was coming to collect more people to take them home. They booked me a place on it, but the matron came round and she said, 'I'm sorry; you can't go, you're not fit enough to travel.' It would have been a lovely trip; the boat went to South Africa and across the Atlantic to New York. I had friends who lived in New York, and it would have been nice to see them. Mind you, I would still have been in bed. It was 22 July when it happened, and I didn't get out of bed until February the following year − eight months, that was.

Eventually they flew me home in a Hastings. We went to Singapore and the Philippines, to Clark Field, which was a big American base. They put me and another chap in this ward where we noticed all the reading-matter was in a foreign language. The plaster on my leg was starting to crack, and I couldn't get out of bed to wash or anything − they just dumped me there. Eventually we got hold of this nurse, and the chap with me said to her, 'This chap's plaster is broken; he's got to have attention. We've been travelling all this time and he needs a wash.' She said, 'You're not telling me what to do,' and he said, 'I've never come across this; we're British soldiers.' 'You're what?' All of a sudden, there was a hell of a lot of action went on. They collected up all the books; they asked us what we wanted to eat; I got washed; my plaster was looked at − all that sort of thing. We thought: What the hell's going on? No one would even talk to us before. Then one of the American guys said that we were in a VD ward; also, they thought that we were Puerto Ricans, and they don't exactly think the world of them. After that, they couldn't do enough for us.

When I got back to England, I was in the Cambridge Hospital at Aldershot; very nice it was. Once I was up and about, I came home. I was on a caliper, but I could get about. I was a bit of a mess, you know. Going back to the night it happened, I must have been very, very strong because where they found me was a long way from where the action had gone on; I had actually pulled myself along by my arms. It did hurt my dad, because I was quite a good sportsman before, but I couldn't play after being wounded. I was twenty-one in the January while I was still in hospital. When I came home, my mum had people round for drinks. She had napkins with my name and all that sort of thing on them, and of course they were two months out of date. Anyway, they felt a lot better with me home, as I did myself. It's strange how it never leaves you, in a way. I get a pension for my wound, but now I've gone deaf in one ear. We had a heavy mortar raid on us one evening. A couple went off very close and I was deaf for two days, and my ears have always given me trouble over the years. I've also found that a lot of the other guys in the regiment have gone deaf as well.

When I was in the hospital in Japan, a couple of the ward maids there had taken a shine to me. They did my shopping for me and bought the little presents for my family — tablecloths, and that sort of thing. We landed at Lyneham when we got back, and when I got my kit all the boxes had been broken open by the Customs. I thought to myself, what the bloody hell did they think I could do? I couldn't even walk; I was a stretcher case.

I never really understood what we were doing in Korea. I must admit they did try to explain to us when we arrived in Japan. An Intelligence Corps officer got up and tried to tell us why we were there. On getting back to our own billets and talking it over amongst ourselves, we realized he spoke a lot of crap really, because none of us knew what it was all about. But at the end of it I thought to myself: Be fair; I suppose the guy himself didn't know what was going on.

I wanted to do National Service. I lived in flats at the time, and a couple of other guys in the flats who were older than me had gone. Another thing was that those who didn't go were the ones who had failed the medical and, of course, I didn't want to be one of those. So I didn't mind National Service at all, and I've always been a good mixer, which made it easier. It was a terrible shock to some guys. I remember one chap tried to undress and dress behind the locker door; he was terribly embarrassed by the whole bloody issue. Now, he couldn't have enjoyed it, whatever they'd done for him.

Even now and with what happened to me, I'm highly delighted I went. I still think it made me a whole person, and it also taught me right and wrong. As a young man, I wasn't a scared sort of person then, but I think it gave me much more courage. National Service showed me how groups all found one another. We had a couple of thieves in our unit; you caught one, you caught them both — because they'd found one another. You get liars and they find their level. I was in with a couple of very nice chaps and

— I know this is patting myself on the back, but — I never thought I was a nasty sort of person, and they certainly weren't.

Gordon Butt

Gordon Butt served with the Royal Fusiliers in Korea 1952-53. He is married with one son, works as a carpenter and lives in Horley.

I joined the Queens, which I did my basic training in. We finished our training and came home on leave, and we all received a letter asking if we would prefer to sign on, or join the Royal Fusiliers in Korea. One of the lads' fathers wrote a letter about this which was published in the *Daily Mirror*, but nothing came of it. Anyway, we reported back to barracks, booked in at the guardroom and not one person signed on; so we were all transferred to the Fusiliers and went to the Tower of London *[the regimental depot]*. The Regiment at that particular time was in Germany. We did a little bit of training at the Tower; then we went out to Germany. I wasn't out there long; it must have been about three months, I suppose. The whole battalion came home and went up to Norfolk to do some training for Korea. Norfolk is absolutely the opposite of Korea, which is all hills.

When we came back from Norfolk, we were given the Freedom of the City of London, and had a banquet at the Guildhall. Then we went up to Liverpool and we got on the boat to Korea — the *Empire Halladale*. The trip itself was very boring; we didn't have a lot to do. We had a bit of weapon training out to sea and everyone had a chore — you know, a fatigue. We stopped at different ports; we got off at Aden and Singapore. We had a very rough ride through the Bay of Biscay. I happened to be one of the ones who wasn't bad, and the few that weren't had to clear up after the rest in the morning. We went into Hong Kong, stayed there a while and then we went off to Korea. We landed in Pusan to an American band playing on the quay, marching up and down in all their finery. Everybody was getting a bit apprehensive then. We were all piled off the boat with all our kit and everything, and got in an old train with wooden seats. We were on this so-and-so train for two days nearly, all getting more and more restless — 'What are we going to do?' 'What's going to happen?' — sort of thing, being young lads at the time. As we're going up, we could see relics of the previous years of the war lying at the side of the tracks; lorries and tanks and all that sort of thing. We eventually arrived at a station and there's this big fleet of American lorries waiting to take us to our first camp. This was August, 1951, and it was *hot*. But we'd been acclimatized coming over on the boat; we used to have forced sunbathing parades. When you went up for your pay, if you weren't brown you had to go and sunbathe under escort. An NCO would stand there for half an hour while you stayed out in the sun and, of course, we were issued with our summer kit before we got off the boat.

In the camp there were just rows of tents — big ones: sixteen to a tent — and of course they all had mosquito nets, which was something new to us. We stayed there, getting acclimatized, and did quite a bit of training. Then it was time for us to take over a position (in the front line); I can't remember who we took over from. I'll never forget the first night. There's all sorts of trenches and you all take up your positions. You've been briefed on what could come up. It's all barbed wire down in front of you and then the valley out to the North Koreans, who'd be about two or three thousand yards away. It was quite scary, I can tell you. Everyone's shaking, and of course there's rats; there's rabbits; there's wild cats; there's wild pigs and there's pheasants — all rummaging around at night in the undergrowth. Grenades and rifles are going off like nobody's business, but no one worried about it; you'd go back and say, 'What are you shooting at?' and they'd say, 'I thought I heard someone coming,' and of course it's these bloody wild things. The next night, we were in this position looking down across the valley, and we were in twos. I was with Ginger Dalton. I'll always remember him. He says, 'There's someone coming with a cigarette.' You're so frightened, you don't realize it's coming across the valley, not up the trench where somebody would be coming from. It was a bloody firefly, wasn't it? In the front line we did two hours on duty and four off. There was a guard corporal, and he was supposed to come along with two more men to relieve you, but he used to get his head down and you used to be left on your own while your mate went to get the next lot. It was a bit scary when you were left on your own.

A lot of the blokes were Londoners. Personally, I couldn't have been in a better regiment as far as being good guys to get along with. They all mucked in together. Most of them were National Servicemen. We were all a bit tensed up but, as time went on, after you'd been there six months you begin to take it in your stride. But I've never seen so many lads wanting to go on church parade when we first got there. It's amazing; when you're in this country, you'll do anything to get out of church parade but, when we went out (to Korea), nobody did. There were a few hard nuts in the battalion. One of the Diamond brothers, he was a real hard nut. He hit someone over the head with a rock one night because he thought he was interfering with one of his mates sexually, you know? He went away to a Canadian detention camp and rumour came back that it was pretty bad, apparently.

29

Ginger Dalton was my mate for a while. We were in the Assault Pioneer Platoon — which is mines and explosives and fortifications and all that: you lay minefields, dig dug-outs, put up barbed wire, breach barbed wire and so on. After a while, Ginger found it too hard physically. It's quite strenuous as far as the manual side is concerned. He put in for a transfer to our own Battalion's medics, which he found a lot better. After he went, my mate was Charlie who came from Croydon, and he disappeared as well. We were doing some blasting for a bunker. It was in the winter, and the ground freezes for about three feet down and we had to blast the top three feet off and then you could dig. We set a pretty heavy charge. We stood back, and the procedure is that you just look up in the sky and if you see something coming, you just stand aside. Charlie said, 'I'm not going to get hit this time,' because little bits used to hit you, but nothing serious. He got in this little hole and he held his shovel over his head, just mucking about really, and we're all standing there, and Charlie's chi-yiking on and he's got the shovel to protect him from the little bits...and a blooming great bit hits the shovel. He got very badly concussed and had to be sent home.

The food was diabolical, at least in the front line. We had compo rations for emergencies. We had American rations — C22, was it? They were always there in case we were cut off by the enemy. We had a field kitchen. It wasn't too bad, I suppose; we had a lot of stew, but we never had a lot of bread. We were definitely the poor relations as far as food was concerned, against the Americans and Australians — they were well off.

I've never been so hungry in my life. I don't want to be as hungry again, either. We used to get a beer ration in the summer of one pint a night. We'd save this beer ration until we had twelve bottles and go over to the Canadians and swap it for food; we were so hungry. We got big tins of salmon, big tins of peaches. It was a court martial offence, but we used to do raiding parties on the cookhouse tent. We'd get under the flap of the tent in the dead of night to get something to eat. Not every night, but now and again. It was pitch dark and you'd rummage around in the boxes and take what you could find, and you'd get back to the dug-out and they'd say, 'What you got?' And — I'll always remember this — once we got a pot of jam and some cornflakes; so we boiled up some water in a billycan and mixed in the jam and put it on the cornflakes. It's all right if you're hungry. To keep ourselves clean, we used to have to wash and shave every day. It wasn't too bad in the summer, because in the summer there's the lovely streams with nice, clean, cool water, and you could go down there and have a good wash down. But in the winter, when we came out of six weeks up the front, our bodies were black, and there again our lads used to have to go and cadge a shower off the Americans. Also, we had white sleeping-bags in the winter, and they used to get absolutely filthy. They were white to match the snow,

I suppose, but we only had them when we were in 'rest'. We wore survival kits: string vest, two pairs of trousers — these were special, fleecy-lined things — and you had a parka with a wired hood. You wore boots one size bigger than you normally took, so you could wear two pairs of socks, and they were these seaman-type socks. I think we were luckier than some of the previous lads who didn't have that sort of kit, just greatcoats. Most of the time, especially when you were 'up', you just lived in it — you never took it off.

Wherever you were, you had to dig a hole for a latrine, and this is one of my pet stories about Korea. In the real depths of winter, you had to go out there with a stick, because it would freeze so quick it would build itself up, and if you weren't careful, you sat on it. You had to knock the top off with the stick. Another thing that took some getting used to when you were in 'rest': down in the middle of this sixteen-man tent there were these thunderboxes, made out of NAAFI boxes, and you'd sit back to back. When you came out of breakfast, you'd go to this toilet tent, and there's all these guys lined up together — no privacy whatsoever. It was all right once you got used to it, but some used to wait until there was no one else in there. The NAAFI truck used to come round once a week, and you could get razor-blades and soaps. They only carried the essential things and, of course, we only had the old NAAFI paper money to pay for it.

The winter was, I suppose, the worst part of being in Korea. They never gave you any heating in the tents, so we used to cut the top off an ammunition box and fill it with sand, and drip petrol or paraffin into it through a funnel. It was a primitive sort of oil stove. Petrol was best; it gave out more heat. It was really an offence to have one but, unless anything happened, they'd just turn a blind eye to it. A few tents did get burnt down, and then there was trouble.

In the wet season, our dug-outs used to fill up with about two feet of water. When you came off guard, you had to wade through it to get to your bunk. We used to be wet for hours and hours, and cold too, but we always had a good supply of dry socks. We lined our bunkers with blankets; at night you'd see the blankets moving and the rats would come out — great big ones — but you were so tired, you just got your head down and, if a rat came running over you, you wouldn't know. Being an assault pioneer platoon, we used to set booby traps for them. We'd put a 27 detonator on a trip, bait it with a cigarette — which they seemed to like — or some food and, when they trod on it, they'd be blown to bits. But then you had to clear up the mess.

I never saw a live enemy; not even a prisoner. I only saw dead ones when they'd tried to get through our minefields and wire. At that time, we'd already lost two or three of our own, so we didn't have any feelings of remorse. The very first one of our lot to get killed, he was out on patrol and he trod on a trip flare; it went right up his leg and he died. They had all these pathways through the minefield, marked with a red triangle, and they used to get blown over, and in the dark it's very easy to go off the path. It was just the first guy who got killed, and everybody saw it as a sort of symbol. After the next one and the one after that, it was just a matter of routine. *[The Royal Fusiliers had thirty men killed in Korea.]*

I did one night patrol myself, when they were short of men. Not being part of a regular night platoon, you're getting tensed up all day, because you know you're going out. I don't know what I felt, really — other than being bloody scared, I suppose. Eight or ten of you go out, faces blacked and with three or four hand grenades and your rifle. You go out there, sit and wait and see if they're coming. It's just the tenseness of it all the time, in the dark. If they're not coming along, you're withdrawn; and they might be sitting and waiting as well, and as soon as you make a move to retreat they open up. But we didn't bump into anybody.

Another frightening thing was that they used to send over these airburst shells. If you were on guard or on patrol, these bloody things went off in the sky, and it all came whizzing down around your ears; that was quite frightening. You'd go into the nearest culvert or whatever to get out of it until it cleared. We had these observation posts manned twenty-four hours a day watching the enemy. Any movement down their regular paths into the valley would be seen. Every infantry battalion had a Centurion tank as artillery dug in on the top of the hill. They had nothing really to touch those tanks, so they sat up on the skyline, as bold as brass. As soon as the observation post saw something, he'd radio across to the tank, and they'd blast the hell out of it.

We were in the front line at Christmas. The enemy crept up in the dark and pinned cards on the barbed wire. When it got light you'd see these cards; you'd been there all night, and they'd pinned them on the wire right in front of you. They were propaganda cards, saying: 'It's not your war, go home to your sweethearts and wives.' That was a bit frightening.

Just before the Coronation *[June, 1953]*, we were out on 'rest' and the Duke of Wellington's Regiment got overrun one night. They (the enemy) nearly got through. They did manage to push them back, but the Dukes were so overrun they had to be withdrawn, so we went and backed them up. The position had been pounded by mortars; all the trenches had been blown in, and it was in pretty bad shape. Being pioneers, we had to go and try to salvage what was left of the position. We went up, and they said, 'There's a bloody caved-in communication trench all along there; you'd better dig it out.' They gave us ten or twelve 'gooks' from the Korean labour force and split them up into four each. When we got up there, they said we had to wear shrapnel-proof vests and keep on our tin hats all the time. They were terrible things to wear, those shrapnel-proof vests — bloody hot. They were made of some kind of fibreglass, which was quite effective, actually, but we were one short and I said, 'Well, I don't want one,' and our Platoon Officer said, 'You've got to have one. I'll get one sent up.' So we were there until dinner time and, when we went off to have our grub the officer said, 'I've got your vest; put it on.' So I put it on.

We went back up the trench and I was with these four Korean guys, digging it out. They'd fill the sandbags and I'd build them up. It's still pouring with rain and, halfway along the section of trench where we are, is a little shelter which was a look-out post. We'd been told, 'Don't throw anything over the top.' Twigs and big stones — anything that won't go in the sandbag — it's natural to throw it over the top. Of course, the enemy are watching, and if they see where we are working they can use it as a bearing for their mortars. I don't know whether one of the 'gooks' did throw something over but, anyway, they're saying, 'Smokee, smokee,' and if you give them a cigarette you get a bit more work out of them, so we've trooped back under the look-out post to get out of the rain. I'm walking along behind them and, with that, over came a mortar. Being behind them, I protected them. My vest was full of it (shrapnel), and I got quite a big piece in my shoulder and it was in my camouflage net on my helmet. I'd heard it coming, but they're whizzing over all the time and you get a bit complacent with them...and suddenly, there's a blinding flash and you're blown off your feet. Our officer was coming along to check us. He got blown over, but didn't cop any shrapnel, because the blast must have gone our way. He said, 'You all right?' I said, 'Yeah, I'm all right,' and he said, 'No, you're not; your shoulder's bleeding. You'd better come with me.' So off I went, and the next thing I know I'm in an ambulance going to this Canadian hospital.

I saw very bad cases there. Mine was nothing compared to some of the people in there. One American had been hit between his legs by a mortar — hell of a state he was in. There was an English guy with his leg all blown to bits. It was a wonderful place, mind you, that Canadian field hospital. I was in there for two weeks and then I went for a week in a rehabilitation centre, where there was a mixture of all nationalities getting over their wounds and getting ready to go back. I went back and took over my duties again. I think those four Koreans saved my life, because that mortar landed right on the sandbags, just after we'd moved away. If they hadn't wanted a cigarette, I might not have been here now.

After we'd been there a year, the Armistice was signed; the searchlights shone in the sky all the time they were talking. Once the searchlights went out, you knew they'd finished. I came back on the *Halladale*. I went to Fayed on the Bitter Lakes at Suez and came home from there by plane, and was demobbed at the Tower. I got malaria when I came home, which I'd picked up in Egypt, I think; you get a bit blasé about taking the tablets (paludrin). We landed at Stansted Airport. We'd been away sixteen months, and the Customs went right through us. I'd got 400 cigarettes for my father; I'd got a watch and a camera. They made us empty all our kitbags – they took the camera and the watch, and they had the cheek to say, 'You can keep the cigarettes.'

When we got to the Tower, we had to have a medical before they would let us go on leave, and I thought, I'm never going to get through this with the malaria and everything; but the doctor was so doddery and blasé, he didn't really examine me – just a matter of passing through, really. But I spent a couple of weeks in the hospital when I got home.

To be honest, I thought being in Korea was a waste of time – it's such a barren, horrible place; just ranges of hills, paddyfields and a few villages – what were we fighting for? But National Service was a good experience, in as much as you come out a much wiser and more grown-up person. Remember, you went in at eighteen, and you weren't all that mature at that age. But I quite enjoyed my service. I met a lot of people, and it wasn't all bad. I remember that for twelve months in Korea we got £19 extra. Nineteen pounds for twelve months' active service – that and two medals and a lot of memories.

Leo Campbell

Leo Campbell served with the Royal Artillery in Malaya, 1957-58. He lives in Newcastle upon Tyne, where he was born.

I was conscripted into the Royal Artillery for National Service at Oswestry on 20 March, 1957. We were there for two weeks: kitting out, medical checks, haircuts and preparation for training. Our training was done at Kimmel Park Camp, Rhyl, and I was fortunate enough to get the driving training I had applied for.

The eight weeks' basic training was sheer purgatory, as I'm sure most people's was. We had square-bashing every morning after inspection parade; driver training in the afternoons; then at least two or three barrack-room and kit inspections every night. Everything you did in those eight weeks seemed to be at the double. None of the officers or NCOs ever spoke; it was all shouting and screaming obscenities. It was so bad that the first week of our training there were eight men out of our troop went AWOL.

The driver training was done in 3-ton Bedford trucks. The first words my instructor, a full bombardier *[equivalent to a corporal]*, said to me were that he didn't like Geordies, which didn't exactly fill me with confidence. At the slightest mistake he would scream into my left ear, and was forever telling me I would never make a driver – and when I passed out (qualified) first time, I think it was more out of defiance than anything else. During this period we were given a list of possible postings of which we could make three choices, mine being Hong Kong, Singapore or Cyprus. After nine weeks I had passed my driving test, got through the passing-out parade and was given an overseas posting – Malaya; no one seemed to get what they had put down, but I thought that was near enough. We were given three weeks' leave, then spent two weeks at Woolwich Barracks awaiting our flight out. We were like pincushions after those two weeks with all the injections we were given. We flew out on 8 July on what I think was a Hermes aircraft that had seen better days. Everyone had to wear civilian clothes, as we had to refuel in some sensitive countries. It took us four days and seven stops, which were Brindisi, Ankara and Baghdad; we had twenty-four hours' overnight stay at the airport hotel in Karachi, two more stops in India – at Delhi and Calcutta – Bangkok and on to Singapore. It was dark when we arrived at Singapore, and I particularly liked the coach journey through the city with the little market stalls, shops, cafés, bars and the oriental smells and music.

We were all aware of the emergency – as it was called – in Malaya and the fight against the spread of Communism in the colonies; we didn't know what to expect but of course, we realized, being in the Artillery we weren't likely to see any close action or terrorists, which turned out to be the case.

After six days in the transit camp in Singapore, being kitted out in our tropical kit – Olive Green denims – we were moved up to the 48th Field Regiment base camp at Tampin, a small town south of Kuala Lumpur. The regiment consisted of four gun batteries, with a mixture of 25lb shell guns and 55lb shell guns, of which one battery was based permanently in the north of Malaya. When we arrived at Tampin, all the batteries were out on operations and the place was very quiet, but burst into life two weeks later when they returned.

Normal working dress was only socks, boots, shorts and beret, but we 'milk bottles' – the new recruits *[so called because their skins were still very white]* – had to keep our full uniforms on for a four-week acclimatization period. The troop and billet I was given had a mixture of old hands and new arrivals, of which three of us had been mates since Oswestry. We had a great bunch of lads; at first when we arrived in Malaya, we seemed to group up – such as Scots with Scots; Geordies with Geordies; Cockneys with Cockneys and so on – but after a few weeks and, especially, our first operation, everyone mixed well. I suppose in every regiment there will be one or two who could not handle the life and spent a lot of time locked up. In our battery, there were three Scots lads from the Gorbals in Glasgow who were like that, always fighting. They were three of the smallest men in our mob, and were quite easy to get on with when sober. Apart from those three, we had very little trouble.

The first two weeks we had jungle training and ambush drill. Our daily camp routine was 6 o'clock reveille, 7 o'clock breakfast, 8 o'clock inspection parade. Gunners worked on gun drill, and drivers were on maintenance mainly and various other small duties, such as ammunition collection, sick parade to hospital, refuse collection in the married quarters and taking out officers on reconnaissance patrols. Everyone was issued with .303 rifles and the drivers were issued with Sten guns.

The local people near Tampin Camp were a mixture of Indian, Pakistani, Chinese and Malay, who were all easy to get on with and do business with. But with bartering being the way they traded, this caused some friction with some of our men when they had been drinking. There was never any violence against them – just verbal abuse, which I always disliked, but it didn't seem to affect them at all, and they would almost immediately forget about it. There were a lot of small businesses in the camp, such as *dhobis*, boot *wallahs*, tailors and shops selling general goods. They were run by Indians, Pakistanis and Chinese, whom I got on very well with.

After about nine weeks, I went on my first operation to a position about 120 miles south-west of the camp. The main purpose of the operation, based on Intelligence information, was for our guns to pound a particular area of jungle where the CTs had been sighted or were suspected to be, so as to force them into one particular direction, to where the foot patrols were operating – which were mainly Gurkha infantry patrols. On the last operation, our battery did some jungle foot-patrols, being dropped into jungle clearings by helicopter, but without having any contact with the CTs. Fortunately for me, I missed all this, being back in base camp on light duties, still recovering from my tropical disease. Apart from that last operation, all the others were the same in as much as the guns were always pounding away – so many hours on; so many hours off.

My particular job – and that of all the other drivers – was of various MT duties, such as ammunition collection; food and water collection; recce duties; twenty-four-hour guards and helping out on the guns, which were regularly short-crewed. Our job on the guns was to manhandle the shells up to the gun crews for loading *[shell and cartridge together weighing 100lbs]*. The vehicle I was given for the trip to our first operation was an armoured vehicle, with a winch and with two REME mechanics and all their tools. We drove at the rear of the convoy in case of breakdowns by other vehicles.

On reaching our position, the drivers put the guns in position, then parked up in the MT section and erected the four-man tents we were going to live in, while the gunners prepared the guns for firing as quick as possible. That first operation, I didn't know this was what they were doing, and was caught unawares when they suddenly fired. I had never heard guns go off before, and I was deaf for hours. Us drivers had to do virtually all the guard duties, for the gunners had to be ready to man the guns at all times. We had two night-time alerts in the first week. The guards thought they had seen a movement in the surrounding jungle. Everyone had to take up arms and lie flat just inside the perimeter of the camp, facing out into the jungle. The second alert was during a monsoon, so we had to lie down in the mud and pouring rain, but they both turned out to be false alarms. It was pretty rough and dirty on these operations, with not a lot of fresh water, which was usually rationed, and there was no one who wasn't looking forward to returning to our base camp.

We lived in four-man tents, which were very uncomfortable, with a groundsheet, mosquito net, a couple of bed-sheets and an improvised pillow made from rolled-up trousers or some other part of our kit. At times, it was almost impossible to sleep, what with the rock-hard ground and the pounding of the guns.

On operations, we all wore long-trouser OGs (Olive Greens); for the rough terrain we had jungle boots which were treaded canvas lace-ups which came up to the top of the calf. The inside of our boots had to be inspected each morning for scorpions, centipedes and suchlike. We always saw quite a variety of snakes at the beginning of each operation, but with the noise of the guns they became scarce.

The food in the camp was, to put it mildly, very poor. Breakfast was usually fried stuff − bacon, eggs, sausage and tomatoes − only palatable if you were hungry enough. The main meals were meat and vegetables and a lot of stews, of which most were curried; but the camp cook was a good bloke and did the best he could with what he had.

The first week back after our first operation, which lasted for eight weeks, all our vehicles and equipment had to be dismantled, cleaned and polished. Then, with eight weeks' back pay, everyone just went bananas the first weekend back, hiring cars and taxis to travel to the nearby small towns, to bars and the red-light districts. Not surprisingly, there were a lot of arrests by the MPs.

In between operations I did pretty well at football, making the regimental team. It was one of the best teams in Malaya, reaching the Far Eastern Land Forces Cup Final, losing to the Dragoon Guards 3-2 in Kuala Lumpur, and so missing out on a trip to Hong Kong, which was what the winners got. Apart from enjoying the football, it also meant I missed quite a few guard duties, which I didn't mind a bit.

The second operation I went on, I had progressed to a 5-ton, left-hand-drive, gun-towing GMC vehicle. This operation involved a six-hour journey. I was given a guard duty the night before we left and, no matter what I tried, there was no way they would take me off it. So, in the searing heat, the journey was a nightmare trying to stay awake. The gun sergeant who travelled in the cab with me had to talk, and sometimes shout, to keep me awake; but the rest of the operation was pretty much routine.

In between the second and third operations, the regimental boxing championships were held, and everyone had to take part. I knew very little about boxing, but my first opponent knew even less, and I won on a technical KO − which wasn't good, for my next opponent knew something about the game and I didn't survive the first round...and that was the end of my very short boxing career.

The third operation was eventful, in as much as our position was only about two miles from a rubber plantation, which had a swimming pool. Near the end of the operation, we were all kindly invited by the owner to use it. We went down, one wagon-load of men at a time, and everyone did the same — just stripped off and jumped in. Not knowing the depth — about fifteen feet — and being a non-swimmer, I just sank to the bottom like a stone. I didn't panic at first; I pushed myself up off the bottom with my feet, just managing to get my head above water but, to my horror, everyone thought it hilarious. After going down again and swallowing quite a bit of water, I was pulled out. I think that was the most frightening experience of my Army service.

My fourth operation turned out to be my last one. We were halfway through it when I went down with a tropical disease called scrub typhus. It was quite common; I know two others who had it before me. It was contracted by being pierced by the ends of the long reeds in the scrub, which had needle-like tips, infecting the bug. I came out in big red blotches and collapsed in camp, which this time was Johore Bahru in the south of Malaya. I was flown by helicopter to BMH (British Military Hospital), Singapore. I didn't know much about it; all I remember was waking up as the nurse washed and dried me, and then rolled me over on to a dry bed.

After two and a half weeks, I was well enough for the nightly bottle of stout, but I got an extra bottle each night, courtesy of my little Gurkha friend in the bed opposite. There's not a lot I can tell you about him, for he could not speak English. He was a very pleasant and happy character, and was given the name Joe, which he was very pleased with. He obviously could not converse with anyone, but would always nod or wave with a smile. He didn't drink or smoke, but would always take his ration of cigarettes or beer and then give it away — me being the beneficiary of the nightly bottle of stout for my last two weeks in hospital. I was in BMH (British Military Hospital), Singapore four weeks in all; then I flew up to the Cameron Highlands and stayed at a servicemen's convalescent hospital for two weeks. On my return to Tampin I was on light duties for four weeks, thus missing what was the last operation. I had two one-week leaves in Singapore; there were four of us together on both occasions. We didn't have much money, but it was great just to get away from the regimentation and the duties and just relax. We stopped at the Brit Club; that had good, clean beds and good food. Long lie-ins, walking around Singapore in the afternoons and then drinking in the UK Club in the evenings, which was for military personnel, and had good facilities and cheap drink.

The 48th Field Regiment's tour of duty was up by November, 1958, which meant that we would be home for Christmas. We sailed from Singapore in mid-November on the *Navasa*. Although it was only a troopship, it was just like a four-week holiday cruise for us, with plenty of leisure time and no duties except for a couple of night watches. The food was very good — much better than Army grub. Queues were forming an hour before opening time at the only bar we could use, virtually every night. I found the sleeping-quarters too hot and clammy to sleep and, like a lot of the others, I slept outside on deck until we reached Port Said.

From Singapore, we sailed through the Indian Ocean to Colombo. I was a bit under the weather, so I didn't bother about any shore leave. The next port of call was Aden, and I couldn't get shore leave because I was on watch. We then sailed through the Red Sea to the Suez Canal, then on to Gibraltar where, at last, I did get shore leave − I can't remember much about it, as I got the worse for wear from drink. We docked at Southampton on a mid-December frosty morning, and were given four weeks' leave with orders to report to the 18th Medium Regiment at Bulford Camp on Salisbury Plain on 10 January. My homecoming was very good; my brother met me at the station in Newcastle − he had got married while I was away − and when I got home they had a party ready, so I had an excellent Christmas and New Year.

I spent my last nine weeks at Bulford camp doing the usual driving duties and I played quite a bit of football, both for the regimental team and for the local Bulford civilian team. I was now counting the days down to my demob, which came on 19 March, 1958; at last I was a free man.

I would never have joined up as a regular soldier, and before my service regarded National Service as two years' loss of freedom, but it was a marvellous experience. I made some good friends and had some good times. I didn't enjoy the Army life in Malaya, but from what I saw of Singapore, I would have liked it there. I liked Malaya and Singapore, especially the climate. I liked the local people; I always got on well with them. I know it will be all different over there now, but I would like to go back on holiday and, with the world getting smaller with modern travel, who knows? − some day I might make it.

I found when I got home I talked very little about my experiences. I suppose this stemmed from my pre-service experience of returning servicemen, who would bore the pants off everyone with their tales. But I never felt the desire to talk much about it; like most National Servicemen, demob could not come quickly enough for me. Although I will always regard it as a worthwhile experience, it was good to get it behind me and get back to living a normal life in Civvy Street.

Roger Davies

Roger Davies served with the RAF in Malaya 1952-53. He is a clock restorer, married with two daughters and lives in Surrey.

In 1951 I had lodgings in Lewisham, just off the Bromley road and opposite Robinson's Marmalade factory. I went to the recruiting office down in Lewisham where I knew a chappie who belonged to our cycling club. Having registered me (for National Service), he said, 'You'll be called in about three months to do your time.' He also said, 'Actually, it's gone up to two years.' So, armed with that information, I was up on Blackheath one lovely afternoon, and there was this recruiting office. I thought to myself: Now, if I went in there, I might be able to do some of the things he said I ought to do. I went in and said, 'I want to sign on,' and they sort of started patting me and calling me 'Sir'. This stopped, of course, after I'd put my signature on the paper. And that's how I came to do three years. I did it for the money, for the additional leave and it seemed that if it was going up to two years, then to do one more year was going to be well worth it — to have doubles of everything.

I went for two months' training at Bridgnorth in Shropshire — at the Regulars Depot. At Bridgnorth, there was a corporal who didn't like me; and the more he walked beside me with his pace-measurer, the more I would lose step and get my arms tangled up. Anyway, I staggered through my basic training and I'd previously said I wanted to do wireless telegraphy, because I'd already started work with Cable and Wireless on the technical side. So I was posted to Yatesbury in Wiltshire and there I learnt about the intricacies of air radar. After this specialist training, I asked for a post at a Fighter Command base at Chivenor in Devon, just the other side of the Tor estuary from my parents' home. And yes — I got Aldergrove in Northern Ireland. While I was in Northern Ireland, there was the odd bit of trouble even then. We were advised to go out in civvies, and the odd hand grenade was thrown at the bus station, I remember. It was nothing, really; we used to hire a car, and four or five of us would go down over the border.

After a while, I was getting firmly dug in there, and I'd met a young lady at the NAAFI, so my feet were firmly under an Irish table in this village; I thought: I expect eventually I shall become an Air Ministry policeman like her brother-in-law, marry this girl and have lots and lots of children. But it wasn't to be; obviously, somebody heard about that and, suddenly, I was posted to Singapore and I had to say goodbye to this dear girl, and that was that.

We went all the way down to Southampton, where we boarded the troopship *Empire Fowey*. But, before we left Southampton Docks, we were in fact sinking. Some of the lavatories were below the waterline, which necessitated two large valves beside each loo – one red, one blue, with written instructions in English on the wall. You opened one valve and the lavatory basin emptied into a sort of chamber; then you shut that one, opened the other, and the drag of the ship removed the waste matter. Well, either they couldn't read, or they were colour-blind; we think it was the Catering Corps blokes that did it. However, both valves were opened and, of course, the sea was coming in. The troop deck was awash with bits of paper and horrible stuff – ghastly. Apparently the guy that actually did it, he did them both at once still sitting there, and this geyser of water, with all the pressure of a large ship behind it, fired him up against the deckhead.

We did eventually leave, and it took twenty days to get to Singapore. We stopped off, but didn't lay against the docks, at Aden. Some Army fellows came out, who were going to where the ship was going to wind up – Kobe in Japan. Probably, they were on their way to Korea; this was mid-'52. We stopped at Colombo and went ashore there, just for a few hours. That was my first touch of the East; I'd never been abroad before. There were lots of strange blokes dashing up to you at the harbour gate: 'This my sister you must meet,' and showing you a photo of Hedy Lamarr or somebody.

Anyway, I got out at Singapore and eventually wound up at Changhi with 48 Squadron, which was a general transport squadron. We were equipped with Valettas, which were a sort of military version of the Vickers Viking. To get to the front part of the cabin, you had to step over the main spar, two foot high and a foot wide – I suppose if you sawed through it, the wings would fall off.

Changhi was a large camp, nicely laid out with three-storey blocks. You could close wooden doors all round on very windy nights, but I don't think they were ever closed while I was there. The food was excellent – in contrast to on the ship, where the food was plentiful, particularly crossing the Indian Ocean, but not very good.

The men I was with: some were National Servicemen, some were short-term Regulars and, of course, some were long-term Regulars. They were very good. We were all, with the exception of a dental mechanic, on our floor of the billet in the same squadron — 48 Squadron. They were a very good bunch; it was fun.

We didn't have a lot to do with the local people. But we had a Chinese *sowsow*, as she was called. She used to come and spend a day every other day on our floor, repairing clothes, sewing on buttons and so on. She also had a small amount of fruit that she sold. And there was a general bearer for our floor, which we all paid 10 cents or something a week for, and he was a very good chap. He was a sort of batman, you see, for the ranks. He would do polishing; he would get some bit of your civilian clothes ironed for you, if you were going out that night.

I've been out to Malaya last year — forty years later — and it's all changed; the narrow, winding road from Changhi to Singapore has gone, and it's straight roads now and they're wide. And the buses are much improved. Leisure was really the cinema and eating, and the usual boozy evenings. On Changhi Camp there were two NAAFIs and there was also the Malcolm Club, which is a club sponsored by the Air Force, but it will cater for any of the fighting services. Like another NAAFI. They always used to keep their beer cooler at the Malcolm Club than the NAAFI's. And it was Anchor or Tiger beer. I was delighted that this last time being out there, Tiger beer could still be obtained.

Regarding my duties: well, I was trained as an air radar mechanic, but the air radar I'd been trained on we didn't possess out there, so I had to sub-learn some again. We had touched on a radar called LORAN; out there, it was called SHORAN, because there weren't so many beacons to get fixes from. (L was for long and SH was for short.) In a way, I became misemployed; being a small squadron, to keep the aircraft flying, we all used to muck in. If there was a whole plug change to be done on an aircraft, then I would help the engine mechanic, even if it was only to pass him a clean, fresh plug as he took one out. I was based at Changhi from mid-'52 to June '53.

We did some flights up country, of course. We did them in Valettas. We had one equipped with loudhailers, I suppose you'd call them — huge loudspeakers slung under the wings, with lots of amplifiers. We had two charming ladies; one was Chinese and one was Eurasian. We used to go up, and we'd have grid references and do a bit of the jungle, these ladies broadcasting suggestions to the terrorists that they ought to surrender, and we would drop them some passes, which they could take to any Army unit or police station and they would be treated well; they wouldn't be shot. When all the broadcasting had been done, then we used to go back over the pitch again, slinging out these leaflets, which said virtually what we had broadcast to them.

On one occasion, we were making a clearing in the jungle. We went up from Changhi to near Ipoh in a helicopter belonging to a neighbouring squadron. We were making this clearing to be used as an airstrip, when there were several shots. I was not armed, and I have to admit that I dived down as flat as I could and wet my shorts. I realized that something was making a noise, which was not the sort of noise we should have. We were there with some of the Green Howards, and they in fact eventually − being soldiers and trained and armed − located these two chaps and got them − killed them. There was no question of calling them down from the tree. I didn't go and see the bodies. That was my one experience of being shot at in anger; it was the only thing that happened to me like that, and I don't like warfare. I'm not a pacifist; I don't mean that. But I wish this country was greater and hadn't given way on everything. But we're only on this earth in this form once, and I don't wish to depart before I absolutely have to. I never saw a live enemy; I did see some photographs of them from a chappie, a friend of mine, who had been stationed in Kuala Lumpur, and he'd been out somewhere and had seen some being brought in. I gather, in the main, they lived by threatening villagers, and it wasn't always very successful.

From the Valettas we also dropped parachutists − Army paratroops. They had a large, old hangar which, I think, had been built by the Japanese. The runway went one way; it was made of concrete, and there was a perforated metal strip (runway) that ran across it, and at one end of that there was a huge, wooden hangar, and there they learnt how to drop. They would use our planes to test out methods of dropping into high timber, and getting out of it without actually being left there hanging by their parachutes. If you could extract yourself from the parachute, you could climb down through the branches, and then you came to perhaps eighty foot of smooth trunk; then they had rope ladders of various sorts. We tried out other Army; we took them, in fact, to Japan...however was it pronounced? That was it: Irikuni. That was an overnight thing; we took them up to try out spades of a particular type. The sand of Irikuni Beach was very fine and dry to quite a depth, and they tried out these spades to see if foxholes could be dug in that sort of terrain should it ever be necessary.

I also had a buckshee trip to the Philippines, to an American base: Clark Field. One of our Valettas coming back from Hong Kong had to put in there with engine trouble and it was diagnosed as a plug change; and I went up with an engine mechanic called Les Boyer, and he lived in Romford. I went up with him, with the tools and plugs, and we did a plug change. The amusing bit of that was, I was handing him up plugs and he was taking them out. There were Americans everywhere, with sort of long-peaked caps and little gold bars, and stripes the wrong way up on their overalls. There were hundreds and millions of them, and one came over and he said,'You're British boys, and you're the plug king?'

Les looked down at him, and said: 'No, I'm an engine mechanic.'

'Yeah yeah yeah, I know; but you just do the plugs?'

'No, I can do any part of the engine.'

He said, 'You can do any part of the engine and you've only got that pissy little two-bladed propellor (leading aircraftmen's insignia) on your sleeve? I'm a Zwecki nozzle king and I'm a lootenant.' It virtually meant he was allowed to put the nozzle into the hole in the wing or the body of an aircraft and refuel it.

I also went to Kai Tak (Hong Kong) several times on buckshee flights. Transport Command were quite good; something would have to go to GHQ, perhaps, and it would go in a Valetta. Anyone who could bum a lift with the crew would go along. The crews all knew their own ground staff, so you could say, 'Look, the little bird in the bakery in Kowloon on the till; if you're going up Friday and coming back Sunday, I'd like to see her,' and this could be arranged. I gather that from some of the flights I did – although they were unofficial flights – because I flew over French Indo-China (which is now Vietnam), I could get the United Nations Medal and the Korea Medal. But I never put in for it, so to speak. I also went to North Borneo…all sorts of places.

Once we were going up country in a Valetta, and I had to go to the Elsan, and I said to a chap – I think he was called Desmond Webb – I said, 'I'm going for a pee.' I went in (to the Elsan) and I closed the door. I had no sooner closed the door, when my feet left the ground and I thought: We've hit an air pocket; but I'm thinking about it as I banged about in this small, confined space with the Elsan, which tipped over, that in fact things had been done deliberately. They'd throttled back, causing the aircraft to dip right down. I don't know if it was an initiation rite, because I don't know of anybody else it happened to. Then things levelled off, and I came out of this small cupboard dripping with urine and Elsan fluid – burning with Elsan fluid, although luckily none went in my eyes; but I was stinking. We had some poles with hooks, which we used to pull in the arresting-straps if we'd done a para pack drop; there was Desmond Webb with one of these poles, and he said, 'You bastard Davies, stay down there!' So I had to sit on the floor in misery in my own pool of muck until we got back. Having a hot bath was a thing you were supposed to do legally out there once a fortnight, but I had three or four hot baths in the space of an hour, to try and get the smell out of me. It was bloody awful! A lot of people have had laughs out of me, but I think the important thing in life is to try and laugh with them.

We used to drop stuff to the Army on agreed drops. They were large packs. They were like enormous bags; about four foot long and about eighteen inches in diameter. The parachute was suspended from one end; it was all packed in. They were all lined up at the door and, when we were ticked off to push them out, you pushed them out. They were on a strap which was fixed to the arresting-wire, so they went back under the tail and pulled their own line. I think I only went on one trip doing that, and we had six or eight of these things to drop. It was a bit risky; you mustn't fall out. There were safety straps for you to wear, but I don't think anybody did. You sort of got used to feeling which way the aircraft was going to bank, and getting away from the door in time.

When I came to the end of my service in Malaya, I was going to come home by sea but, in fact, I came home by air in a Hastings, which was coming down from Kai Tak in Hong Kong. It called on us; I got on it and we went from there to Nicobar, which is in the Indian Ocean, a tiny island where there was an RAF unit commanded by a flight lieutenant. We went from there to Colombo; to Karachi; then on to Habbanieh in Iraq. Then from there to Fayed in the Canal Zone. I was under canvas there for over a week, while they repaired the aircraft, which had broken down. It wasn't successful because, when we took off, we had to turn back. So they sent an Avro York belonging to Scottish Airways, and this took us to Luqua in Malta. Finally, we landed at Stansted, and eventually went out to Inkerman Barracks at Woking, which was an Army place. Then I went home to Devon.

Being back was very different. In fact, I wasn't all that pleased to be back because the one thing, you see, that was in my mind was that I'm going to have to find a job. I was determined, by then, that I wasn't going back to Cable & Wireless in London, where the prospects weren't very good. I mean – I'd changed a lot from the age of eighteen to twenty-one.

But I did enjoy my service. I did a lot of things that I'd never have had the chance of doing before. There were curses, of course, but on balance it was good; it was a terrific change from living in digs in London.

Ian Edwards

Ian Edwards served with the South Wales Borderers in Malaya in 1956-57. He now manages his family business in Blackwood, Gwent.

It was January, 1956, when I went to Malaya. We flew from...I think it was probably Gatwick; we travelled as a draft from South Wales. It was the only occasion I travelled on the railway from Brecon to Newport, and at one point I was very near home and didn't realize how near I was − it was only about three miles away, and there we were, travelling 8,000 miles or whatever it was to Malaya. I can remember when we got to London; we were then put up in what turned out to be a sort of disused underground station, and we went many miles, it seemed, under ground. The next morning we were taken − maybe by bus, − to Gatwick and we flew to Malaya. It wasn't a jet aircraft because I can remember later, when we were in Singapore, seeing a VC10 flying over. It was a prop, a Viscount, I think. It took three days − it was three days by aeroplane and three weeks by boat and, of course, we would like to have taken three weeks by boat to get out there and three days to come home but, in fact, we did it in complete reverse. They treated us very well; it was my first experience of flying any great distance, and it took three days' solid travelling to get there. I know one night we stayed at Karachi; stayed at a very nice hotel there. I can't remember the other two places we stopped at overnight; anyway, the last point we touched down was Bangkok and then on to Singapore.

When we first got there, we'd travelled out in civilian clothes, and we'd obviously taken our jungle greens with us. We must have got into that fairly quickly, because I do remember we were at a transit camp called Nee Soon and, before they shipped us up country, we had to prepare an area in this camp for the battalion that was coming in. We were involved in erecting tents and carrying beds and all sorts of things, and we were instructed not to strip off at all because of the fierce heat − we had to wear jackets all day long − and that we had all to try and take it easy; we mustn't perspire too much! But of course in the Army they soon forget things like that; they worked us into the ground, I think, within a couple of days.

47

From there we were shipped up country to a place called Kluang. We went by train. From now on we were on active service and, of course, everywhere we went we carried a rifle, the No 4 rifle. In fact, although it was dying down slightly − the actual terrorist activity − they were still very much in evidence, and the security was very tight everywhere. The train actually had an armoured car on the front of it; which went up in front of the steam engine as it was − to give some sort of protection, I suppose. We did six weeks' jungle training at this camp, before we were shipped out to the various companies within the South Wales Borderers. The normal pattern for the day was − once you had acclimatized − from the feet upwards: you would be wearing your boots with socks rolled down, then you would wear shorts, which invariably were sort of black or navy, with a webbing belt and your beret. That was it. Then if you were on an official duty, or you were going maybe into the jungle, you had to wear long trousers, a jacket if you were on guard duty − much the same. But for work that went on around the camp, everyday work and in the training, that was what we wore. We wore long jungle-boots with the lace-ups when we went on operations.

In the basic training − as I say, it was over six weeks − in that period they started off by giving you a twenty-four-hour operation; and then I think it was a three-day op; and then you finished with a five-day. So, I suppose, out of your six weeks you had nine days when you were actually in the jungle, when you were actually on operations. We carried all our food and ammunition and supplies on our backs and, obviously, it depended as to what sort of member you were in the platoon whether you carried something like a rifle or a Bren gun. We were given compo rations; it was the time when they were experimenting with a thing − it was a tin of soup and you pulled the gadget underneath and it was a tin of self-heating soup. Otherwise, we simply used to cook with these little blocks we set light to.

Then they decided − the powers that be decided − that you were being shipped out to the various companies in the battalion. Now I was attached to B Company the whole time I was in Malaya, which was fifteen months. We started at a place called Yong Peng which, at the height of the emergency had in fact − before the South Wales Borderers got there − been shot up, that particular camp, by the bandits, the Communists; they'd sort of marched in one day and sprayed the NAAFI, I think, and killed so many British soldiers, actually in that particular camp. I remember arriving there on a Saturday afternoon, and my first greeting was from a sergeant major who I didn't particularly like − I don't think anybody did, really. I'd gone away to school, and he looked at me and he looked at my record, and he said, 'Oh yes, you're Edwards, are you?' I said, 'Yes Sir,' and he said, 'We have another educated idiot amongst us.' He was one of those types of fellows, and from the first day to the very last day that I was in his Company, he wasn't a particularly nice kind of man.

We simply settled down into the duties. When you actually joined the company you've got to realize that they live in various permanent or semi-permanent sites, which may be in jungle clearings, coconut groves — that type of thing. We were in tents; but it varied, actually. When we did the basic training, we were in a more permanent hut which was constructed out of bamboo, I suppose. But when I went out, we were in tents, then, with eight or ten — something like that — to a bell tent and, because of the heat, the sides were rolled down and we had some sort of construction of a fence, with a large monsoon ditch around the tent. The fellows I was with were very good; there was quite a mixture, obviously, although I would say they were all Welsh and mainly from the valleys; there may have been one or two from North Wales. I felt very much at home with them. They seemed to be from this area in the main.

We were fairly fortunate with our platoon sergeant; these people varied considerably, but the chap we had, a fellow called Holland, he was a very nice type of fellow. I got on well with him, exceptionally well. Our platoon commanders were National Servicemen and they were very young. That was the thing about those fellows; they were second lieutenants and they were really very raw, there's no doubt about that. One really felt, I suppose, that when you went out on a patrol that the sergeant was with you, the platoon sergeant, and you had more confidence in him than you had in your platoon commander. I suppose as time went on and they really got more used to it and experienced, then one had more confidence in them. They changed around quite a bit, because obviously if they were National Servicemen or short-term commission people, they would be temporary. The first one we had, he was actually, I think, sent back home after six months, and we had a new fellow came along then. They swapped and changed around a lot. The company commander of B Company, when I was there, was somebody called Major Alun Gwynne Jones, who is now known as Lord Chalfont. He was the company commander, as I say; a very nice type of fellow. I got on very well with him. He was a very good soldier.

I didn't do too many operations in actual fact. I was designated a job when I got to the company, and I ended up in charge of the ration stores. But, having said that, you were totally committed so that if one of the three platoons was short of a man going out, then you simply joined the platoon going out on operations. Plus the fact, of course, that if the Company was out on operations, either you had the situation that maybe the company itself was out, or maybe it was joining the rest of the battalion who were out; it depended on the size of the operation. But then, if you were one of the people left in, you could find yourself on a twenty-four-hour guard; you'd be twenty-four hours on, twenty-four hours off and that sort of thing. In the camps, they were very security-conscious, obviously, and the people who were left had quite a hard time, because they were the ones who were left with the responsibility. From the time that I first joined the battalion, I went out to an operation fairly quickly. It absolutely scared me to death, being my first time. The operations started through various ways; usually they picked up information of some sort or another — either bandits had been spotted, or they had various ways and means of intelligence of finding these things out. I do remember there were certain sorts of ploys that went on whereby we would be put into a position and then, shall we say, it may be five miles ahead of us, that position would be shelled, hoping to drive the bandits into our positions, flushing them out. I can remember the first occasion, having joined the battalion; within a week we were out on one of these operations, and we actually went out in the night; and it frightened me to death, because we were in the ambush, or walking over ambush positions and, as we were actually walking in, they were actually — the mortar platoon behind — were already sending in the mortar bombs. And you could hear these things whistling over our heads and going however far they were into the darkness.

A lot of these operations came to nil, but they obviously served a purpose. In actual fact, that reminds me of the very first time when we were doing our jungle training and out on the twenty-four-hours op. We were walking through a coconut grove, and we didn't know it but we disturbed some bandits in there because, when we got back to our trucks later in the afternoon, expecting to be ferried back to the camp, there was an almighty flap on and, as completely new boys, we suddenly found we were in ambush positions again, having actually been responsible for flushing out these bandits — and we didn't even know it at the time. That sort of thing happened fairly often, that one found oneself in ambush positions....There were obviously more unpleasant things that I wasn't involved in. If they knew through information received that there may have been a camp — and you've got to realize that some of these bandit camps were miles and miles in the jungle — and they'd been bombed by air or mortared, or whatever, certain people would have to go in and try and find if there was anybody left there. I saw one or two of the enemy who had been captured, but I never saw any dead ones — only photographs. The prisoners were sent back to HQ, not within the company; they went back to battalion headquarters, I imagine, where the Intelligence people or, maybe, even the Malayan police — I'm not quite sure who — would have interviewed these people.

The politics didn't really come into it. We'd been told when we did our basic training in Brecon, right through to the time we did our jungle training, you knew what you were going to be about. It came home to you particularly

50

if you were on an operation and you were confronted with an enemy. As I say, I can remember the first occasion when we were in this ambush position, and I thought: If somebody suddenly crosses the road in front of me, and I'm confronting the bad guy, what do I do? I suppose I pull the trigger on him. I would have done it, if it had been necessary. There were people in the battalion when we were out there who had had that situation, because the battalion was there fifteen months, and I'm certain that within that time they killed forty-odd bandits. I don't think the battalion lost many men; not to my knowledge. I certainly don't remember anybody being shot at all. As I say, the emergency was dying down a little bit. One of the main policies that they had was trying to starve these people out. They were from these little villages, the *kampongs* as they call them, and they either had friends or relatives in these places. In the early days, they simply went in and they took whatever food they wanted and went back to their jungle places in hiding. Eventually all of these villages − each village was surrounded by a fence with very large gates, probably at either end of the village − and these people were in a curfew situation, whereby they weren't allowed out of the village, probably from six o'clock in the evening until six o'clock in the morning. They were all rationed; they were all allowed a certain amount of rice, being the staple diet. We used to, on occasion, surround a village; we would be there at first light and, when the gates opened up, we would be in the village then, and every house had to be searched. I didn't feel terribly happy about that, to be perfectly honest; the fact that you found a container full of rice, and you looked around and you saw a family with three or four children or whatever. I don't think it was our function actually to measure out the rice; if we found it, then we had to call the police in, who measured it out, and if they found they had more than their ration, then they simply confiscated what they weren't entitled to. No, I wasn't happy over that, I must say.

We also had to do these escort duties, and we'd have an armoured car in the front and then so many trucks, and these fellows would be dropped miles from whatever to walk to their position. I can remember; we were coming along, the edge of a swamp it was, and one of the trucks broke down, and I can remember thinking: What a perfect set-up now for the bandits, if they're there; they could ambush us. As a corporal, I was in charge of the convoy, and I was shipping these fellows off to guard positions and whatnot. Fortunately, the chap got the truck started fairly quickly and we were away; but I remember being pretty scared that time.

There were all kinds of horrible things which went on. There was a chap who lives in Maesycwmmer; I see him now, quite a lot. There was a bombing raid going on on a particular bandit camp, and they had the job of going in afterwards and finding the remains − that's all that was left. They had to get down under the water in the swamp and feel, and he felt an arm or a leg. I've got a photograph, actually, which is pretty weird, of just the head of a bandit. Because they found they were so far into the jungle that it was too far to carry the body out for identification, they just chopped the head off. Now, whether that was legal or illegal, I don't know; but then, again, it varied. This was a particular captain there; he was a pretty hard nut, this bloke – he sort of had his own rules to a degree, this particular guy.

A platoon had gone out on an operation, and the Company Commander had gone out with them, with the Sergeant Major, and they had actually killed a couple of bandits. And the Company Sergeant, who was a pretty hard guy...one of the bandits was wounded and he wanted water, and he wouldn't give him any at all. But the Company Commander came in and said, 'You must give him a beaker of water'; and the Sergeant Major had to turn round and give the shot man a cup of water.

The camps we were in were invariably near a Malayan village. They had occasional people who came in to work, to clean up; you can imagine sanitation was pretty primitive in these places, and these people used to come and clean out the toilets and dispose of it in whatever way they could. But apart from that, I'm not really aware of us actually coming into contact with the local people, other than occasionally; if you were on an operation, and you were in a rubber plantation, you'd see the rubber-tappers there.

We didn't get an awful lot of time off and, again, it depended on where you were situated; but we did have the opportunity to go into certain villages or small towns, but we had to go under escort. Wherever we travelled, because we were on active service we had to carry our rifles. There was always a scout car in the front and a scout car behind, guarding the three or four lorries we were in. When we got to the town, we had to hand our rifles in at the local armoury; and there were only bars there – we'd have to wander round the bars, and we'd be picked up again at ten or half-past ten at night and taken back to our place.

I don't think there was ever a question of actually being bored; there was a definite excitement about it all the time. There was something happening all the time; even if you weren't involved yourself, the company was constantly involved in operations, whether it be training or a proper operation – going out on escort duties or being dropped into jungle clearings and this sort of thing. We never had occasion to be bored, and we moved around quite a good bit, in actual fact. I can think of at least three camps we were in, in the fifteen months. Then, fairly regularly in Singapore, they would have the student riots; and I can remember we were shipped down to Singapore to help with the riots. It was quite hairy, in actual fact, because we had to do a fairly quick training schedule; I mean, there is a particular sort of box formation that is taken up, if I remember rightly. Then again, we were involved at checkpoints, and we were actually involved in being rushed around various parts of Singapore where there were problems, and moving these people on, or dispersing them. We did searches; I did in fact take a large sheath knife off a student on one occasion.

The one thing I did remember about that time was that we were coming off duty at five o'clock one morning and being taken back to the barracks in Singapore, and the headlines on the banners for the paper were: BRITAIN INVADES SUEZ; and, of course, at that time I probably had less than six months to do, and my immediate reaction was: How much longer have I got to be here? Because we thought we might have to be there for another twelve months or two years. As it happened, that didn't occur.

At the time, probably given the choice of staying home or going to Malaya, I would have stayed at home. Having done it, I thought it was a marvellous experience and, from the point of view that we travelled that part of the Far East fairly extensively and you did it at the government's expense, looking back on it now, it was a marvellous experience. And, as life is, you tend not to think of the bad times; you tend to think of the good times: it was a marvellous, marvellous experience. It's easy to say now; it's going back a very long time ago when you were young and tough, but it was character-forming, and it did teach you to take orders and accept responsibility.

When I came back, I talked about it very extensively both with my family and friends, and people were fascinated. They wanted to know what you'd done, what you'd been involved in while you were out. I remember somebody telling me some years later what a good Army it was at that time. When you think we were eighteen-year-old fellows who, after three months' basic training, turned out to be the soldiers that they were.

Having gone in to do your National Service, you were initially in with a group of people that you did your training with; and then, what was fascinating was what happened to those people. Although you all did your two years, what you actually did, and your commitment in those two years, varied considerably; there were often positions left as permanent postings back in Brecon, and I can think of one fellow who lives locally, and I see him from time to time − and he was left behind as the Company postman in Brecon − and we went out to Malaya, and we considered that to be fairly tough, compared to him having a very cushy posting.

I've not been back to Malaya since; I would like to; it would be quite fascinating to go and see some of the places we went, but I would doubt now that they're still there, some of the sites. I often think I'd like to go back.

Rex Flowers

Rex Flowers served with the Lincolnshire Regiment in Malaya, 1955-56. He is a retired farmer, married and lives in Cowbit, Lincolnshire, where he was born.

In common with most men of my generation, I didn't want to be a soldier. World War II was too recent a memory and, like previous generations of my family in my home village of Cowbit, I wanted to be a farmer. War, for a lad of my age — I was born in 1935 — was a nasty memory, talked about by the older lads in the village who had come home after the defeat of Germany and Japan.

I was called up for National Service in 1955. I joined the Lincolnshire Regiment, and was sent to Malaya after an all too brief training period. Of that I have always been highly critical; conscripts were taught a few of the skills of classic war on the European plains, and it did little to teach us the guerrilla skills which would keep us alive and fighting against a largely unseen enemy in the jungle.

I did a brief period of jungle training in a supposedly safe area shortly after my arrival; then began the tedious business of patrols and guard duty in what seemed to me to be some of the roughest, hottest, most humid country in the world.

Few soldiers in this situation saw any action, but our unit had been trained by an ex-SAS man, and that was probably why we got picked for jobs which looked likely to end with some shooting. On two occasions we were in the thick of it, and I will tell you about both of them.

The first action came while I was a corporal, stationed at Simpang Pertang, and it happened like this: a Tamil Communist surrendered to the police, and he provided information on which our platoon was to act. To perform the planned operation, Lieutenant Surtees, our leader, picked a team of nineteen men from our 12 Platoon, plus a section from 10 Platoon. We were told to draw rations for a week; then report for briefing.

At the briefing, Lieutenant Surtees told us that the surrendered Communist was an important man and that his mates had been treating him

54

rather roughly. As a result, he had agreed to take us to look for his old comrades, one of whom was a man called Chi Ying, a State Commander member. The key to this operation would be speed, as we had to find the Communists before they packed up camp and moved to another location. At the time, they were believed to be four or five miles deep in the jungle in some very mountainous country. In addition to the Tamil, we were to take a Chinese translator with us, because the surrendered Communist didn't speak any English. He did speak some Malay, and for that reason one of the Iban trackers joined the party, too. We were all driven to the next village to the north, from which we began the operation.

Now, we could never be sure whether a surrendered Communist was honest or not; our man could have been telling the truth, or the whole thing could have been a set-up and, somewhere along our route, there could be a reception party waiting for us. At the time, all we knew was that we were a good fighting team, and that we would have to accept whatever the operation held in store for us.

To begin with, the country was very open, without trees or shade, and for that reason it was very hot. I was pleased when we got to the borders of the jungle because, once inside, the temperature dropped several degrees and we got some shade. But soon we began to climb – gently at first, but soon steeper by the yard – and this difficult country seemed to go on for ever.

Naturally, our Bren-gunners tired first, so we began to pass the heavy weapons from man to man. Remember that we all had our personal weapons – mine was a semi-automatic shotgun – plus full packs and equipment, so soon we were all wet through with sweat. Not a word was spoken but we were dreadfully tired, so it was a relief to be ordered to rest for a few minutes. It was great to rest the weight of the pack, take a mouthful of water and wipe the sweat from your eyes. Then we carried on again, and was I pleased to see the top of that hill! After that, things got easier, although the country was still mountainous, but nothing we came across was quite as bad as that first hill.

By this time it was quite late in the afternoon, so Lieutenant Surtees decided we should *basha*-up and form a base camp for the operation. Here we would leave our food and carry on with just weapons and water-bottles. We set off after the quickest of meals – a cup of tea and a bar of chocolate – leaving the camp in the charge of the men from 10 Platoon and their own NCO. Our Tamil told Lieutenant Surtees that there was just a mile to go.

As we moved off, our section under Corporal Clowes led and, in anticipation of needing some firepower, we kept our Bren-gunner, Sandy Powell, close to the front. There was great excitement when we found some fresh tracks, but we were so tired that all we could do was smile.

We advanced with great caution, travelling slowly, with our eyes about us in the fading light. It would soon be dark. Then we heard the sound of a waterfall and, when we descended a small hill, we found ourselves on the bank of a swiftly flowing stream. The water was as clear as crystal, so we had a quick drink before crossing to the opposite bank.

By this time we were very close to the enemy position, but night was falling so quickly that there would be insufficient time to press home the attack. The only thing to do was to spend the night where we were, standing up. There would be no ferns to sleep on because we couldn't risk any chopping noises, although our Iban did manage to cut himself a few leaves with a knife.

Few men slept very much. I know I didn't, and the stink of my clothes was terrible. I spent most of the night thinking of my folks back home, although I did have a break when I had to do an hour's guard duty. Even this was a bit of a formality, with pretty well everyone awake anyway.

At first light a few men crept back to the stream to get water. Then we checked and loaded our weapons – a full magazine and one in the breech – took another swallow of that lovely cool water, and we were ready to go. We began by climbing a little higher, on to the top of the hill, and we knew we were getting very close indeed. We could see where the Communists had been digging for roots, while the waterfall couldn't have been very far away because the sound of it was so clear.

Lieutenant Surtees went forward with the interpreter and the surrendered Communist and, when he returned a few minutes later, he told us we would have to move fast. The Communists were packing up camp and would soon be moving out, so the plan of attack would have to be put into operation quickly. One section, under Corporal Fletcher, was sent to circle the camp to the north while the other section, which included me, went to the south so that we could attack the camp simultaneously from two sides.

I remember our section moving forward slowly in single file. There were no smiles now; it was for real. Kill or be killed. We didn't know what weapons we were facing and, when I looked down at my gun, I noticed that my knuckles were white. There was not a lot of cover on the hillside, and suddenly the enemy was in full view. That last forty or fifty yards seemed to take for ever as we crept from tree to tree. Twenty yards away and we paused for everyone to catch up, praying that nobody would tread on a twig and give the game away. Then Lieutenant Surtees calmly said, 'Fire.' The whole line of us opened up together. Two of the Communists never had a chance. Their bodies were blown back two or three yards by the power of our fire, and they fell. Then the order came to charge, so we ran down the hill into the Communist camp, ready to fire as we ran. I remember shouting to our men to be careful where they shot, because we had another party closing from the other side.

When we got to the centre of the camp it was empty, so a follow-up party was organized from one of the other sections. Private Finney was in this section, and it wasn't long before we heard his Owen gun in action, so we set off to investigate. It looked as if the Communists in this area would have to elect a new State Commander, because Finney had just killed the current one. He caught him with a carbine in one hand and a grenade in the other, so he let him have the whole magazine from the Owen.

Two other Communists were so badly injured from our first attack that they were soon forced to surrender. We felt a little chuffed with ourselves after the day's events; certainly we had outnumbered the Communists, but we had beaten them on their own territory without loss. In fact, we didn't have as much as a single scratch between us. Soon the men were laughing, and enjoying being able to talk out loud.

Our relaxation couldn't last long, and soon four of us were sent down the hill to collect the body of the man Finney had shot. It seemed strange to me that he was so full of holes, yet he had managed to die with a smile on his face. Next job was to fully check out the captured positions, and I remember one of the lads shouting out with laughter that the buggers actually carried french letters with them. Then we found out from one of the surrendered men that there had been some women living in the camp; all the comforts of home for the troops, so to speak!

We didn't know then, but one of the CTs who was to surrender a few days later was a woman. She had been shot through the arm and the wound had started to go gangrenous, so she was rushed back for surgery. Her friend had been shot through the leg; I don't know what happened to him, but the woman was later to join us and help us find some of her old mates. So much for Communist principles; it seemed that they would do anything for money, including shopping their old comrades.

What followed was one of my most horrible, disgusting experiences of the whole campaign. For me it soured the success of the operation, but for one of our lads it was worse. It left him in such a bad mental state that, for weeks afterwards, he used to cry out in his sleep. This is how it happened:

We had to take the enemy dead back for identification, so first we cut stout poles to which the bodies were lashed with vines. The bodies were wrapped in ponchos, which was just as well, because what were once yellow-skinned men were by now black with flies. The carrying was heavy-going and we progressed slowly. Sometimes a man would trip and a body would be dropped. We couldn't make base camp that night, and when we stopped to make temporary camp at dusk, we were careful to place the bodies some way away and down wind. That night we dined on a little chocolate provided by the 10 Platoon men before sleeping on the ground once again and, in the morning, we felt a little better.

The bodies, however, were in a worse condition than on the day before.

When I was sixteen and on the farm back home, I could carry an 18-stone sack of corn on my back, but this body-carrying was ten times worse. I was in the lead with the first body, and behind me I could hear groups of men stumbling and cursing. Then, thank God, we were met by a group from 11 and 12 Platoons, who took over the carrying duties from us. They were under the command of another lieutenant, a man whose name I was to remember for a long time. Unexpectedly early, his platoon arrived at the base camp. As Private Houchin walked past me, I noticed he was carrying a large, round object, wrapped in a poncho, on his back. He usually had a ready smile, but this time he looked a bit grim and, when I asked him what he was carrying, he just said, 'A head.' I couldn't believe it, so he explained.

It seems that the bodies were proving so difficult to carry that the lieutenant had ordered the Ibans to chop the heads off, so that just the heads could be brought out of the jungle as evidence. The Ibans, although their ancestors were Borneo head-hunters, had refused this grisly task, so the lieutenant had ordered some of his own men to do it. Poor Private Houchin seemed full up with emotion, so I went over to have a word with Lieutenant Surtees.

When I got near to Surtees, I saw that the other lieutenant was with him, and they seemed to be discussing the very issue I had come to talk about; so I hung around within earshot. I didn't hear all that was said, but I heard Surtees tell him that such actions would give the men nervous breakdowns. As far as Houchin was concerned he was right, for he was the man who was to cry out in his sleep.

Much later in my service, while based at Taiping, I saw action again, and once more it was due to information provided by a renegade Communist. One night a Communist informer told the local police that a band of CT were coming out of the jungle to make contact with the local people. The problem was he didn't know exactly where, but it would be in one of two places. Dan and I were told to report to the CO, and he put us on the operation.

The plan was for Lieutenant Earl of 10 Platoon, with a full corporal and two men, to ambush one position while Dan and I, plus Sandy Powell and Bob Hind, would take the other. For the first time that I could remember, Dan elected to carry a Bren, and for Sandy a second Bren was the natural choice. Bob took an FN rifle, and I got myself an automatic shotgun. Transport was due to leave early in the morning, so that we could be in position before first light.

That night we had a couple of beers in the NAAFI and went to bed early. The guard woke us early with a cup of tea; then we loaded our kit on to the lorry. Nobody spoke, probably because we hadn't quite woken up, but this was the last chance to check weapons before we started out.

After about twenty minutes we got off the lorry and set off to do the last half mile on foot. We pressed on through wet grass, left Lieutenant Earl's party at their ambush point, then pressed on to ours, which was about a quarter of a mile away. The Lieutenant came with us to ensure that we were in the right position, then returned to his men. Our position was above a tin mine, about forty yards from it on the north side and hidden in the wet grass. We knew that we would be dry as soon as the sun rose. We just sat there, talking quietly and, as it became light, we saw an RAF aircraft near the horizon dropping supplies to another unit deep in the jungle, and I began to get the impression that this was going to be just another failed ambush.

After a while, I felt a great need to go for a shit, so I left the men and went up the hill. While I was squatting down, I noticed a great activity at the tin mine. There were a lot of people there and some had long hair, a sure sign that they had been in the jungle for a long time. So, when I had finished the job, I went back down the hill to Dan and the men, and we continued the surveillance through binoculars. Dan confirmed my suspicions, so I left him and Sandy with their Brens to give us cover, while Bob and I set off around the hill to confront them on the ground. Before we left, I told the two Bren-gunners to open up if they heard any gunfire on our side of the hill. Bob cocked the FN, and we were off.

We headed north, away from the tin mine, and moved as fast as we could without showing ourselves. Then we crossed over the top of the hill and started to run down the other side. Bob was about six yards behind me, still in the long grass and, at this point, the jungle edge was about forty yards away.

Then it happened! Shots whistled past me; in fact I heard the bullets before I heard the bangs. I remember shouting, 'Fucking hell!' and falling to the ground, and within a second Bob was with me, asking if I was all right. I said I fucking wasn't, so he asked me if I was hit. I wasn't, but he damn soon would be if he didn't hit the ground. Then the Brens opened up over the sides of the hill. It was a hell of a racket but, in those circumstances, the most lovely noise I had ever heard. I looked up and saw a CT running for the jungle, so I fired at him five times. He hit the ground, then got up and started to run again, so Bob emptied a magazine at him. By this time I was re-loading the shotgun; I just couldn't cram the cartridges in fast enough. Bob and I were now standing, and the CT started to run again. I treated him to another shower of lead. I had never seen a dead man run before, and it was a bit unnerving. By now Bob and I were down to our last rounds of ammunition, so I told him to keep a couple for our own defence, because we did not know what was going on around the other side of the hill, and the fight could be far from over yet.

As there was no more activity on our side, I told Bob that we should go back up the hill and find out what had happened to our two mates. So we retreated back, moving one at a time and covering each other until our two mates came into view. Once we had established that they were unhurt, Bob asked me if he could smoke a cigarette. 'Sure,' I said, 'and give me one.' As we lit up, I remember saying to him, 'This game's for real — that bugger was trying to put holes in me that Nature never intended. It made me mad, which is why I tried to make a sieve out of him, but still he kept running.' I still couldn't understand why he hadn't fallen for so long, but he had dropped dead at the jungle edge. In fact, the operation had been a great success, with two CT killed and ten captured.

I finished my service as Orderly Sergeant at Taiping and, when the time finally came for me to go back home, I joined a party on a bus in the camp. As soon as I got on, Colour Sergeant Roberts came running out, called me off the bus, shook me by the hand and thanked me for what I had done for the Company. As the bus drove out of the barracks I saw our Company Board, and remember wondering how many more stars it would bear before this wretched war was over. All companies kept a board, bearing a star for each Communist killed. A day or two later we were on the train to Singapore, and it was then we were told that we would be flown back to the UK.

Before I left the Company, I went to find our two Ibans. I found them sitting in the Iban tent, smoking and making a fishing-net, and they were as pleased to see me as I was to see them. They were truly good friends. I had just enough money left to buy them a beer, so we went down to Chinatown, had a last look at the dancing-girls, then came back to barracks with no money left. Next day I flew home — 10,000 miles without a penny in my pocket.

On the first part of this journey we flew northwards over Malaya, and as I looked out of the window the memories came flooding back. As we crossed Johore State, I remembered my first journey northwards, by road, when we had to stop the truck on the road because our way was blocked by a fallen branch. Lieutenant Walters, the SAS man who had trained us, had made us all get out and take up defensive positions, because it might have been an ambush. The branch had been so heavy, it had taken twenty of us to lift it.

Over Negri Sembilan I looked out and realized that I had walked through most of the jungle I could see. In the distance was the elephant and crocodile country I remembered so well. Nobody on the plane was saying a lot.

Even though I am sure the Malayan experience was responsible for the health problems I was to suffer later in life, I was proud to have had a part in it. Another thing it left me with was a hatred of guns and, although I live in a country district and many of my friends shoot, it's a sport in which I wish to have no part.

Robert Gretton

Robert Gretton served with the Royal Engineers at Suez and in Cyprus in 1956. He is a journalist and lives in London.

About six months after I had completed my National Service in the Royal Engineers, I was working in Smithfield Market as a canned-meat salesman when I received a brown envelope containing a letter which said I was being recalled to the Army. This was on 13 August, 1956, just before my twenty-first birthday. I first of all thought that this meant the two weeks' camp that you had to do if you were in the Army Emergency Reserve, but it worried me, so I showed it to my boss, and he laughed and said, 'No; they want you back for permanent service.' He was an ex-soldier; he and everyone else at Smithfield seemed to think it was a great joke, but to me it was devastating. I'd already done almost two years in Egypt, and had never even begun to think that I might be called back. All my friends also took it as a great joke, gave me a huge party and then drove me, rather drunk, down to Southampton, which is where our camp was. When I arrived there was, in fact, no camp, and we had to build it there and then with tents.

In our unit, the 25th Port Operating Regiment of the Royal Engineers, most of the men were dockers, and a pretty bolshie and undisciplined lot we were. It was pretty clear right from the beginning that the officers and NCOs didn't have a lot of say or control over us. We more or less took leave when we wanted at the weekends, and the few occasions we appeared on parade we were fairly scruffy and had our uniforms arranged as we liked them, rather than as the NCOs might want. We were kept doing virtually nothing for several weeks and we used to take longer and longer weekends; and we all began to think that it wouldn't come to anything and we'd be discharged.

Morale was steadily getting worse, and we were getting more and more difficult to handle, when we were suddenly summoned into the biggest tent on the camp, a sort of marquee, and told that General Somebody-or-Other was going to talk to us. We sussed right away that this was meant to be a morale and discipline boost. The General was late and, during the hour or so that we were waiting for him, mutterings and general bolshiness began to grow. Then from the back of the tent, furthest away from the officers and NCOs, little showers of stones started to come over, plus jeers and boos. They were getting distinctly edgy and were looking round and wondering what they could do about it when, suddenly, the General did arrive. They tried to call us to attention; everyone just booed and greeted the General with a shower of bigger stones. He looked distinctly alarmed, and obviously was wondering whether to go straight out again; but the Sergeant-Major encouraged him to stay, and he stood on a chair and started off something like: 'I want you men to know you're doing a valuable job.' Of course, that was absolutely the wrong thing to say, and was greeted with absolute yowls and shouts of derision and yet more stones. He looked frightened, got down off the chair and scuttled out of the marquee. There was then just a general milling around and shouting, and we were sent on leave almost straight away, because they were worried we might pull the camp down. Amongst us reservists was a *Daily Herald* journalist, so next day it was on the front page that there had been this incident, or mutiny, at one of the reservist camps.

So we were all on leave but, when the weekend came, we all got these telegrams recalling us; and then things moved more quickly. I was asked – as a lot of us were – if I could drive, and I said, 'Yes' – anything to make things less boring. Thus I found myself driving – I think they're called TCVs (Troop-Carrying Vehicles) – in convoy to Southampton Docks, which was a terrifying experience. When we arrived, we loaded this boat and, as a lot of us were dockers, it was work we did quite cheerily. But we still hadn't been told where we were going or, indeed, if we were going anywhere. Because none of us had been given any military training whatsoever since being recalled, or even fired a rifle on a range, it didn't occur to us that we could be going anywhere on active service.

Anyway, we sailed from Southampton in a small vessel, not a traditional troopship. Mainly, it seemed to be carrying the heavy equipment that we'd loaded. We went straight to Malta, and as soon as we got there we transferred to a proper troopship and set off again. It seemed like no time at all before we could smell Port Said, which is a smell which anyone who has been there never forgets; a terrible smell. A foetid sort of earth and shit smell, basically.

We were with 41 Marine Commando and other assorted soldiers. I remember we were pulled on to the deck to get this talk about what was happening. Of course, by then rumours were rife: we were going to Cyprus; we were going home; we were going everywhere. We were all in a fairly jumpy state. We'd been issued with twenty-four-hour rations and we were armed with the old No 4 Lee Enfield. We'd pointed out, fairly vociferously a number of times, that none of us had fired a fucking rifle for years, and what were they giving us a rifle and live ammunition for? Still in a fairly recalcitrant mood, we were told we were actually going to land at Port Said. Some of us just couldn't believe this, because we'd been cut off from news from home, and didn't know what was happening.

There was a lot of air activity, and a thick pall of smoke over the area we were heading for. Although we couldn't actually see the land, there was this unmistakable smell of Port Said just over the horizon, perhaps ten miles away. The Marines we were with were all in high spirits, really hyped up, saying things like, 'Kill the wogs'. Even the rough lot we were with found this extremely alarming, especially when they transferred us with them from the ship to the landing-craft. I had this uncomfortable feeling that my parents didn't know where I was, because they were abroad when I got called up and I hadn't had a chance to get in touch with them. I felt I might go in there and get killed and no one would know where I was.

When we came in sight of Port Said, there was a lot of black smoke and the sound of heavy gunfire which, we were told, was our own ships bombarding the shore. There was a certain amount of small-arms and artillery fire coming our way; although it was nowhere near, as far as we could tell, it was near enough to be scary. What with the motion of the landing-craft and everything else, we were all feeling distinctly queasy, and quite a few of us were sick.

Port Said looked surprisingly normal. The firing appeared to have died down, or was happening a long way beyond us. The landing-craft scraped up on to the beach; and then the platform thing wouldn't go down properly, so we had to climb up it and jump about twelve feet, carrying all our gear; so a lot of us landed with sprained ankles, and found it difficult to move up the beach. I remember thinking: It's not like John Wayne, limping along like old men and not knowing what we were meant to do, anyway. The Commandos did seem to know what they were doing and had gone ahead of us, although I gathered later that Port Said had been secured by then; it was only a question of mopping up. So none of us Engineers used our rifles at all, at least at that stage.

The first people we encountered was these Military Policemen shouting, 'Get a move on – down that street!' – just like policemen directing traffic. We could hear small-arms fire ahead of us, so we stayed close to the side as we ran down the street. We got to a block of flats, and the officer and the sergeant stopped to talk to each other and decided that, because of the firing, it would be safer for us to go into the flats and work our way down on the inside, rather than down the street. We had no trust whatever in our officer, who seemed very jumpy and more panicky than us, which didn't inspire confidence at all. Anyway, when we got in, there was this huge sort of ceremony. It had no people, obviously, but there was a wedding breakfast of some sort, laid out with silver and food. To our astonishment, the Sergeant said, 'All right, lads; help yourselves, but don't be too long,' and I said, 'Isn't that looting?' and he told me to get on with it. Not all of us did; we were too shocked by what we had seen − but people were stuffing their packs with silver candlesticks and things. Thus the first real action I can describe was looting, actually encouraged and ordered by an officer, which I found pretty demoralizing. Not that we were better than any other soldiers; it was just an automatic assumption that was what we could do.

When the noise of the small-arms fire had stopped, we went back into the street and moved up, going from block to block. We could hear a lot going on ahead; we discovered after that it was the Marines or the Paras moving down the canal road, with the eventual aim of sweeping all the way down to Cairo. Down the canal and turn right at Ismailia.

Our objective was to find a house for the night before it got dark. After we'd gone about three or four blocks into the town, I was beginning to recognize streets that I knew from when I'd done my National Service in Egypt, and I began to worry that I would meet some Egyptians that I knew. Then we stopped, bizarrely enough, by an Egyptian street photographer, who took some pictures of us, so we had our photographs taken in the middle of all this uproar.

Eventually we came across this building which was clearly a school, and the Colonel of our Regiment, who had joined us by then, said that he was going to bring the various platoons in, so the Port Operating Regiment would all be centred at this school. Then he ordered us to smash up all the 'wog bogs', as he called them; ordered us to destroy them completely, because of the danger of disease from anything to do with any sanitary arrangements the 'wogs' might have. We knew this was nonsense, but we did as we were told, using rifle butts and anything else we could find. We were ordered to throw the desks and other equipment out of the windows in order to clear the building, so that soldiers could sleep on the floor. Then we constructed these sort of cots with strips of canvas.

The next three weeks were a nightmare, in so far as it was terribly uncomfortable. A lot of us got the shits. We dug trenches in the hard tennis court to use as latrines − just open ones; no building around us.

Once established in the school, we spent each day down at the docks unloading equipment, knowing all the time that we'd probably be loading it up again quite soon. The rumours were going round that various things were going to happen; that the UN were coming, and we'd be home by Christmas. There was a tremendous panic one day; we heard sirens and a helicopter with a loudspeaker passed overhead, warning us to expect a rocket attack, and this really shit-scared us − we took cover for some time, but nothing came of it. Our duties, apart from unloading boats, was also the unpleasant job of fishing dead bodies out of the harbour. I suppose they had been killed in the air raids, but I couldn't face looking at what had been the reason for their deaths. It was just a question of getting it done.

As usual, the main thing which obsessed us soldiers was the terrible food. As well as doing daytime duties, we were on guard most nights. One night we thought we were being attacked. There was all this shooting, followed by a lot of shouting and laughter. A whole lot of French soldiers appeared, trying to barter with us for our food. We said, 'You can have it.' They seemed to like Army biscuits, for some weird reason. They were drunk; the firing was them shooting in the air. They were a pretty rough-looking bunch, paras, as far as I could gather from their dress. They told us that there were pigs running loose, so we went out on a marauding party. I found a pig; someone shot it; we brought it back and shared it with the French. They also showed us a Czech-built field kitchen that had been abandoned by the Egyptians. It was much better than ours, so we wheeled it back to our unit. As far as our unit was concerned, we came out on top in that encounter. But those twenty-four-hour rations we had were absolutely disgusting, and most of our talk was about when we were going to get some decent food.

I remember I'd sent several letters from the troopship and, in fact, I had a letter delivered to me within a couple of days. I was writing to a friend who worked for a Canadian press agency, trying to give the details he'd asked for before I left. Oddly enough, none of those letters was censored, although the ones to my granny — which were much more innocent — had great blanks where our Platoon Commander, who was a complete idiot, had censored them.

During a daytime patrol about two days after landing, he wanted to go into a part of town that was obviously unsafe. We said, 'No, you go; you can test it.' He drew his revolver and said, 'I'm giving you a direct order.' We just stood there and said, 'We're not going.' We also made it clear to him that if he tried to push us into situations we didn't trust, not only would we not go but we'd see to him. Yes, we'd kill him. I can say for sure that from that moment he was finished as an officer for us.

The NCOs, on the other hand, weren't too bad. They were similar sorts of men to the Sappers; there wasn't the big gap there is in some regiments, because both Engineers and Sappers were usually technically qualified in some way. The same with uniforms; we wouldn't put up with Army bullshit, which was different from my National Service time.

Anyway, further rumours arrived that the UN were coming and that we'd be home for Christmas, and we started to cheer up. Then we actually saw the blue helmets of the Yugoslav UN troops, and that cheered us up still more. We started re-loading the boats with all the stuff which, only a few days earlier, we'd finished unloading. Our mood by then was getting quite high, because we really thought that we were going to go home straight back to England. However, when we finally set sail, we were on a little flat-bottomed boat, not a landing-craft, and we were all terribly sick. I think this was just before Christmas, so we'd only been in Egypt something like a maximum of four or five weeks. All the time we were in Egypt I don't remember seeing an Egyptian soldier, but we did see a lot of people who'd clearly changed their clothes fairly rapidly, because we found their uniforms, and in one case they were actually still warm. As well as uniforms, there were boots and rifles and even grenades. There were men sitting around wearing new-looking *jellabas* (robes). We thought they were soldiers, so we rounded them up and passed them back, I suppose, for internment. But I never saw an identifiable enemy.

As we approached Cyprus, we were given a very stiff talking-to by an officer who was in an infantry regiment on Cyprus, warning us that what we had just experienced in Port Said was nothing compared to Cyprus. He said that the security situation was very bad, and that we could expect bombs and shooting and, generally, that things would be much worse. Our morale of course then rocketed down. Everyone said, 'Why aren't we going home?' We were in a really recalcitrant and bolshie mood, but we were so seasick we could hardly raise a shout against him.

When we landed — I think at Famagusta — thoroughly scared, we were told that from being the 25th Port Operating Regiment we were going to join 35th Field Engineer Regiment. This meant proper soldiering duties, not loading and unloading boats; and we weren't too keen on that, and we let it be known to any officer or sergeant who dared to come anywhere near us. By then, we had acquired a fairly unsavoury reputation as an unruly and ungovernable lot.

My memories generally of Cyprus are pretty sketchy, except that we seemed to spend a lot of time doing patrols, but not knowing quite why we were patrolling. Really just showing that you were around. I remember going up into the hills in trucks or, more usually, in Land Rovers. Curiously enough, it was being in trucks that made you feel more vulnerable. We weren't ever ambushed; but once we came to a village where there were a lot of schoolchildren who, as soon as they saw us, promptly picked up stones and rained them on the truck. We were stopped at the time, because of the traffic. It was scary, because we were then ordered to put one up the spout and prepare to fire. They were kids, eight and nine years old, and some a bit older than that. We had helmets, so the stones weren't hurting particularly; it was just alarming because we had no training about how to deal with rioting children, or any other sort of rioting people, for that matter. When we got back, we made a hell of a fuss about not having had training for this — and immediately regretted it, because they gave us a lot of drill and that sort of nonsense. You know, practising soldiering. So we wished we had kept quiet.

At least the food was better than in Port Said; there was plenty of fresh fruit, the first I'd had for about three months, and the usual sort of Army-catering food which can, in fact, sometimes be quite reasonable. We were living four to a tent; they were quite comfortable, with electric light, and Cyprus in winter isn't too bad.

Whenever you got in a taxi to go anywhere socially – and that was pretty restricted by the time I got to Cyprus – the taxi always seemed to take you first to this brothel, whether you asked to go there or not. Out of comradeship rather than the need for sex – although that, too – I joined a friend called Jock; he was very enthusiastic. It was all very clean, just a little suburban bungalow. We went in; the woman who ran the place gave us coffee and some of the girls were sitting round; you chose one of the girls and went to your respective rooms. Both our girls were extremely young, probably only fifteen or sixteen and, I think, Turkish, because that was felt to be safer because they were less likely to be terrorists. You had to clear with the madam whether you were going to stay all night. We decided that would be much nicer, because we'd heard you got breakfast and the papers in the morning. Anyway, the first time was fine, and we went back again a few days later. We were settled in with the same girls, when there was a terrific noise outside. The madam came in and said it was the MPs. She showed us the way out at the back, and we ran straight into the arms of these waiting military policemen. It was such a routine matter to them, nobody was cross or angry or anything. We were told we would be charged with 'behaviour prejudicial to good order and military discipline' and sent back to our unit. We never went back to the brothel, so it had the desired effect as far as the Army was concerned. In the Canal Zone, it would have been much more serious. There we were on no account to go with any Egyptian women, because there was this British Army fear that anything the Egyptians had or did was dirty and disease-ridden.

Eventually, and quite suddenly, after a period in which we became more and more rebellious, we were told, 'Right; you're going home.' We were taken out to the troopship, either the *Windrush* or the *Dunera,* in one of these awful flat-bottomed boats. The mood of exhilaration was just extraordinary, and I hardly remember the trip to Malta, where we transported to an aircraft, a Hermes. It was absolutely jam-packed. It's a terrifying take-off, anyway, at Malta. It seemed extraordinarily cold and foggy when we got back to England – that must have been about March, 1957. We were taken from Blackbushe Airport to Barton Stacey, which is where the Royal Engineers used to go to get demobilized.

I still remember the hut where we were given our discharge, and the mood that the Army 'had better not delay anything now, or we'll tear it down and burn it.' When we got outside the camp, we tried to burn our uniforms, but they were either too damp or fireproof, and we didn't manage that. We were given a £5 bounty, and I remember being strongly tempted to tear it up and throw it in the face of the officer handing it over; but £5 seemed too much to throw away.

I didn't feel all that close to the men who were with me at Suez; only in the sense that we all had to put up with this terrible inconvenience. What was worse, we had a stupid officer. The NCOs were all right, we could tolerate them; but the contempt for officers was absolutely total, and we identified them with the politicians who had sent us on this ludicrous mission. But although I had feelings of disquiet, I wasn't particularly politically aware, so I was astonished when I got into circulation with my friends to discover that there had been these demonstrations in Trafalgar Square. People were very interested and wanted me to talk about it, and asked why hadn't the soldiers refused to take part. I said, 'Well, we did have a mutiny, but it was nothing to do with politics; it was just because of the Army.' Most reservists felt that the Army was a stupid and ridiculous organization that mucked you about anyway. National Service had taught us to lie, swear, cheat and steal; and having another spell of it made us even more cynical and more liable to violence.

I went to a political meeting where a Tory MP was speaking, and I couldn't believe it when he said the British Army hadn't invaded Port Said; we'd gone in to 'separate the belligerents' — that was the phrase he used — and 'it wasn't a war', and a load of other nonsense. I was so angry, I stood up at the back and said that I'd been a soldier and that wasn't why we were there. He was a bit taken aback. It was somewhere like Chislehurst, down in Toryland; it wasn't Edward Heath, but some other old duffer. He looked at me, and a thought clearly came into his head, and he said, 'Well, I don't know what regiment you were in or why you were discharged, but I'll let the audience draw their own conclusions.' They all cheered and clapped; I couldn't believe it. Typical — if you can't think of an answer, you attack the person who disagrees with you.

The feeling of being cheated out of my youth was very strong. For a long time after that, I almost sought conflict with any authority figure, and in a way I have never done since — got involved in fights, not over Suez or anything but because I had become an aggressive sort of person. I got drunk a lot for a long time after coming back but, oddly enough, didn't like talking about Suez at all. My future in-laws had been very anti-Suez and had quarrelled with their best friends over it. They thought it was the most ridiculous military campaign Britain had ever been involved in.

My own feeling was shame that we had inflicted death and destruction on the Egyptians through the vanity of a few politicians. I still feel it when I meet Egyptians; I have a sort of compulsion to tell them about it. I suppose

I'm half-wanting forgiveness. If I'd been more politically aware, I wouldn't have gone. I did try to register as a conscientious objector; after this second spell in the Army, I was determined never to go again. I went to whatever the pacifist lot are called, and I wasn't a pacifist, so it was just a cynical action. They said, 'Sorry, but as the law stands, once you've been a soldier they can call you up and court martial you if you refuse.' There was that thing in 1960 when they were talking of calling up people; I remember thinking: Right, I'm going to move; I'm not going. I meant it in my heart. By then, I was married and had one child, but I was absolutely determined — and my wife was with me on this — that I wouldn't ever be a soldier again. I would do whatever lying, cheating and breaking the law that was necessary to not be a soldier — that's all.

Ron Harper

Ron Harper served in Malaya during 1952-53 with the Royal West Kent Regiment. He is a bookbinder and lives in London, where he was born.

I was called up on 1 November and I spent my two years with the Royal West Kent Regiment. I wasn't particularly keen to go into the Army, and I suppose I was a bit naive. I can remember a chap at work getting some tickets for an international football match at Wembley – England were playing Austria – and I said, 'Keep one for me because, with a bit of luck, I may be able to get home on that afternoon.' I can remember the date; it was 28 November, and I think by then our feet weren't touching the floor.

Basic training was at Maidstone, which was the Royal West Kent depot, so the four or six or whatever weeks of basic training were done there. We weren't allowed out of camp until the last weekend there, and then we had a strict inspection to make sure you were fit to be allowed to join humanity. We did a further ten weeks' training, and then we were just waiting about for a boat and a draft to go to Malaya. I can still remember the draft number – DAJPH – which for some reason still sticks in the mind. We were given the option of staying in the West Kents and going to Malaya, or of being transferred to the Royal Fusiliers and going to Korea, and some did transfer to the Fusiliers.

Before we left for Malaya we were given some idea of what life might be like when we joined the 1st Battalion in central Malaya. Illnesses such as malaria, scrub typhus and dysentery were mentioned, plus the added warning that we could expect to be bitten by any snake or scorpion that we might annoy. All this *plus* the jungle made my future as a National Serviceman seem a very unhappy one indeed – and no one had even mentioned the enemy.

After embarkation leave, we sailed from Southampton on the *Empire Windrush*, which was a good ship; a pre-war German boat. It had been used to take the Hitler Youth on cruises. It was a bit claustrophobic down below, and myself and a few others used to sleep on deck. I should think that previous to this I hadn't been any further than the south coast — Ramsgate or whatever. Our first glimpse of the East was Port Said, which was pretty exciting. We weren't allowed off the boat at this particular time, because there was some trouble on shore then. But there were some vendors who came out in small boats, and some even came aboard. They were conjurors and sort of street entertainers; a first glimpse of the East, which to me was a bit of an eye-opener. Then we went down the Suez Canal to the Red Sea, one of the hottest spots on earth, I should think. It was quite easy to cook an egg on any metal part of the ship. We stopped at Aden and then went on to Colombo, which was the last stop before Singapore.

Most us were glad to get ashore after four weeks at sea. The first impression of Singapore was of all the bustle and activity going on there; it seemed so much was happening. We did a bit of sightseeing that day and then at six in the evening we got on the train to Kuala Lumpur, which was probably a journey of about 250 miles but, for fear of derailments or ambushes, the train took about eighteen hours over the journey, which was made mostly in darkness and was not a very comfortable trip.

We reached Kuala Lumpur about midday the next day and we were taken by lorries to a camp, which was just on the outskirts, where we were fed and watered and kitted out. Everyone was issued with the old Mk V Lee-Enfield rifle, jungle webbing equipment and whatever, which was all jungle green, including the uniform and a floppy hat. I've read in recent years that it annoyed some of the top brass apparently, when they saw the way British soldiers were wearing the jungle green hat; it was the only part of a soldier's equipment that he could mould into individual shapes — some of them turned them into Robin Hood-type hats, or Arthur Askey trilbies. But if you look at a photo taken at that time of a Gurkha regiment or the Malay Police, you'll see them wearing the hats as they should be. We were also issued with a lace-up boot that went almost up to the knee, which was made of canvas and rubber. They were comfortable, but in the jungle they would soon be torn, and get worn out. It always amazed me that leeches could get in, because they were tied round the top and tightly laced down the front, so you'd think it would be impossible for anything to find a way in; but you'd probably get five or six if you had to go through any wet area.

We left the camp we were in and went up to the West Kents' main camp in Northern Selangor. We did two weeks of training to get used to jungle activities; mostly at night, strangely enough. It was just sort of to get you acclimatized to different conditions and what to expect. We certainly never had any trouble from the enemy in those two weeks. Basically, this training was to learn how to live in the jungle, make a camp, how to cook and whatever. We'd all trained together as a draft, but at the end of this time we were sent to different companies so, unfortunately, the group that I'd been with for most of my training were split up and sent to different platoons.

The strength of a platoon at that time would probably be about eighteen to twenty men, and this in turn would be split into three sections. Apart from the platoon officer, there was a sergeant and two NCOs, so each of them would be in charge of a section.

Then we were sent out on operations. I suppose the maximum time you could spend in the jungle without support would be about five days. That would be as much supplies as you could carry. We used to drink from the jungle streams and rivers; they were crystal clear. There was no fear of drinking any of that water, and it was nice and cool. These rivers or streams originated in the hills. There was no trouble about water for brew-ups or any of that; there was always plenty around.

You'd probably go into an area that hadn't been patrolled for some time, and the job was to see if there were any signs of camps or terrorist activity in that particular region. Basically, of the three sections that went in, one would stay in the camp that we would make, and the other two would go into different areas to see if they could see anything in the way of camps that were being used by terrorists. The following day, the group that had gone out would stay in camp, and so on.

We were a mixed bunch; we even had two Scots. God knows how they got put into the Royal West Kents. They probably couldn't wear a kilt—didn't have the right-shaped legs for it! We had quite a few Londoners, Kentish lads, and there were some in other platoons from Wolverhampton and Derbyshire. They were a good crowd, 4 Platoon that I was with; they were...yeah...a good bunch of blokes. Mr Jackson — Jacko, our Platoon Officer — was a National Serviceman. He was probably twenty or so; might have been a year or two older than us. He had a hell of a lot of responsibility and, when you think of that, they did a hell of a good job, all of those platoon officers.

Sometimes we would go into an area where the local villagers weren't supposed to know there was any military activity going on, so you'd probably go out in the early morning, say at two o'clock, go past the villages at night and get into the jungle before their work-day began; they were rubber-tappers and that sort of thing. It was probably a difficult secret to keep, because any lorries going by carrying troops at night would start the dogs off, but even then the villagers wouldn't know exactly where you were going. When you think—it was pitch black, quite often no moon and our drivers had to get to a designated area on time. This was OK on the trunk roads but, when you think they were going down rubber-estate tracks, and tracks leading off of them, which had quite a steep drop on one side and a high embankment on the other, and the track just about took the width of a 3-tonner, I think a lot of credit should go to those drivers. I don't think they got the credit they deserved. And then, of course, they had to make their own way back.

When we were de-bussing once, I can remember an incident where one of the lads in our platoon thought he couldn't take it any more. We were getting off the trucks early in the morning to go into the jungle. He just couldn't take any more; he was just shouting, 'No, no, no!' He was taken back to the camp, and we never saw him for some weeks after that. Apparently, he'd been sent to the Cameron Highlands, which is a sort of convalescent place. But he must have showed a hell of a lot of guts prior to that, because we never had any inkling that he was in that condition; really, we just didn't know. I suppose there's a point that most people reach, and that lad had reached his.

There were some tragic things out there with accidents anyway; there was one in particular, where an ambush had been laid for a couple of days and the terrorists never turned up. This officer who was in charge of my platoon— I can't remember which company it was — anyway, this officer was going down the track calling the men out to go back, because it wasn't worthwhile staying there any longer and the Bren-gun team, hearing footsteps coming towards them and thinking it was the enemy, just opened fire on him and killed him. I suppose twenty-four members of the battalion died out there, some in action and some in tragic accidents. That was in the three years the battalion was out there.

Another time, a sentry of our battalion took a shot at a car that had gone through a roadblock he was on and, by sheer chance, the round went through the back of the vehicle and killed the driver, a European. Anyway, the sentry was within the law, but he was so upset that they sent him home. It must have preyed on his mind so much that he committed suicide before reaching England.

A friend of mine in another platoon was accidentally killed. He was coming in from a patrol, and an Iban tracker thought he was a terrorist and shot him. I thought of going to see his parents when I got home, but I didn't know how much they knew about their son's death, so I wouldn't have known what to say to them. I just couldn't bring myself to visit them.

It's very difficult to say how many days you spend in the jungle and how many miles you trudge. In my time, I only missed one three-day operation. It's difficult to say what my total was; we used to do three, five or perhaps seven days, which was the longest time I ever spent in the jungle at one stretch. It's a pity that I never kept a record of how many days I did altogether.

In all that time, I only saw the enemy once. Our officer said that the area to the north of our camp, which was quite hilly — probably the beginning of the Cameron Highlands — hadn't been patrolled, and it was decided to send our platoon up there just for three days or so to have a look round. I can always remember the very first morning. I was the last one in the patrol, and I suppose forty yards away in a clearing to my left there were three khaki-clad figures coming along, talking quite loudly in Chinese — not aware that anyone was around, of course. Then they did a U-bend along what must have been a regular route, I should think, and went back into the jungle. No one in our patrol said a word; mostly we were dumbstruck that we'd been so near; they must have been about thirty yards away. We never even opened fire. We should have spent the rest of the day marching to the spot we'd been given, but I think our officer radioed back, saying that we'd made contact, and we'd been given the go-ahead to stay in that area to watch the track. They thought we must have been near a camp of some sort.

I can always remember that earlier that day one of the lads in the platoon hadn't been feeling so good. In fact, he was pretty ill. During the night he hadn't improved much. The following day, the lad was even worse and the officer said, 'He'll have to go back, and we'll need two volunteers to go with him.' Yours Truly was the one that volunteered. I think it must have been a time when I was scared, because I cannot for the life of me remember now who was ill and who the other bloke was that I came back with. But most of it was just boring, not frightening; just routine, boring, tiring patrols — exhausting at times, really. But there were situations when you felt a sixth sense that something was going to happen, but then it didn't. It's a difficult thing to describe.

We were also at a place called Sungei Buloh and — providing you weren't on duties of any sort, patrols or anything — Sunday at that camp was quite an easy, cushy time. But one Sunday morning at about eight o'clock, one of the terrorists walked into the camp to give himself up. As we were acting as stand-by patrol, we thought it wouldn't affect us, but apparently he'd just left a camp with his colleagues still there, and he could take us to an arms dump. So everybody who was able in the camp that particular morning went off in trucks with him in the back, with a blanket over his head so he wouldn't be recognized going through the villages. He wasn't too popular with some of the lads, because they'd just come off a week of jungle duty but, as it turned out, it was quite a sizeable haul of weapons we got on that occasion. It was probably stuff that had been used in the Second World War; there were old Lee Enfield rifles, as well as Bren guns, and there was quite a lot of ammunition recovered, too.

We put an ambush on the track to the arms dump for the rest of the day. We were told that some of his colleagues may not have known he'd given himself up and would come back to the camp, so there were groups of us dotted all along this track, keeping our eyes and ears open. It was late afternoon when we very distinctly heard footsteps from where the camp would have been, at the top of the hill; stealthy steps, quite distinct, but in no hurry. As they got nearer, we got quite tense, because there was obviously someone coming, but it turned out to be a wild boar. We shouted at it, and it ran away. We never saw anyone, and at the end of the day we were just called in. I should think the terrorist's colleagues must have realized that he was thinking of giving himself up, so they didn't trust him and beat a hasty retreat.

Our spell at Sungei Buloh Camp lasted for some weeks, most of the time being spent on routine three-day patrols. However, in our operational area was a leper colony – the only one in Malaya, I believe – and, when possible, we used to go in there to check if things were all right. Food supply was always a problem for the CTs and they sometimes got into the lepers' compound to steal chickens and the vegetables that were grown for the patients, many of whom were a sad sight; but some would wave as we passed between the huts where they lived. Poor people; it was felt that something must be done for them.

So, one day, during what was to appear as a routine patrol through the colony, eight or so of us stayed inside when the rest left to go back to camp. The idea was to set a trap for the CTs, and we stayed hidden in an empty hut until it started to get dark; and then formed a semi-circle facing the gateway that led to the compound; the plan being that, if they turned up, Sergeant Garratty, our platoon sergeant, would fire a flare illuminating the target area. As we were only about fifty or sixty yards from the gateway, it should have been a perfect ambush position for a 'result'. We were there for some hours; by then it was pitch black. There was no moon and, with the jungle as a background, the eyes didn't really become accustomed to the darkness. Eventually, sounds could be heard near the gateway; no voices, just movements and the sound of the gate being slowly opened: our guests had arrived. At this stage Sergeant Garratty was to fire the flare pistol so that we could pick out the CTs in the glare. I can remember the plop sound on my left as he fired the pistol but, unfortunately, the flare had got wet so that the bloody thing didn't ignite. Those few seconds lost between the sound of the pistol and us opening fire in the dark were sufficient for the CTs to disappear. At a guess, I wouldn't think there had been more than three of them; three very lucky guys. We missed them completely; you'd think one of us would have had some luck. But after this incident, we never had another report of theft from the colony.

I suppose most of our successes were sort of off-the-cuff with small groups. There was a larger operation which, I think, was called Operation *Sickle*.

They had information come in that there were some top-ranking Communist leaders going to meet at a particular hill. For some days our troops were encircling it. The 13th/18th Hussars were also involved, with a 25-pounder gun battery. We came out into a clearing and there were three of these artillery pieces lined up; I think it was the first time we'd seen real guns and real soldiers.

Anyway, the Australian Air Force bombed the hill; they did a couple of runs, and the artillery shelled it for some time. Then we went in, hoping that there might be some joy after all that activity. At the top of the hill there was a camp site that had obviously been used for some time − Chinese papers strewn around, and so on. It had been occupied, probably up to a dozen days earlier. They must have got wind of the operation and legged it. If it had been done more stealthily, with small groups, we might have got some success from it; but with 25-pounder guns being brought up so close, they must have twigged. It's not a thing that can be done quietly.

There were a lot of other regiments in Malaya at that time; there were Gurkhas, the Worcesters, Suffolks, Somerset Light Infantry, Manchesters but, although you might be involved in operations with them, you rarely saw them. It was basically your platoon, within your battalion. There were also Iban trackers out there. They were headhunters. Everyone said they were cannibals. New blokes used to be told, 'You're in no danger, mate, they're vegetarians; they only eat greengrocers.'

When we were at Penang, they decided to do an early-morning swoop on the workers going out, because food could be smuggled to the guerrillas in the frames of bicycles and bicycle pumps. So we decided to stop everyone that went out. It was quite a sizeable operation, actually; there must have been hundreds of workers going out to work in the rubberfields. Men and women had to be separated to be searched, but we never did any of the searching; the Malay Police did that. I always remember having fixed bayonets while we were doing this; they were just simple people, and it just seemed as though you were a bit brutal. But I think there was a lot of kindness shown to them; there was a hell of a lot of sympathy from the British troops, to the Malays especially. It was just one of the searches you did out there, but that was the biggest we did. You couldn't help feeling sorry for those people; they'd probably been threatened to make them supply the terrorists. Although we weren't politically minded, there was always this tremendous sympathy for the Malay people. They only made up about half the population; the rest was made up of Indians, Chinese and Tamils. They are the most easy-going of people, and it seemed that their country was being taken from them. That, basically, seemed to be the British Tommy's attitude.

Then I came to the end of my fifteen months over there. No one was more glad to get out of the Army than me. I went round the hut to say goodbye to the lads I'd been with all that time. You'd shared that mucking-in spirit which, before or since, you don't experience. They were a great crowd. I just couldn't speak when I said goodbye; it was a pretty emotional moment, really. But I was glad to go home.

When I got back to England, me and another bloke, called Jack, had to report to the Queen's depot at Guildford. Jack lived in Guildford, and his father worked it so that Jack on his first night back could have a meal and an evening out with his folks and his girlfriend. They kindly tried to get me to join them, but I declined; as it was his first night home, it would be a bit much having me tagging along. They invited me back to their home as well. They were good people. The depot staff treated us like outcasts. I don't know why; perhaps they thought we'd be a bad influence on the new recruits. We were treated rather like *janker wallahs*. We even had to deliver coal to the married quarters. It was a place I was glad to see the back of.

When I was finally demobbed, I went by train to Waterloo and from there took a Number 1 bus to Surrey Docks, and from Surrey Docks a single-decker, which stopped opposite where I lived. I was laden down with a kitbag and equipment and whatever. When I got off the bus, there was a rather embarrassing banner that said WELCOME HOME RON with Union Jacks on it. The bus driver gave me an old-fashioned look. If he'd asked where I'd been, I would have said, 'Bloody Guildford, mate.' My parents weren't sure of the exact day I'd get back. They were round at the pub that Saturday when I came home. They didn't really ask me about my experience; they were just glad to see me. But they can't have been more glad to see me home than I was to get home.

David Hartley

David Hartley was an RAMC doctor attached to 1 Para during 1956-57 in Cyprus and Suez. He is a retired consultant gynaecologist and obstetrician, and lives in Avon.

I joined as a National Serviceman and, because I was medically trained, was commissioned as a 2nd lieutenant in the Royal Army Medical Corps. I then discovered that by taking a Short Service Commission (three years) I could become a full lieutenant, with much better pay and conditions. So that's what I did after my first three months. I also went on a Para training course, because I wanted some excitement...and also because you got an extra six bob for every day you had your parachute wings, which was a lot of money in those days *[a National Serviceman's basic pay was four shillings a day – 20 pence]*.

What I can remember is that in about May or June of 1956, the whole of 1 Para, plus supporting arms, was flown out to Cyprus in a fleet of Shackletons. They put me in the tail in the gunner's position, so I was lying on this piece of Perspex, which was completely transparent, 12,000 feet above the Mediterranean. I had a very good view. I'd just finished my Para course and they wanted me out in a hurry, as the battalion was two doctors short. We arrived in Cyprus and went to our camp which was on the Morphou road, about five or six miles out of Nicosia. But in fact, when I got there, the battalion had gone out on a cordon-and-search operation in the hills north of the Troodos Mountains and they were searching two villages, called Kambos and Chakistra – fancy me remembering that! – and I went to join them there. A most appalling fire had occurred in the forest there, in which twenty-two soldiers of the Norfolk Regiment had been burnt to death. This had happened just hours before I landed, and I found myself going up to the scene of the fire because a lot of my kind of people – medics – were helping. But there was nothing I could do. And that was my introduction to Cyprus. No one knows whether it was an accident or started deliberately, but the whole place was as dry as tinder. There were no injured; they'd either escaped or been burnt to death. I didn't see the bodies; they had all been removed. I just saw the smoking ground and everybody looking a bit shattered. I was a bit dazed myself with the journey, the flying; and so much was happening, anyway.

Our camp was tented; the tents were big and square and comfortable. I shared mine with a fellow-officer; I ought to be able to remember his name, but I can't. I can see him in front of me now. I shared the tent with this guy for six months. He was non-medical; one of the Regular Army officers.

When we went out on operations I had two roles, actually. The first was to treat any soldiers that got hurt, which happened rarely. Most of those who got hurt were injured in accidents. There were two fatal shootings; one was a chap who was on escort and killed his driver with a Sten gun, and another a guy who got shot by one of our own patrols. There was a chap killed diving into the sea; he hit his head on a rock − and I can't remember how the other man lost his life. There were about thirty accidental discharges of firearms while I was there so, in fact, the chance of being shot by one's own side was far higher than actually being shot by EOKA. We lost no men to enemy action; not to my knowledge. None whatsoever.

There were a lot of young National Service drivers in the Army at that time and they did drive too fast. They drove these 3-tonners with twenty guys in the back, and they *were* driving dangerously. I was in one that overturned; we were out on a mountaineering expedition and this chap was driving much too fast on a twisty road but, fortunately, he chose an inward bend to overturn on, so that all that happened was that the truck fell sideways against the upward slope of the mountainside. Had he taken the next bend too fast, we'd have rolled down 300 feet into the sea. This was just an immature, eighteen-year-old National Serviceman, who just had no idea about momentum and so forth, and he was just obeying orders to drive faster. Nobody was hurt, actually; we all got a fright, but no one was hurt.

So my first role was to look after the soldiers; apart from anything else, they used to get sick and suffer minor injuries and so forth. The other role was to look after the local villages. The word had got round that there was a doctor with the battalion, so they would roll up for treatment during cordon-and-search operations. Most of these little villages had no doctors, so most of the villagers would see a doctor once or twice in their lifetime, provided they could go to Nicosia by bus or car or what have you. Even if they could get there − and it might take all day to do it − they might see a doctor who they couldn't afford to pay. So a lot of these villagers never saw a doctor, and suddenly there was an Army doctor in their village. OK, he was a foreigner; but he *was* a doctor. They knew every battalion had one, and they'd come to see, and I very quickly had a surgery full of them. I remember seeing extraordinary things; quite pathetic, really. There was so little you could do − people with very bad arthritis, wanting you to cure them. Subtropical disease, particularly gastro-enteritis, was a common problem. It was awful, really, especially the sick children one occasionally saw. A friend of mine who was one of the other medical officers – he delivered a baby in a house once; there were chickens and pigs and the whole family in the room throughout, and a dog ran off with the placenta.

I'm rather embarrassed about the following incident, really. The whole time I was there, which was about six months, there were only two Para officers who were ambushed; one was myself, the doctor, and the other was the padre. We had very little sympathy from our professional soldier colleagues, who wished they'd been there, because they could have done something about it. We were probably rather asking for it, in my case. We went off to climb a mountain called Pentadactylos, which anyone in Cyprus would know; and to get to this mountain by road from the south, as we did, you have to come back down the same way – there's only the one road. So we went up there and climbed this mountain, and I got benighted on it...which is another rather embarrassing tale, which we won't go into at the moment. Five of us got down safely, but one of the young officers slipped; a great lump of rock came away and he fell about fifteen or sixteen feet. We thought at first he'd been killed but, in fact, he was unconscious with a fractured skull. So we got him on a stretcher to the Land Rover, which had a big red cross on it, and so on. There was myself as his medical officer, a driver, and an escort with a gun in the front, next to the driver. Because it was a hot, sunny day, the whole vehicle was open. We set off to drive to Nicosia with this chap in the back on a stretcher. I was taking his pulse from time to time and wondering whether he was going to live or die. Then, going round a corner next to a big stone barn, there was this tremendous blinding flash and a colossal bang. Three things happened. The driver let go of the wheel in shock and the vehicle promptly swerved towards a big deep ditch – and had we gone into that we might have been in big trouble. But as it was, the chap sitting next to the driver very calmly got hold of the steering-wheel and pulled it back straight. The next thing that happened was that he (the escort) said, 'Fucking EOKA up to their fucking tricks again.'...actually, he said, 'Fooking EOKA oop to their fooking tricks again,' because he came from Yorkshire. Finally, my patient – who I thought might be dying – sat up and started fumbling for his pistol, which he didn't have, and this last was very good news as far as I was concerned. We went round the corner, stopped and scattered in all directions. There was an olive grove; I made sure the patient was OK and stayed with him, while the other two went into the olive grove with their guns looking for and expecting a fight, but nothing happened. They found a battery, which was obviously a firing point. The mine was fixed in the fork of a tree, and what actually saved us was the fact that it was placed at just the right height for a 3-ton truck and we were below this; so the blast went just above and behind the Land Rover. That was the other thing; the terrorists couldn't actually see exactly where we were, because their vision was blocked for a moment by this big, long, stone barn round which the road curved. Had we been a 3-tonner, they could have seen it over the top of the barn; they got the timing wrong by half a second or so, and that saved us. Of course, EOKA never used to stop and open fire − at least, not very often; they just used to leg it. After all that, we got this chap to hospital in Nicosia and he recovered.

The other ambush involved the padre. Sadly, he was actually conducting a funeral of one of those poor chaps who had died; I think, the one who had died swimming in the sea. He was driving quite slowly through Nicosia and someone tossed a hand grenade into the back of the Land Rover, and the soldier who was sitting there calmly picked it up and threw it out again. It went off with a bang, but nobody was hurt.

I was very happy in Cyprus. I was twenty-five years old, but the fact is, going straight from school to a highly-specialized education actually shelters one from the world. Looking back on my time in Cyprus, I realize that I was very immature and had been insulated from the harsher realities of life. But I did get on with people, and I certainly didn't throw my weight around in intellectual ways. What I enjoyed very much was that it was the first time that I was on my own amongst 800 blokes, who were non-medical. I felt I had a duty to them, so, whatever they did, I wanted to do the best I could for them, because I felt they'd got a trust in me.

The officers I was with were a superb bunch of blokes. All the junior officers, the lieutenants, were National Servicemen. They had gone through the parachute course, and the Regiment did select a particular type of person. Those who were captains and upwards were Regulars. At that time, all our officers came from other regiments. They served a term of two or three years, and then they went back to their units. This actually created a special camaraderie; there was a lot of friendly badinage about the particular regiments they'd come from.

The ORs were a good mixture, like the world's made up of. They were nearly all National Servicemen, so all the private soldiers and some of the corporals were NS men, and they used to beef like mad about being in the Army. It was the thing to do; to moan and to look forward to the day you were out. But they were so good at doing everything; they pretended not to be enthusiastic but, when it came to doing something, they always came up with the goods. They had the most marvellous sense of humour − which didn't often rise much above the navel − but they were very funny. They were also very loyal; the thing about the English soldier is that, although he will respect senior rank, he will never be afraid of it. His seniors have to

81

gain his respect, whereas I think in some armies the soldiers are frightened of their officers, actually.

When the Suez thing blew up we went by sea. One battalion was earmarked to go in by air and capture Gamil Airport, which was the airport for Alexandria. The RAF only had enough planes to drop one battalion and its supporting units; 3 Para was chosen for this, and 1 and 2 Para went by sea in a large number of extraordinary ships. Crazy, isn't it? – all that training wasted. I went in some old tub; I can't remember what it was.

When we went ashore, the Commandos had already landed some hours before, but the fighting was still definitely going on. We landed in Port Said harbour, or what there was left of it, and got off at the quayside. The Commandos had already taken possession of the northern part of the town. We had to dig in along the sea front just a few hundred yards from the sea. Well, I dug in; everybody dug in along about 300 or 400 yards. Fighting was still going on, and we could see things burning to the south of our position. We heard that 3 Para had captured the airport and were fighting to link up. The most exciting thing that happened to us at that point was that a 3-ton truck full of tank shells caught fire just near us. The driver proceeded to try and drive it into the sea and, when he got half-way down the beach about 200 yards away, somebody pulled him out of it and dragged him away – as, in fact, these shells started to go off. Several hundred soldiers sat very tight in front of this incredible fireworks display. There seemed to be an awful lot of shells. The trouble was, it was a bit like a giant bag of popcorn; you didn't know when the last one had gone off. At the end of it, all I remember is my CO saying, 'My God; that was a real stonk.' *[An artillery barrage, perhaps from the noise made by a mortar shell leaving the barrel?]* It sounds a bit conceited, but I don't think I was ever really frightened; I was too interested to be scared. Anyway, 3 Para broke through, and the Egyptian Army retreated down the Canal at great speed. They were followed by 2 Para and tanks, with some of the troops travelling in commandeered buses. It was rather like going on a Sunday picnic, driving at 25 or 30 miles an hour. This was our advance, and I remember the Egyptian radio saying that they were fighting a hard rearguard action. Suddenly, we were simply told to stop, because at this point the UN had insisted that we do so – and also the Americans had put their spoke in. It was all very bewildering. At the time we were slightly indignant, you see, because the Canal by legal agreement belonged to Britain. France had some shares in it, too; and Colonel Nasser had stolen it – he'd grabbed it; this was the thing. We were simply getting back what was ours, and this was perfectly legitimate. But, of course, it was far more complicated than that, because the Israelis were involved as well. That was the end of Suez for me. I wasn't there more than about four or five days, and I received a campaign medal. I was most embarrassed by it all, because I did nothing at all, except to have five days of rather wondrous happenings. A combination of interest and chaos, but very little danger.

Anyway, we came back from Suez on HMS *Bulwark*, an aircraft carrier, subsequently scrapped. I had my first bath for ten days on *Bulwark*. I do remember being impressed by the courtesy of the Royal Navy; they filled the ship up with thousands of soldiers and made us very welcome. We went back to Famagusta, I think; I really can't remember. There was a terrible feeling of anticlimax about Suez, of a job not properly done. I felt pretty angry towards politicians in general; not just ours, but the whole lot – the Egyptians, the French, the British – everybody. That common soldiers had killed each other because politicians had ballsed it up; that made me very angry.

But I felt differently about Cyprus. I didn't feel that we had a right to be there, simply because it was part of the British Empire. I felt we were wrong. Some of the older officers – one man in particular, whom I liked very much – simply said, 'It's the British Empire and it always was and always will be.' Well, I disagreed with him, but I felt also that the Greek Cypriots were going about it the wrong way, and that's certainly been borne out by what subsequently happened, because they've lost half the island to the Turks. When I look back on the whole *enosis* business, what an example of human futility it was – because in fact Greece didn't want *enosis*. I'm told that, if a Greek wants to insult a fellow-Greek, he calls him a Cypriot. It was some of the Greek-Cypriot fanatics who wanted *enosis*, and they wanted to be rid of the British – which is fair enough. But the price they paid was losing their island to the Turks. The whole thing was futile and unnecessary – and they never achieved their *enosis*.

Really, my service in Cyprus as a medical officer wasn't very dangerous. I had a lot of free visits to beauty spots. We used to sleep out at night in a tent. That is a memory I shall always treasure – being in such beautiful countryside and with such nice companions. There was a lot of compensations for being away from home.

On returning to England, my feelings were mixed; there was a sense of relief that I was returning to a more normal sort of medical milieu, as far as my job was concerned. But I had a vague consciousness that a very important part of my life had come to an end, and I only appreciated later how important it had been to me. I had made some good friends in the Army. My family were keenly interested in hearing about my experiences, but that's about where it stopped; the average acquaintance was supremely bored by it all, totally uninterested. That's amazing, really.

It was a tremendous privilege for me to have been able to help – even in a minor way – people who were in physical danger. I was also very fortunate to be with non-medical people. At the time, my medical colleagues were quite scathing about service life; they saw it as a professional dead end and a waste of time. But my Army service taught me to communicate with all types of people, and it subsequently helped me to communicate with members of the public — a skill which young doctors don't seem to have.

Altogether, my Army service represents some of the happiest years of my life. I am very lucky and very happy that it happened.

Ron Hawkes

Ron Hawkes served with the Royal Irish Fusiliers in Korea after the Armistice and in Kenya, 1953-54. He is an electrician, married with two daughters and lives in Orpington, Kent.

Being from South London, I put down for the Royal West Kents, who were at Maidstone; they sent me to Northern Ireland. When I went up to − is it Euston? to catch the train to Liverpool to go to Ireland, that was as far as I'd been. I'd never been across that side of London even; that was a foreign land to me, because I come from South London. I was called up to the Royal Inniskilling Fusiliers but, halfway through the training, they changed us over to the Royal Irish Fusiliers. I took to the Army; I thoroughly enjoyed it. I was young and fit and I enjoyed the comradeship.

After training, we went to Berlin; then the whole battalion came back for embarkation leave, and then went to Korea on the troopship *Empire Fowey*. Most of the lads, we didn't see them until Gibraltar; going across the Bay of Biscay, they were just lying in their bunks, absolutely dying. We went to Kure in Japan, to the United Nations Battle School, and that's where I did my assault pioneer training. We learnt how to lay booby-traps, and how to identify various types of mine and how to pick them up. Actually, I was nearly killed one time in Korea; we were doing battalion manoeuvres and we had to lay out plastic charges and gun cotton to simulate artillery fire. Some idiot threw a charge of plastic explosive at me and set off my explosives. They sent me back to the next hill − it's all hills there − and I think that, walking back through the paddyfields, the coolies must have thought I was a throwback from the actual fighting because I was all bandaged up. I'd damaged my eye, a bit of cordite or something like that.

We used to maintain the trenches [*the Kansas Line*] in case the Chinese attacked again. We used to look after the minefields. At one place the minefields were where the 'Glorious Glosters' did their last stand. They mined that off and nobody went in there after that. We also did guards on the Teal Bridge. Usually we only stayed in the trenches for one day at a time; you go out, do your work and come back. They weren't actually trenches;

85

they were dug-outs as big as this room; like the old pillboxes but much bigger. They were criss-crossed all across Korea. So the idea was that if they — the Chinese — tried to come forward again, the crossfire would wipe them out. Another thing that used to get us was that the main defence was a massive big minefield, and two or three times we had to turn out in full battle order in the middle of the blooming night. Then we'd go up to the dug-outs; we didn't know if it was the real thing — it used to frighten us. All the flares used to go up and, nine times out of ten, they told us it was blooming wild boar tripping the wires.

We were living in winterized tents with sandbags up the side. We slept in sleeping-bags which came completely over your head, and there was wire holding it open around your nose and mouth. Although it was only the beginning of the winter, you'd wake up and your breath was frozen around the face-hole in your sleeping-bag...and that was *inside* the tent. You wore the full winter clothing: you had longjohns, a quilted trouser, a waterproof one over the top of that, and then you had your big parka. You wore ordinary gloves with mittens over the top; the mitten had just a firing finger, but you couldn't get it through the trigger guard (of your weapon). You'd have to wear your ordinary gloves all the time, because your bare fingers would stick to the metal of your rifle.

I remember, our sergeants used to invite the American sergeants down to their mess and our sergeants used to go up to theirs. I think the Americans were Green Berets; they carried pistols all the time. One night, they were all drunk, and one of the Americans tried to shoot the hackle off the beret of one of our sergeants. He shot him in the head. I can't remember now whether he actually killed him; I know he shot the top of his head, but he only just missed the hackle.

I saw some Americans once when we were picking up rations at Seoul. There were loads of these Americans; we thought it was a full brigade *[about 2,000 men in the British Army]*, about three battalions, maybe. We found out after that it was only one, sort of, battalion. They had *everything* you could think of; they had flame-throwers and everything. The equipment they had was magic; we'd never seen anything like it. We used to like getting their rations. You used to get a packet of cigarettes in every tray, and all the biscuits you could think of; oh, it was marvellous. Our own rations weren't too bad when we were in camp, but we used to have field rations when we were at the front.

The local people were funny. I could never understand how they could squat down for hours and hours, and then they'd get up and just walk away. If we'd have done it, we'd have been all aches and pains. These were quite old men, too.

I was in Korea for about five months and, after about two months, they sent us to Tokyo on R&R (Rest and Recuperation). Oh dear, that was great, that was; we had beds with sheets. We hadn't seen sheets since we left England. We got in with an Australian who was an ex-Londoner. Because we didn't have any money — I think we had about ten bob (50 pence) between us — he kept us for seven days. We had a smashing time. We saw Tokyo, and we went to Hiroshima and saw the devastation there; I just couldn't believe it. We went to this bridge, and you could actually see the shape of people on this bridge, where the heat of the bomb had burnt their shadows into the concrete.

From Korea, the battalion was posted to Kenya. We went on the troopship *Dunera*. We weren't allowed ashore for two or three days because the Irishmen in our battalion, they really tore up the NAAFI on the last night. They were throwing MPs (Military Police) out of the windows, and I think they had to get reinforcements in to quieten them down.

We got to Mombasa and took the train up from there, which wasn't very comfortable, because it was all wooden seats. When we got there, we were issued with the No 5 Lee Enfield rifle, a lovely weapon. It's a beautiful rifle; you can really hold it. But most of my time in Kenya I was with a Bren gun, No 1 and No 2; we used to take turns each. My idea was that if we were going to come across anybody, I'd have good firepower. Attached to us was a bloke from the Kenya Rifles. He was our tracker. He was an ex-Mau Mau, a Kikuyu; we didn't trust him one bit. He kept saying, 'Me up front (give) me rifle.' He just wanted to blooming get hold of a weapon and make off with it.

We did patrols in the Aberdare Forest; it was about 11,000 feet high. The climb to the top took us over a day, I think. We had mules carrying our equipment, and they used to get jammed on the rocks and we used to have to lift them off. We had big packs ourselves to carry all our stuff. At one period, we had a good view of Mount Kilimanjaro; that was lovely. Right at the top, it was freezing at night, and even during some of the days it was cold enough to wear our big green jerseys, and we had a sort of parka, but not as heavy. We didn't find it too bad, but it was cold.

The object was, when we were up in the Aberdare Forest, to drive the Mau Mau down towards the African Rifles or the Kenya Rifles, who were coming up the other way. The first sweep we went out on, our officer shot one. He was the only one in the battalion who had one of the new FN rifles. We came across this hut and we all surrounded it. He went in, the officer with the rifle; shouted a command to surrender and the man who was inside the hut — which was only made of mud — he just had it away through the side of the hut. As he went through, the officer fired at him and got him. There was this little hole in his back, and in his chest was this great big hole...a powerful weapon; he was dead, all right. Actually, we left him there because we were going on, and apparently — so we heard afterwards — there was a big rumpus about it. It turned out that he was a quartermaster in the Mau Mau, supplying money to the groups throughout the forest. When they did search the place, they found all sorts of paper and money. Our officer got a real rollicking for that, because we didn't do a proper search. We had to go back and pull the hut down, and destroy everything.

That was another thing we had to do; whenever we had iron rations — cheese, or whatever — we had to make it impossible for the Mau Mau to use the tins. We'd make holes in the bottom and screw them up. We used to have to bury them. The trouble was that, nine times out of ten, we used to get in a row because the monkeys used to watch us, see these tins glinting as we buried them, and they'd come down and dig them up.

Our corporal of our section was out on patrol one night. I don't know where; I must have been doing something else. Anyway, I wasn't with them. He sent one of the lads back to say they'd come across a hut, and the stones round the fire were still warm; so what he did was, he sent one lad back and three of them waited in the hut, waiting for whoever was using it to come back. During the early hours of the morning — he was telling me — they were sitting there; the corporal had the Bren gun, a rifleman and a Sten-gunner. They heard someone coming and what they do is, they come down and they stop; they keep stopping and they look to see if anything's been moved — a blade of grass, even; they can tell. Anyway, this Mau Mau chap came in and Dennis, our corporal, said that as the Mau Mau bent over to come in, he (Dennis) opened up with the Bren gun. The weight of the bullets pushed the Mau Mau back; but when Dennis stopped firing, of course, with the momentum, the Mau Mau started to come in again. So Dennis shot him again. When we saw him the next morning, oh God! he was shot to pieces; but Dennis was telling us they could still hear him moaning out there after they'd actually shot him. The corporal said to the rifleman to go out and finish him off. This little lad, a Londoner, he said he went out there and put the actual muzzle of the rifle on his forehead and pulled the trigger; but the next morning, when we got there, we saw he'd actually shot him in the throat, he was shaking so much. He would have been dead, anyway; he had his kidneys hanging out — you imagine, half a magazine of Bren. But these men were tough. We were told by a Kenya Rifles bloke that he had personally put a whole twenty-eight rounds of a Sten gun into one Mau Mau, and he'd still run away. To look at them, they were only wiry little people; but they certainly were tough.

We were on ambush one night. They'd found a track that was being used for supplies, so we had the job of laying an ambush. We lay there all blooming night; it was cold and damp and boring. The trouble was, it was a moonlit night and every time the moon came out, you thought something was there. A tree was there; the moon went in and came out again, and you'd forgotten the tree was there − oh dear, you know − the old heart starts pumping. It was just breaking daylight and we heard these footsteps. My mate was Number One on the Bren, and I was lying alongside him; we were right ready to go. They've come along with these big loads on their heads; we didn't know how many there were. Now, in the Aberdare Forest you were allowed to shoot any black man − if he's black, you shoot him because he's a Mau Mau − it was a prohibited area. Anyway, he pulled the trigger, and there was a 'clonk' and they were gone. You couldn't get anywhere near them; they left everything and they were gone. We captured what they'd left; it was only clothing, it was rags, more or less. There was a bit of grub there, but nothing we could touch; cor! it was shocking.

Down on the plains, when we weren't in the Aberdare Forest, our job was to lay ambushes. When they attacked those farms, most of the time they attacked them to divert attention while they pinched some of the cattle for food. Then they take the cattle into the bush, cut the meat all up and hang it in the trees to dry. Our people used to find it, and we'd wait for them (the enemy) to come back and get it, but they never did. Apparently some of our people used to inject it with poison, so it didn't do them − the Mau Mau − any good. I don't know who did this, but that's what we were told. It was never official; you never heard anything official − it was always word of mouth, you know.

Another time, we were out on patrol; it was on a flat plain. We'd been out half a day patrolling, and we came across this load of people. We did the action, what we were meant to do...and they turned out to be baboons. They were walking about like humans, upright. We were told if there's enough of them, they'll attack you. As a section − eight to ten men − there weren't many of us, so we cleared off. Another day, we saw these buzzards circling around and we thought: There's something on there, like. We travelled for miles before we actually got there, and all it was was two blooming dead horses. Some farmer took them out in the bush − I suppose there was something wrong with them − shot them and just left them there.

The whole company was on patrol once, and our tracker smelt smoke; miles away, it was. We saw these three guys, Mau Mau, in a bit of a dip around a fire. The officers decided it was their shoot. We're lying around with full battle order, with the old spade in the back. The officers surrounded the enemy and, of course, they were shooting across us. None of us had ever got so close to the earth as we did that night; you could hear their bullets pinging off our shovels. Those blooming officers; they thought it was a sport.

While we were up in the Aberdare Forest, all we found was gas pipes and door bolts; they used to fashion these rifle butts out of wood, fix this gas pipe on; one bullet used to go in the pipe, and they'd have this bolt on a big elastic band. Half of them used to blow themselves up. It was quite a big camp we found.

I suppose we were after these Mau Mau because they were terrorizing the white people, and their own people. I heard a little story from a Masai who was one of our trackers; he said they had offered the government to kill all the Mau Mau (Kikuyu) men so that they could have their women, because all their own women had syphilis. They would have done it and all; they were a vicious lot, those Masai. Our trackers used to live in a row of tents opposite; they used to come over and talk to us. One time, one of them passes round a bottle, and we drink from it. We found out later it was cow's blood and milk, their staple diet. Made us all feel ill.

When we were out, we used to see monkeys and giraffes and zebras, and we were always finding zebras knocked over on the road. And birds; there were all types of birds. One bird used to come and perch on our wireless aerial in the camp, and sing like the clappers. I don't know what sort of bird it was. That's a part of my experience that I always regret; that I never took more of an interest in the wildlife. As eighteen- and nineteen-year-olds, all we wanted to do was go down the NAAFI and have a few pints. But we did have a couple of lads who were interested; that's the only way I've got these photos. It's only what other people took; I never had a camera − couldn't afford one.

Another experience we had up in the Aberdare Forest − a lot of it was completely bamboo; you couldn't move for it, it was so close together. We used to see these tracks coming down the side of the hill. Our tracker told us it was the elephants. The only way they could get through it themselves was they used to sit down and slide down, and smash everything out of the way. I would like to have seen that. Another time, we were on patrol and we went off the track to camp for the night, and we laid guards − you always had to lay guards. The next morning, there were tusk marks in the clay at the side of this blooming track, so the elephant had actually walked past and our guard never heard it.

I liked Kenya; a lovely country. I keep saying to Pauline, my wife, we are going to go there some time. The climate where we were at Naivasha, about fifty miles north-west of Nairobi, was just like a glorious summer's day in England. We were only there a couple of months when we got seven days' leave in a farmhouse. Apparently the white settlers coming back on leave to England used to let their houses to the Army, for the British soldiers to spend their leaves in. It was a single storey, with the main living-quarters in the middle and wings which went off for bedrooms and bathrooms. We had waiters who waited on us, but we had to sleep with our weapons. Everywhere we carried our weapons, and the first night there they (the authorities) took the cook away — he was a Mau Mau.

I was in Kenya about five months. I thought we were going to leave about two or three weeks before demob and have a nice sail home; instead of that, two days before we were demobbed, they flew us out in a Britannia to Blackbushe Airport. The Customs there went through us like a dose of salts; every single thing came out of our kitbags, all our socks were unrolled. Christ knows what they were looking for; I bought my sister a watch and I couldn't pay the duty on it at the time; and I had to leave it there.

It was strange, really, when I came out, because I missed my friends; I missed the fun we had together, the laughs and the jokes. When you come back, you're on your own; you miss having company all the time. It's not even the same as leaving your mates you had back before you went in the Army, because you were never a team; you were always an individual, even if you were in a gang. Yeah, I missed the companionship and the travel. In two years, that battalion really travelled; I'd been to Ireland, Germany, Japan, Kenya — with all the stops in between.

We had some great chaps in our unit. They were first class, you know, real buddies; help you out, you wouldn't have to ask. The comradeship was fantastic. You can understand the British Army being so good as it is, because they instilled in you a comradeship and pride in the regiment. About two-thirds of the battalion were Irish and the rest were Londoners. Most of our lads came from Shepherds Bush and Islington; they were teddy-boys in real life.

After National Service, I felt more of a person, more confident. I had experiences. I know you look back on the good times — and there were some bad times — but I enjoyed it.

Brian Hughes

Brian Hughes served with the RAEC in Malaya in 1950-52, and was subsequently commissioned in the Royal Artillery. He is retired, married with six children and lives in Aldershot.

I was a willing National Serviceman; I wanted to be a soldier. I wanted to go to Sandhurst and be an officer. I passed the written examination, but I failed the interview. That was the first time I'd ever failed anything. I went back home and worked for my father while I waited to be called for National Service.

If, as I did, you had a Cert A from the cadet corps at school and a decent School Certificate, you could select the Education Corps; so I filled in the appropriate forms and eventually I went to Bushey Camp in Winchester – the Greenjackets basic training depot – for, I think, six weeks' basic training. It was a shock; yes, it was a shock.

We lived in wooden huts and were a mixture of grammar-school boys like myself, university graduates who were not officer material for some reason, and Rifle Brigade and 60th Rifles men. Now, the Rifle Brigade in particular tended to recruit from London and, predictably, they were a bit rough; so it was a bit of a baptism for me. It was my first exposure to really nasty bullying, the pure sadism I met from some PTIs – and that's the only word for it. Quite shocking; quite shocking; and I think others probably found the same.

After six weeks, we were given leave and sent on to the Education Corps. This time, we were in Nissen huts in the grounds of this rather large hall near Beaconsfield, which may also have been a German officer prisoner-of-war camp. When we came to the end of our training there and became Education Corps sergeants, we set off back to Bodmin, which was the Education Corps depot. The staff there made the point that Education Corps sergeants were not really sergeants at all, and life was *not* pleasant. It was a very unhappy place to be while we waited to go abroad. Korea was just starting (1950) which meant, of course, that gaps on troopships had to be filled by unimportant people like us.

So off we went; I can't remember which ship it was. It might have been the *Empire Windrush*, or it might have been the *Empire Fowey*. On the way we had *cabins*, a cabin for three; not a lot of room in it, though, three Education Corps sergeants together – too many for buggery and not enough for cards. God, what a trip that was; a cross between idyllic and boring. There were only three or four (gramophone) records on the whole ship, and these had been brought by a WVS lady. One of them was ' 'Tis the ivy, dear Mother, upon the wall tapping'; hearing that always takes me back.

We didn't go ashore at Gibraltar, but we did at Port Said. Some of the people on board were going to Korea, and they had to go for hardening-up marches in the desert. The Education Corps 'schoolies' had to go with them. We stopped at Aden – that was hot and horrid – and at Colombo. Then down through the Straits of Malacca, where the water changes colour; it's yellow and nasty. It was there I saw my first floating body. Then into Singapore Harbour, where we disembarked.

There must have been about fifteen or twenty education sergeants. The command education officer's staff came aboard at Singapore, had us all in one of the lounges and gave us papers to read and forms to fill in. This was to decide where we would go. Three of us were to go to Malaya. The Singapore ones went to their Singapore units straight off the ship. The three of us going to Malaya – Atherton, Cherry and myself – were sent to Nee Soon transit camp, which is the site of Leslie Thomas's book, where we shared a tent with a chap from the French Foreign Legion. I never worked out why, because my French wasn't good enough at the time. We stayed there for maybe a week, and then we were detailed off to go to our postings. By this time we were wearing jungle greens. We went by train to Kuala Lumpur overnight. We were issued with arms and ammunition before we went there.

We were carrying our personal documents. Cherry, being Cherry, opened them up and had a look inside, and for each of us the CO of the Education Training Unit had endorsed it 'Likely to do well in an operational theatre.' And that is how I got to Malaya, I feel sure.

We had a 'crash train' with up to three cars running in front of the train itself, each loaded with rails, so that, if the fishplates had been pulled, that would go off the track – not the main train. There was very often a *kubu* (small tin fort) on the front of the train proper; it had people inside it with instructions to shoot. One of the difficulties of my first posting – the 26th Field Regiment (Royal Artillery) – was that we used to patrol the railway on foot with instructions to shoot anything that moved, and these boys on the train had the same instructions, and one had to get out of the way. I only did a couple of these, to be honest; really, because they were short of men.

We arrived at another small transit camp near Kuala Lumpur. Nothing much happened at all. Atherton, Cherry and I shared a room, but Atherton was taken off almost immediately to the military prison as the education man there. We were actually in the camp over Christmas; and the sergeants' mess families were very kind, and invited us to their quarters for Christmas dinner.

Eventually, Cherry and I went on to the 26th Field Regiment of the Royal Artillery. They had their guns parked, and just acted as infantry. I was given a tent and a load of planks from the sawmill, and I was told to floor the tent as my school. I shared a tent with a bloke called 'Topper' Brown and a man called 'Busty' Bridges. This was my home for six months. I did a few foot patrols with the 26th Field, largely in a spirit of exploration. If you asked ever so nicely, they'd take you with them. Sometimes I was CO's escort (Major Boyle) and used to go out with him in his jeep; that way, he wasn't stealing a man from any of the troops. His battery was divided into three troops; so you'd have one troop in the jungle, one troop resting, having been in the jungle, and one on standby – each, really, in charge of a sergeant. Bridges, who I shared a tent with, took me out on my first one, which was a follow-up after a civilian bus had been burned. What happened was that the OCPD (Officer Commanding Police District) had talked Boyle into talking the Chinese into not paying protection money to the terrorists. Then he started to lose buses so fast it was unbelievable; and this was the second or third bus he'd lost in about a fortnight. The moment we got the message, a light patrol (eight or ten) went out to see what had happened. We found a camp. We were led, of course, by an Iban tracker. I loved them; I used to share a tent with one, a bloke called Singka Anaka Melaya. He showed me a photograph of his wife, wearing a grass skirt and a Guards sergeant's cap, which he'd been presented with from his last unit. They had this hair that went all the way down to their bottoms, with a fringe across the front, huge earlobes and huge tattoos. They carried a long *parang* (sword), and they could peel an onion with it.

One thing about sharing a tent with an Iban; it went up quicker than anyone else's. The thing you had to watch about them was that they were very, very superstitious. They carried a bandage – it looked like an old lady's stocking – round their waist, full of bits of bone and God knows what else. Sometimes they would say, 'Not going out today – bad dream,' and, if there was a bad dream on, you were wasting your time. But they could look at a track and say, 'Two men going that way yesterday,' or 'A pig going that way just an hour ago.' One of the problems was that you couldn't always understand what they said; they did speak, most of them, Bahasa Malay.

So you just followed the Ibans. We followed up and found this camp. There was virtually nothing in it, but they'd obviously lived there for some time. We located it, brought out a big patrol, and Bridges and I burnt it.

We were just an instant response, carrying 24-hour rations; that was all. We were in 1-ton trucks and away; it was a whistle and it meant run, and you did bloody run. You hopped on the trucks and you were away. One reason I could go on these outings was that my school work was a bit intermittent. Whenever I was allowed to teach them — and it was a bit ragged; it didn't follow a syllabus under these circumstances — your class would meet. They're fully armed with their packs behind them, and the whistle would blow and they'd be gone. I learned a lot; I did a few general patrols and escorts for the CO.

I went on to the Cameronians, when the 26th Field went home, under the command of Colonel Bill Henning, subsequently DSO. A very old man of about forty, you know. The battalion was principally National Servicemen. I was responsible for two companies: A Company was in Batu Pahat, an old town but thriving, and D Company in Bukit Sarempang, in a planter's bungalow with tents all around it. In rubber, you'd hear the rubber-tappers go out every morning, and we were behind the wire down a long laterite track; ruddy miles in. A bit boring, to be honest. They ran it the same as the Artillery did; one on, one off, one in the wash — and my education bit was really a welfare bit. The odd help with letters home, supply of books and a little bit of current affairs; I mean, there was little point in trying to follow any logical sequence of teaching in that situation.

The thing I noticed about the Artillery, and also about the Cameronians when I joined them, was the Regulars; to me — at eighteen or nineteen — old men. They were all just about on their '22' *[22 years of service]*. Now, if you look at their '22' in 1951, it meant they joined in 1929, and that was Depression year. To me, it appeared that they were the quality of men who would possibly have done something better if they hadn't got caught in the Depression. All these chaps had two, sometimes three rows of medals, very often with a DCM or MM amongst it; very impressive, solid soldiers and, as I say, old enough to be my father. I learned many, many things from these chaps.

Occasionally I would go on little jobs with them, nothing serious. We had an attack on a village called Pekan Jabi, where they (the enemy) had cut a hole in the wire you could have driven a 3-tonner through — they went through. The police were, traditionally, asleep; they were lovely chaps, the Malay Police but, well....They went past the police *kubu* where the two policemen were asleep, and in to the police sergeant in the headquarters, which was just a long shed with an office at the front, and said, 'No heroics; we just want the guns.' They woke up the sleeping policemen and told them to push the weapons to the end of the bed, and a hero in the corner started to make a fight of it; and when we got there, it looked like a butcher's shop. There was only blood when I got there; the bits had been taken away.

95

Templer (Commander-in-Chief) arrived within six hours. He put a twenty-three-and-a-half-hour curfew on the village; this is a resettled village, you understand, mostly Chinese tappers and a few Indian storekeepers, about 1,000 or 1,200 people altogether. Every man between seventeen and seventy would be in the Home Guard. A little Scots sergeant – to say he was a disciplinarian would be understating the case – was put in charge with eight or ten soldiers, and he was the arbiter of who was seventeen and who was seventy. These were marched about, taught rifle drill, taught shotgun drill. They made life very unpleasant for about six weeks. Then, after that, he was withdrawn, and I was put in as burgomaster with the soldiers. I arrived at about 5.30 each night, and took over and ran the place until about 7 in the morning, when I opened the gates and searched every man and woman who left the place, and then handed it back to the police. This was a sort of active command, if you like. But, although we took over at night, there was still a full Malay Police section of a sergeant and about ten men there during the day.

I was actually attached to Support Company, which were in the headquarters, although they were a fighting unit; so you got your four companies out (in the jungle), each with their own area and support company again within an area, but based on the headquarters with the Old Man. Support Company was commanded by Major Kettles; now he deserves fame as the man who de-poisoned the 'poison dwarves' when he later became Commanding Officer of the Regiment in Germany. Kettles was the tactician who masterminded 'the big kill' that was on Radio Malaya *[recording of a large-scale successful ambush]*. One of his sergeants was Sergeant John Hannah, now Sergeant Hannah MM; very young, very green and very, very nice. He was taking out a patrol, to lay an ambush, and I asked the company commander for permission to go with it, and he said yes. I accoutred myself and marched proudly away. I'd done lots of little ones previously; but this was different.

We went off together in a truck down to a *kampong* with a truck driver and *his* escort – because, you understand, the truck had to come back. So off we went into rough rubber, not trees in lines like the Dunlop plantations; this was lighter rubber with a certain amount of high grass. We walked for, I suppose, a couple or three miles, and Hannah went off with some of the others to look at this cache or whatever it was that the enemy were meant to be picking up. When he came back, Hannah said, 'Right, we sit here, six in a row. They're supposed to be coming from that way to the cache over there, and you're stop-man, Brian; when the last one comes past you, you hit him.' The zone, I suppose, was knee-deep in tallish grass with trees here and there, with a bank up behind with jungle up it – well, not jungle, really; thickish stuff. Behind us, there was more light stuff. I said, 'What about a backstop, Johnnie?' and Hannah said, 'That might be a good idea.' So we put the automatic shotgun....we had this automatic 8-bore shotgun with us; a particularly nasty piece of work when it hit you. But we had to hit with the first one, because it usually jammed after the first round. It had about six up a tube; it was a horrible bit of work. Anyway, there were two men behind us and six of us in a row in a sort of arc, expecting people to come past at between twenty and forty paces.

I lay down and covered my side with branches and so forth; I learned a bit about camouflage after that one, too. I could see across this ground; it was more or less flat. We set up all day; we took the ambush down at dusk. We pulled back, cooked up, changed into a second set of gear − you always did during the night; if you were in wet gear during the day, you changed into dry for the night. The character test was changing back into wet in the morning because, if you didn't, you slept in wet clothes the following night, because you now had two sets of wet gear. Happily, it didn't rain on us. We lay there all day; we could hear the tappers chattering. They were all around us; some of them were within 100 yards, but we never actually saw anyone. We slept at night in a row under ponchos, one man awake on duty with the platoon sergeant's watch. When the hour was up, he would wake the next man up, give him the watch and slip into his place, as it were. It was like a huge family bed. Up at about five; dig your own little hole for ablutions, then tea and biscuits. We used to have the ten-man, one-day pack. We had three of these, I think, big biscuits; one of those and a cup of tea, and you were full. Then back in position, and we lay there all the second day.

On the third day, round about noon, there was a rustling noise behind me I didn't recognize. I was bored, half asleep and very frightened at every noise I heard...and it was Hannah. He said, 'I've got a raging toothache; I've got to go for a walk.' I said, 'Well, don't walk in front of us, John. Take two men with you, in case you get a bump, and tell our backstop what you're up to, in case you bump them.' I suppose we were in an area about the size of the lawn out there; altogether, about seventy yards by twenty yards. We could all talk to each other, if you raised your voice a bit. So off goes Hannah, and there I sit, not realizing that I have now accidentally assumed command of this party. Well, command is a bit much; two at the back, two with Hannah − that left three of us with a Bren-gunner in the middle. John hadn't been gone long, and I hear these footsteps, and I think, 'Bloody Johnnie; he's in front of us.'

Not from left to right as it said in the book, but from right to left where I hadn't got any cover at all, just laying there, there appeared three men; a little fellow with his rifle under his arm, rolling himself a cigarette, one behind him and, to be honest, I didn't see the third man. Knowing that there were to be three, but not being able to see the third one, I let the first one go as far as I dared – bear in mind that this is the first time I'd ever fired anything at a man. I lined him up, and whether I went first or the machine-gunner went first, I don't know; but we certainly spun him, we rolled him around. We went for the second and, I'm ashamed to say, we hit him but he didn't stop; he was away up the hill virtually opposite, going like the wind. But I still didn't see the third one. I remember, while I was doing this rapid fire after this running man, nothing happened; it must have been two seconds before I realized I'd gone through all ten shots. I amazed myself at the speed with which I got another five in, and probably fired three of those at moving branches, when it went quiet. Then there's this hush; deadly quiet, all the tappers' noises stopped, all the birds stopped. Then holy bloody Moley, it started coming back at us. Automatic fire, and rapid single-round fire, and I thought, 'Oh, shit; we've hit a regiment.' Then it stopped, and a voice said, 'Sergeant Hughes?' from where the shots were coming from. All I could muster was, 'Aye.'

Hannah shouted down to us, and the machine-gunner said, 'Sar'nt Hughes; Sar'nt Hughes, are you all right?' I said, 'Yeah; I've answered him,' and he said, 'Well, I can't hear you.' So I shouted, 'What you got?' He said, 'We've got two up here; one appeared wounded, we got him and there was one other and we got him. What have you got?' I said, 'There's one in front of us, but I'm not going to say he's dead, because I can't see.' Hannah said, 'I'll come down,' and I said, 'Come round; sweep and watch the backstop.' I shouted to them, 'Watch out; Hannah's coming round.' Of course, it was bad discipline; had the CTs been the advance party of a regiment, we would have all been there together and massacred when the rest came up. However, round comes Hannah, and we decided to toss a 36 grenade in where he (the man we'd shot) was lying. It was the first time I'd seen one thrown in anger, and they don't half make a bloody bang, don't they? It landed about right and, at this, we decided we'd sweep gently in, and there he was. He wasn't quite dead. I found him with one of the Jocks, and then he finished him off on my instructions. I don't think I had the bottle for it. He wasn't going to last very long; he was bubbling through holes in his chest...and that was our three. Of course, we couldn't wait to get on the radio and tell the Old Man. Jubilation was out of this world. This was the Regiment's century: numbers 98, 99 and 100. One of the ones we had got was the district committee member for Tungu Tiga and he was the third, I think, who had been appointed in two months. As they'd been appointed, they'd been killed. We'd had first-rate information, except that they'd come right to left instead of left to right. It was perfect. It was the first time I'd seen a live enemy, and the first time I'd seen a dead enemy.

We got a message to the Old Man, and he said to stay where we were; they'd bring a carrying party. So we cut three long boughs, and put the gentlemen on the boughs, and brewed up. The carrying party weren't very long. They weren't very far away; they probably could hear the fighting. They were largely odds and sods as they tend to be, took one look at our trophies and were very, very sick. In the end, we carried the gentlemen ourselves out to the track where they could get the vehicles in. The not-very-pretty bit was, we did tend to string them on the front of our vehicles and drive them back through the village — which we did, back to the police headquarters in Segamat, where we were debriefed. John Hannah shared out the $800 that was in the pocket of the man that dropped in front of us; a measure of our greenness was that normally one goes through the pockets, and we hadn't. I had the *parang* off one as a souvenir; so that was the end of that.

Incidentally, John Hannah went on several other actions after this, his first. In a campaign where physical contact with the enemy seldom lasted more than forty-five seconds, there wasn't much chance of deploying tactics once the action had begun. However, there were young officers and NCOs whose steadfast patrolling brought results, and the Army has traditionally rewarded these men with medals. Thus John Hannah, when he returned to Britain with the Regiment, went to the Palace and was presented with the Military Medal by HM Queen Elizabeth. The action cited for his decoration was the one described, although the medal was really for long, productive work in a hostile environment.

I'd now done eighteen months of my service, and I didn't know what I was going to do when I came out. Quite honestly, I was a very happy man where I was. I was living in the sergeants' mess of a pretty decent regiment, I'd been presented with my spurs and I was accepted by the Infantry. I did in fact do some education work at this time; I got a few through their second and third class certificates, and I briefed a few on their first class. It's a ticklish business briefing sergeants, wearing DCMs, on their map-reading; but I'd like to think I negotiated it well. I was happy and fairly well paid, and I applied to sign on for three years. Eventually I was signed on by the colonel of the Cameronians the day after the King died — almost forty years ago today.

I came home by ship with the battalion, but this time it was six to the standee [*bunks in pairs, three deep*] on a deck God knows how far below the waterline. I didn't like that much at all, but at least we were coming home. I didn't talk much to anyone about my experiences; I think this sort of information is normally best swapped soldier to soldier, because they know what you're talking about. If you are overdoing it, they'll bloody soon let you know.

During my time in Malaya, I was never there when one of our chaps got hit; but people didn't come back. That was thought-provoking, but not terribly. That age group, we were all the right age to be a fighter pilot. It helped me to grow up; my horizons had been a school, really. Knowing what I do now, and if the whole thing started again tomorrow, and my younger son was sent out there, I'd be sick with worry. But I must admit, I did enjoy my soldiering.

Tom King

Tom King CH MP served with the King's African Rifles in Kenya, 1952-53. He is married with one son and one daughter.

I was called up to the Somerset Light Infantry; I went to the Light Infantry Training Depot at Borden — that would have been in September '51 — and then it was moved to Strensall in Yorkshire. I then went to Eaton Hall for officer training in February 1952, and passed out of there in about June. I had imagined that I would go straight back into the Somersets. What then happened was that the Somersets were in Malaya and were due back quite soon and, because of the training period involved, I would be too late to go to Malaya. The prospect for me was being attached to some other Light Infantry regiment, I knew not what, in Germany. But in my squad at Eaton Hall there was a friend called Charles Thatcher, whose father was a District Commissioner in Nyasaland (now Malawi). He had already made up his mind that there was a way to get back to Africa; he had discovered that you could get seconded to the King's African Rifles. He applied and I applied. Not many people knew about this, so there was no difficulty about getting in, and I went out there in about August 1952.

We set sail on the troopship *Empire Ken*. Time didn't seem to matter. There we were, going to serve for a year in Africa, and it actually took a month to get out there. It was a very leisurely trip, a very gentlemanly cruise out and it finished in Mombasa, I was attached to a Tanganyikan battalion of the King's African Rifles based at Dar es Salaam, which was something like 200 miles from Mombasa, down the coast. The only way you could get there was that you had to go inland by train all the way to Arusha on the slopes of Mount Kilimanjaro. You'd hardly believe it. Then you'd turn round and go back towards the coast, have two nights on a train, a 200-mile bus ride in the middle; it took two and a half days to get there.

We arrived in Dar es Salaam, a wonderful place, a good camp, and were immediately thrown into the life of the King's African Rifles. The first thing was that all the officers had to be able to speak Swahili, and in fact I had started to learn it on the boat coming out. They hand-picked a platoon of people who spoke no English at all, except one platoon sergeant, who spoke a few words. I was put in command, and I took them out on patrol, I forget how long for; perhaps three or four days. The idea was to throw you in the deep end and get the language going, and that regiment certainly had a very high standard of Swahili-speaking; I still speak a certain amount now. The practice of the King's African Rifles was to mix the tribes in each unit, so my platoon came from a range of what were then Tanganyikan tribes. Swahili was really the *lingua franca*. The Tanganyikans spoke good Swahili, and they were full of contempt for the Kenyans, who spoke a sort of 'kitchen' Swahili.

Many of my memories of that time are of what I call peacetime soldiering, which was about to be shattered by the changes brought about by the Mau Mau emergency. Peacetime with the King's African Rifles was *very* civilized. We used to get up and start work at 6.30 in the morning, because of the heat. You finished work, I think about half-past twelve or one o'clock and that was it, finished for the rest of the day. There was a small British officer element. Each company had one British major, a British subaltern and a British sergeant major; otherwise it was entirely Askaris — entirely African; African sergeant majors, African sergeants and officers. That was how it was in those days.

It was a pretty gentlemanly existence. I remember my Company Commander was also president of the mess, and there was a regimental tradition that on Wednesdays curry was served in the mess; it took him the whole of the morning to go to the market and organize all the ingredients that were needed. It was a matter of regimental honour, and part of the fairly leisurely and agreeable life of the Regiment then.

We were due to move as a battalion to be the garrison for Mauritius, and we were preparing for that when suddenly Operation Jock Scott — which was the Mau Mau emergency — occurred in Kenya. There were killings and murders of European settlers in Kenya, particularly in the White Highlands, as they were called. So there was a great upheaval, and it was decided that two companies would go and give help in this emergency; so two companies went to Kenya, and two companies and the colonel went to take over garrison duties in Mauritius. I was in one of those companies, and so we set sail in another troopship — a frightful journey right through a cyclone and God knows what; it was really terrible, I thought it was the end of my military career. We arrived at Mauritius, a wonderful place now much better known to holidaymakers, but in those days pretty cut off. An amazing part of the world. We were there some three months; then we had a switch over, and we replaced our two companies that were in Kenya for the emergency, and they came back to do garrison duty in Mauritius. For some reason, we never switched again. So from about January '53 through to September — nine months or so — we were totally committed on the emergency in Kenya. So back we came, again by ship, up to Mombasa, train on to Nairobi, then out by truck into the Rift Valley. We started at Gilgil, a military base near Nakuru; then we came over to Nyeri and out on to the Aberdares, and were based with the brigade that was in the area. For the rest of my time, I was on the Aberdares or on Mount Kenya.

What happened thereafter was that we, a 120-strong company, separated from the other company. We were therefore a detached company, responsible to the brigadier commanding the brigade, but he had plenty of other things on his mind. We had no colonel; he was still in Mauritius. We had one British company commander, and myself, and a British sergeant major; and then we had three locally-enlisted Europeans from the Kenya Regiment as platoon officers. (This was a local TA type of regiment.) I then took a platoon up on the edge of the forest, the Aberdares, from where we conducted patrols, ambushes and sweep operations in the native reserve outside the forest, and also inside the forest, by day and by night. We did night-time ambushes in the forest. I had thirty or forty chaps; I was living out in this heavily defended camp, barbed wire, ditches, spikes in the bottom of the ditches and all that – the traditional way of making that sort of camp – and was really responsible for giving some confidence and peace to the people, including the loyal Kikuyu in the area, and protecting them from terrorists. It was very much based on a relationship with the Kenya Police; nonetheless, I was in sole command of that area. I was then nineteen. There was an extraordinary sense of responsibility, being right on your own in a native area.

We had some nasty incidents. On one occasion, we had a loyal headman and a small sort of 'home guard' group that we'd tried to form in one of the villages within my area. The terrorists came out of the forest, surrounded them and got them in a great big *boma* – a mud hut with a grass roof – and burnt them all to death. We did lose a few home guard in that way. We had one or two active encounters, and we did kill a few terrorists, but it was pretty much needle-in-the-haystack stuff and, of course, the forest – which was much bigger then than it is now; a lot of it's been cut down – was also full of animals.

We had contacts with the enemy on patrol. I remember one – an unsuccessful one – in a village where we caught up with some terrorists who were, I think, about to kill a local headman. We just managed to stop them. One of my Askaris shot one of them, but the other two got away. On another occasion, we bumped into them in the forest. We were on patrol and there was a clearing, and suddenly we saw these boys on the edge of it who had weapons. They fired one shot at us and then tried to disappear as fast as they could, because their aim was to keep out of contact with regular forces. We fired back; I had a few Askaris with me who were blazing away and who got over-excited, I think. They didn't hit anything. But we were reasonably successful in keeping that area quiet. While we were there, other areas were not nearly so good. There was Fort Hall, which had all sorts of trouble. There was still the murder of farmers in some of the other areas. That led to an increase in troop numbers, which led to the Lancashire Fusiliers coming out, the first British Regiment to serve out there in that way. But we managed to have reasonable success in our area. There were various problems, but we were in some ways more acceptable (to the local people) because we were a Tanganyikan regiment, and we didn't give rise to some of the tribal hostilities encountered by other units. There was a very nasty incident with one of the King's African Rifles regiments where one company commander, who had an obsession about Somalis, did something that was absolutely against all the rules of the King's African Rifles, which was that he managed to filter the recruits coming in so that he formed a total Somali company. Then, of course, you saw exactly the wisdom of the King's African Rifles' founding fathers − what happened was that it turned into a tribal war, where quite clearly the Somali view was that the only good Kikuyu was a dead Kikuyu.

In terms of relationships with the local communities, it was tremendously important not to blackguard them all, and not treat all Kikuyu as though they were Mau Mau. But what was interesting about that was the responsibility that it gave me at a young age. It was interesting that we were trying to conduct an anti-terrorist campaign of a different kind, where the terrorists tried to live within the local community. You never knew, even in the European areas − someone could be a houseboy by day and a terrorist by night − that problem of knowing where the loyalties were. There was a huge amount of this oath-taking (by Mau Mau recruits), which was designed to destroy people's self-respect and build allegiance to their cause, and there was a lot of intimidation and threats, and killing children to force African people to support the cause. Intimidation is always there in terrorist organizations, as indeed I saw later with the IRA − with a lot of intimidation of the local people to get support.

The other interesting thing about Kenya was the presence of all the animals. You'd be patrolling quietly through the forest, and suddenly there'd be this huge eruption, and you'd find it was a rhino or a buffalo or an elephant. There was a huge amount of game there; very much more than there is now. We felt by then that we were pretty hardened Africa hands, and seeing new people coming out, and new senior officers who organized great sweeps rather like organized drives on the Malayan model. But what you could always tell was that, if the animals were there, the terrorists weren't, and you were in the wrong place. That lesson was learnt the hard way, because a new company commander from another company came out from England – he was very keen and anxious to show a lead. They were searching on Mount Kenya and came to a great big bush, and he decided that this must be properly checked to see that there was nobody lurking inside, and he started crawling in, and a huge great rhino came crawling out. The rhino tossed him, but fortunately it had a broken horn, or it would certainly have killed him – but even that put him in hospital for three months for his enthusiasm!

What then happened was that our British Company Sergeant Major's wife had a miscarriage in Mauritius, so he got compassionate leave. He was top priority to get to Mauritius, but he didn't seem to have the same priority to get back again. Anyway, he didn't reappear. My Company Commander then got jaundice, was quite ill and was laid up, so I was then left to command this company as Acting Captain – and paid as one, I am pleased to say! I was then nineteen, commanding a company of 120 Africans on active service. I had no Colonel, because he was still in Mauritius, so I was answerable direct to the Brigadier – but he had plenty of other things to worry about. So basically, having agreed the territory for which I would be responsible, we just got on with it. It was a tremendous experience to have such responsibility at such an early age.

What made it even more remarkable – the way we operated, we really were genuinely on detachment and we went off into the forest, conducted ambushes and patrols and all the rest of it. We had base camps, but we had camps out as well. We had our own transport – 3-tonners and jeeps; we were totally self-sufficient.

We used to come back from the forest, come into Nyeri, and it was rather like the Wild West. We practically hitched up the trucks at the hitching rail. There was in fact a hitching rail, which was used by people coming in on horseback. There were various Indian traders who operated there. I would order the stores; maize meal for the Askaris, meat, sugar and salt and all the things we needed. I would just sign a chit for them, then we'd load up the trucks and we'd go off for another week or two weeks in the bush. So there was this total responsibility for running an operation.

We came under attack once or twice. We had murders in our area; it was such a big area to cover. It was a wonderful country and, again, full of game. And yet there was this evil that stalked at night, and sometimes by day as well.

A later base I had was at Nyeri Station. I was based at a place called Doig's Farm, which was a typical European farm in the highlands. The farmer and his wife – I think their parents had come from England and found this bush area – cleared the bush, built themselves what was a very nice ranch-type house, had a wonderful English garden, 700 acres of first-class farming land, good fences, excellent stock cattle and all that. They

105

had created, out of what was nomadic grazing, wonderful farming country. Years later, I met the son in my constituency in Bridgwater; I gather that the farm is now almost back to the condition that it was in when the grandfather arrived in Kenya.

So that was my service. There was a certain amount of incident; we lost one or two people. We had some terrorist attacks; we lost some loyal Kikuyu, and the headman, the home guards and one or two terrorists were killed. It was like all terrorist campaigns; you spent a lot of time chasing and not finding.

At the end of my service we flew back, with quite a few stops. It must have been just about the time when they started to troop people in by air. It was wonderful to get back. I was going to Cambridge – an exciting new life. Seeing my friends, they had been in different places; some in Malaya, some in Korea. The 'Koreans' were the ones who really had a hard war and had lost people. You could tell that; they were a bit wild, quite a lively lot.

I came back with an abiding affection for Africa, but, sadly, Africa is not what it was. But the truth was that it's always been changing. It was changing when the Europeans got there, and it changed again when the railway arrived. One of the biggest changes was the arrival of the Lancashire Fusiliers; that was the first time outside the war they had ordinary soldiers who were whites. Before that, the Europeans tended to be only officers and warrant officers, and the European settlers got very worried at their impact on African attitudes. All in all, it was a wonderful country, and I came back with an abiding affection for the King's African Rifles, who were wonderful; quite mercurial, but they had a wonderful sense of humour and were very loyal and quite keen. In the Army, they did well, even under the old traditional disciplines that the KAR maintained. When I was there, they had the *kiboko*, a rhino-hide whip. I remember, an Askari was had up for drugs – *bhang*, they called it: cannabis. The regiment formed a hollow square, the Askari was marched out, made to hand over his rifle, his hat and his belt and lie down. An African sergeant major gave him three strokes from one side, right turn, left turn, three more strokes from the other side; then the Askari stood up and marched up to the colonel, asked permission to rejoin the regiment, got his rifle, hat and belt and marched back to camp. Though it may appal people nowadays, what Africans liked about it, in those days, was that there was no nonsense about detention or long entries on your conduct sheet; it was expunged in that way.

Altogether, Kenya was a completely new world to me. It was a challenge to put my training into effect in a real situation and have real responsibility. I remember some years ago Peter Drucker, an authority on modern management, was asked for an illustration of outstanding management practice. I think people expected him to say IBM or Exxon – he's an

American — but he said the British Indian Civil Service, because *they gave responsibility to people very young.* There's no doubt I was the beneficiary of that same philosophy. I had that responsibility very early in life, which has stood me in good stead right through my life, whether in industry, running a large factory, or in government with the various tasks I have been given and, most recently, as Secretary of State for Defence. One final memory is of standing in a clearing on Mount Kenya, being inspected by Field Marshal Sir John Harding, the Chief of the General Staff, and little thinking that I would find myself later nominating his successor.

Owen Parfitt

Owen Parfitt served from 1955-56 with the First Battalion Parachute Regiment on operations in Cyprus against the EOKA guerrillas. He was also at the Suez landing in 1956. He is a schoolteacher in Blackwood, Gwent where he was born and still lives with his wife and family.

What I remember was that just before going to Cyprus I was ill, prior to the movement of the unit from Aldershot to 'holding and drafting' which was in another camp on Gun Hill in Aldershot. I was very anxious to get back in time to catch them before they actually went to Cyprus, because I hadn't been issued with any kit or anything. I was in a hospital in Southampton, and I hitch-hiked back and got there a day before they were due to leave, and got issued with my special clothing.

In London, we stopped in an underground station which was used as a transit camp. It was an old station which was in Tottenham Court Road. I think it was on a high level; they had a train tunnel going underneath it. We stayed there on the Friday night and Saturday, and we were flying out on the Sunday. I remember a contact with a friend of mine, Sandy Gray, who moved from Blackwood to London. We went to the cinema and saw *Ill Met By Moonlight*, which was about Crete. We then went from one of the London airports to Malta in a Hastings, and stayed there the night. We just got out of the plane, slept on the floor, you know; then back into the plane and landed in Cyprus, in Nicosia. I can still feel the heat, which I'd never experienced before at that time (the early spring of 1956). From there, we travelled to our camp which was just a plain, a dirt field with some tents which hadn't actually been completed at the time. Ridge tents, I think they were – four-man tents.

I joined the corps of drums, and Alun Pask went into C Company. I can't remember exactly what happened next, but we started a routine of actually preparing for our duties on the island, which were mainly internal security duties. Our camp was on the Famagusta-Nicosia road, actually opposite an RAF unit; I remember during Suez the Vulcan bombers used to take off from the end of the runway and keep us awake at night.

In the camp, the rations were pretty basic – pom (I'm not fond of powdered potato, or powdered anything else, for that matter). It consisted of pom and fried corned beef, and Spam, and Spam fritters. The one luxury was grapes, which we'd never seen growing before, and watermelons and things like that. I can remember, we went to Famagusta, gave them a small amount of money and ended up with this Ali Baba-type basket, full of grapes – it was amazing.

The routine was totally different out there, of course. There was 'gunfire' (early morning tea) at about 4.30 a.m.; the tea was brought and placed in the path between the tents. We went out and helped ourselves, and then we'd start our duties. We'd have tea, work for a while, then have breakfast, and then work. Initially, all recruits going out to Cyprus with the battalion went into training–fieldcraft I suppose, preparing for an ambush, where to set an ambush and what action we should take in an ambush. We did this in an area which the Army, I believe, used as a sort of shooting range. You couldn't call it a desert, because it was all shale and stone, though it had all the characteristics of a desert – no trees; nothing there at all. And it was really hot. Then we went into the Kyrenian mountains and we did some mountain training in the woods, climbing trees and setting ambushes. I remember one particular occasion, where Alun and I were still in the same platoon, because we joined together. We were up in the mountains, and we started off in our shirtsleeves. We got up into the mountains, and we had lightweight blankets with us – I don't remember if we had our Army smocks with us – certainly lightweight blankets, and we had camp rations. We settled down for the night, and it snowed, and we were lying under these very, very thin blankets, you know – and trying to shave in freezing cold water....and we went up in blazing sunshine.

We were prepared for what we had to do. When we went on internal security duties, what would invariably happen would be that we would go into the Troodos mountains and the battalion would have a base camp; and then we would operate out from the base camp, searching the area. I remember one occasion when we actually came across the Kykko monastery; we went in and did a little search there and, as it happens, this was exactly where Grivas was hiding at one time.

We would be in the mountains for a few weeks on internal security duties. We would actually have specialized sleeping-bags; they were like a roll, you know, the cowboy roll. It was quite a heavy thing, but you could put all your equipment in it, roll it up and tie it. A sleeping-bag with a waterproof base; quite sophisticated, quite a good thing – not suitable for carrying, but if they were transported, it was excellent. We'd go off in patrols and cover an area.

In Nicosia one day, I wasn't on duty; I was just out with a group of friends.

109

When we went out, we had to carry weapons. I carried a Browning pistol, and somebody else a sub-machine-gun. We went in groups of four, and each carried a personal weapon. So I carried a Browning pistol. We used to cover one another, and somebody was actually shot near the old city, near the wall. I remember helping to get this body that had been shot in the head; he was a Cypriot, he wasn't a British soldier.

I'm trying to think now whether I actually witnessed this next incident, or whether it was hearsay afterwards. I can remember we took potshots at someone who was moving during curfew, and one fellow was shot, and it turned out the poor devil was deaf, and he hadn't heard the 'Halt! *Stomata! Dur!*'

One thing that really sticks in my mind: the drill sergeant took me with him as a runner, and in an isolated village we came across what I can only describe as a sort of café. He and I went into this café. It was full of men of various ages – nineteen, twenty, thirty years of age – and we got them all lined up against the bar. We were going to search them, and then the lights went out. I don't know whether it was a power cut or whether they'd done it. I was frightened then, but he was a marvellous fellow, and said, 'Don't go panicking, now,' and we continued to search, and the lights came back on. We didn't catch anyone, and we didn't find anything, but that was one sort of moment that actually made you realize how vulnerable you were.

Another occasion when we got very close to the enemy: there had been an incident in the mountains – a party of our Regiment had been mountaineering, and somebody had fallen and broken their leg. It must have been in the early hours of the morning that we had a call, a stand-to call. We collected our kit and we surrounded this village, rounding everybody up, and I was left guarding, with a Turkish policeman, two or three Cypriots who were suspected of being involved. These fellows were very stubborn, and they wouldn't say anything at all; so we were holding them in this mill, and there was a mill-race, and above the race was a sort of ledge where the Turks had put the prisoner, and we heard these thunderflashes – not dynamite, but simulated grenades. So they questioned him, and would count to 10, and by the time they'd got to 10 they'd drop one of these on him, and it would explode and fall into the race. I think he eventually spoke. I was in this part of the mill, upstairs. I remember the wooden floor and the roof, and hardly anything else, except this fellow sitting on a chair. The Turkish policeman was quite vicious. We had these toggle ropes we all carried, with loops on one end and a toggle; we linked them together to make a long rope. The Turk took his off, and he was hitting this fellow.

At the time, you think: My God, this is wrong; but you're so incensed about the incidents that have gone on. I think it was about that time that a soldier had been shot, and people coming out of a church just walked by as

110

he lay in the gutter, and spat on him — these sort of incidents. You want to find out what's going on and, when you look back now, you're probably ashamed of it. I'm not proud of it; perhaps I will talk about it when I've had a couple of drinks. Having been to Crete and the Mediterranean, and knowing what nice people they are, you tend to be concerned about it.

We ended up putting a bullet in the barrel of a rifle. We appeared to be doing it but, by keeping hold of the trigger, it didn't take up the bullet. Then we questioned this man and told him if he didn't speak, we'd pull the trigger. Of course, he was in a terrible state of agitation, and obvious dread and worry. He did speak in the end, and he was one of those involved, and we felt this justified the action. To be honest, all the time I was there — and I don't know if this is just retrospect — I just couldn't understand what it was all about, mainly because it was such a beautiful island and the people had been living together for centuries. OK, they'd had their differences, the Greeks and the Turks, over the thousands of years, but they'd lived quite happily. Why they couldn't all call themselves Cypriots and get on with it I could never understand, because it was a beautiful place. And reading Lawrence Durrell's book — I think *Bitter Lemons* — afterwards, it makes you realize what it must have been like. But really, it was a marvellous experience for me.

We did things, we went places, we even got caught up in forest fires where people were burnt to death. I don't think we actually lost anyone in that. But we lost some men in accidental shootings where I think patrols had been set. The standard rule when you'd go out at, say, dusk, was that you wouldn't move until dawn or an hour after dawn. I know one patrol that did move, and was accidentally shot down by their own men, and a man was killed; the first man was killed, and the bullets went right through and hit a second man. He was shot more than once in the pelvis.

Another fatality was in the mountains. With a Browning pistol, if you put pressure on the barrel, it will project slightly from the body of the pistol, and if you held that, it would stop it firing. Somebody tried this, but they could never decide if it was an accident or whether he committed suicide — but he blew his brains out. Another incident in the camp was when somebody — I think it was a lance-corporal — was explaining the Browning action, and he actually blew a hole through his hand. So there were these incidents, and they had their funny side. There was one chap — God! he was a wild character — he shot up a taxi. He got a taxi to bring him back to camp and, you know, the fellow charged him too much. He carried a Sten gun, and he riddled the taxi, and he ended up inside, and my God, it was hard. They do everything at the double. He actually escaped from the compound and found his way to Limassol, swam out into the harbour and got on a boat. Thinking the boat was moving off, poor fellow, he gave himself up, but, it was just changing berth, so they handed him back. But he was a good soldier – lots of initiative, and he had a lot of guts.

There was one incident when we were up in the mountains. We'd been there for four or five weeks, and I was coming back. We'd go up into the mountains in these lorries, and there were times when we'd have to get off the lorry, because the outer wheels would be off the road, and we would have to bounce it to help the driver. After a while they stopped taking 3-tonners, but we were in this particular lorry to bring our Company back. I got on the first lorry, and just before it pulled away, I said, 'No, I'm not getting on this one,' and jumped off. About three of my friends came with me, and we got on the second lorry and we were off the tracks, got on the tarmac road and I can remember looking out and the lorry in front, for no reason, didn't make the corner...and it wasn't a sharp bend, it just went straight on. I can see it now, sailing into space with all the bodies spilling out. I think there were about four or five killed. I was one of the first down there to help, and I got out one fellow; he was dead in the water. There was another with his face smashed on a rock. I climbed up into the lorry, and there was a big pool of blood, and there was a fellow, Private Ward, there. I was in field dress, and I took off my camouflage scarf – it was like net – and I washed his face, and saw he had a broken nose and, as I lifted his head, his scalp fell back on to the back of his neck. So I lifted it back on and tidied him up, and looked after him for a couple of hours, until they got a helicopter and took him back to camp.

In August, it looked as though something was happening about Suez. We then started some simulated training. If I could say something first of all, which is quite interesting, because it happens now: we also started practising how to use helicopters. You know, climbing down ropes; so the helicopter would hover, and the platoon would come down ropes – which obviously was used later in Vietnam, and is quite common practice now. The news was building up about Suez, what was going to happen. We started to have sessions of training; in fact, I think there were only one or two parachute drops when we were in Cyprus. I don't know if it was the heat or the lack of aircraft; there was some problem there, anyway. We'd have formations of lorries over these plains, and we'd always be sitting on the backs of lorries with the tail-back down, and we'd have the same signals as you would in an aeroplane. You know: green on, stand, the door opens, red light on, go – and everybody would roll off, and you'd all form up into your Companies and march off. And we'd do this a lot in readiness for a drop in Suez. I can remember the French Paras were there as well, and we'd have shooting competitions against them, but they were more hardened than us because, I think, a lot of them had been in Vietnam anyway, and Algeria and Dien Bien Phu – a lot of them were there. So there was this build-up, and the para reservists came back, and this added another dimension.

The medical officer, Hartley, might remember this: I was ill and in the medical tent waiting to see the MO, and this fellow was rushed in; he was a reservist. He'd been on a run with a Captain, who'd left this fellow behind, when he collapsed. It turned out he had dysentery and heatstroke. They brought him in, and I helped to cover him with blocks of ice, because he was dehydrated; but the poor fellow died in the end, and there was an enquiry afterwards. I think there was an enquiry in the Houses of Parliament about it. I think he was a cross-country champion, and he'd run off when this fellow was so obviously ill. There was a lot of ill feeling about it, actually, because these reservists had come back, and they obviously weren't acclimatized, and they just kept it quiet.

And then there was a disappointment that we weren't actually going to drop. It seems strange now, but when the Falklands were on, and people around were saying, 'Oh, it's terrible for the soldiers,' I said, 'Look, they're as happy as Larry, because at last they've got the chance to do something they've been trained for.' You know then it's different; I remember feeling thoroughly apprehensive, but we really wanted to go. We'd have these briefings with this Captain of Intelligence, a tremendous fellow. I spent a lot of time with him as his personal bodyguard. When he went out in the Land Rover, I would ride shotgun. As a matter of fact, he took my name and address, because he wanted me to go out to the Argentine because, when he left the Army, he was going to start up a ranch. He wanted me as a security officer on the ranch − a totally different life.

There was this build-up to Suez, and then a decision was made. Partly because we didn't have a commanding officer at the time − we had an acting commanding officer only, and there weren't enough aircraft − it was decided that the Third Battalion would do a drop; and there was a lot of ill feeling about that.

They dropped on Suez Airport. We went out on a troopship of some sort; I can remember climbing down the nets, which is a frightening experience. This was offshore in Suez. You could see the silhouette of the town and the fires behind it, and this sort of thing. We went in on these small craft, and settled on the beach for the night. I never saw the enemy − no, wait a moment, I remember they caught a sniper, who was dealt with in an unceremonious sort of manner. We were under fire, but it wasn't very frightening as it wasn't concentrated; it was spasmodic sort of firing. But we were nervous about it.

The following day we were detailed for various duties. We were on this road junction; there was a very tall building, and the corner on the ground floor was sort of open − it was as if they hadn't completed it, you know − and we had to dig in there with Bren guns and some rifles. I can remember thinking it was a bloody stupid place to be. There was talk that the Russians

113

were going to be involved, and I thought that if a Russian tank comes up here, or any form of tank, one shot and the whole building will be down on us. But that's where we were told to go, and that's where we stayed. But I must say, I was highly relieved when the Regiment turned up and we were able to get away from there.

I think I was in Suez for about three days; then we were taken out and shipped back to Cyprus on HMS *Ocean*, which was an aircraft carrier. Back in Famagusta, back to our camp, and we were on stand-by there; we had all our kit packed, and we waited there for perhaps four days. It seemed that this infantry battalion had gone further down the Canal — was it El Kantara? — and they'd been surrounded by Egyptians. If the conflict had gone on, they would have dropped us right on this position; but, fortunately, it blew over.

After Suez, everybody had some sort of extra weapon. Alun had a Lanchester sub-machine-gun. I remember, I had this Russian rifle with a folding bayonet, but nobody could figure out how to make the rifle work — but a very nice weapon it was. But when we got back to Cyprus, there was this big search for weapons. Everybody who didn't hand these weapons in was in serious trouble, you know. It was funny, because you had these toilets — these latrines — which were dug out of solid rock; rows of twelve latrines with seats on, and you all sat down at the same time. There were all sorts of weapons and ammunition dropped down there. Within a matter of days, it came through that we were going to fly home, and we just left and came back. We were overseas about eleven months; I never got my campaign medal, though.

I had a remarkable two years...going in the Army, I think, changed my whole life; I'm convinced it did. Where I'd always considered myself an 11+ failure — which I was — I put that behind me, mainly through the experience in the Army, and went back to art college, and qualified as a teacher. I think, if I'm in situations now, I've always thought of myself as an ex-Para, sort of in inverted commas; not as somebody who is particularly tough, or whatever, but who would get out of situations, or could cope with situations, you know. Certainly, it was something I wouldn't have missed.

Alun Pask

Alun Pask served with the 1st Battalion, The Parachute Regiment in Cyprus and at Suez, 1955-56. He was subsequently captain of the Welsh Rugby team and a British Lion. He is a retired schoolteacher and lives with his wife and family in Blackwood, Gwent, where he was born.

I think the biggest impact I can remember is that when you went from school into the South Wales Borderers. It was tough. Just going into the Army was tough; the military discipline was hard to take. But when you went from the South Wales Borderers to the Paras, then it was like going from the Girl Guides into the Army. Brecon was a nice, friendly little barracks, and we were all Welsh boys and all from the Valleys. But the Paras was different.

Owen (Parfitt) and I had been together all our lives, and then we'd been together in training in Brecon, in the same platoon and all the rest of it, but when we went to Aldershot to join the 1st Battalion of the Parachute Regiment, Owen was put in, I think, the 2nd Battalion, and I was put in the 1st. So, for the first time ever, we were being split up. So there we are in Aldershot, home of the British Army and there was a famous Sergeant Major called 'Snowy' White — three or four rows of medals; he knew it all and he was the tough Sergeant Major. I went to him and I said, 'Look, Owen and I are old friends; we lived next door to each other. Is there any chance of us being kept together?' A little *[Alun Pask is 6'3" and probably 15 stone]* squaddy, a little National Serviceman and unknown person, is saying this to this famous Sergeant Major Snowy White. Even so, they changed us over and, instead of being split up, they put us both in the 1st Battalion. So then we went out to Cyprus; we flew from Stansted out to Cyprus. When we arrived, they said, 'Right, Parfitt; you're going to Headquarters Company and you, Pask; you're going to C Company,' and I nearly wept; three or four were in this company and three or four in that, but I was the only one sent to C Company.

We were living in tents; little bivouacs at the end of the runway at Nicosia Airport. Two to a tent to start with; we lifted the tents up, lifted the pole up and put cardboard boxes round the sides to make a wall. We weren't permanently there; we could have been in Saudi Arabia or back home at any time – you know the sort of battalion it is. Anyway, when I went to C Company, I joined the real men now. I was in a tent with a fellow called Jock Adams from Glasgow; another one was Taffy Dean from Barry and another was Jock Marshall, who joined us from the Queen's Own Highlanders. C Company had the reputation of being tough nuts; you'd got real, hard men there from Liverpool, Birmingham and London, and it frightened me to death. They had broken noses, scars, medals – and there I was, in amongst this lot. It literally broke my heart inside me, I'm sure, being placed in this company with the real tough nuts.

Owen and I must have been the best soldiers in the battalion, because we were so naive, so keen, so innocent; I was never on a charge. We were the perfect soldiers; we'd had the top awards up in the South Wales Borderers. We had the top awards in the Paras; we were promoted; we never put a foot wrong, and the reason was that I knew I was going to Loughborough College when I came out, and I was told that if you were ever on a charge, your time inside was added on. So I was the perfect soldier, because I didn't want to lose my chance of going to Loughborough. There was a chap from the Royal Welsh Fusiliers who joined us, and he was going to Manchester University to study metallurgy and, again, being an innocent, intelligent schoolboy, he was a good soldier as well. He was up in the Troodos mountains and put his Sten gun down; Brrrrtttt....off it went. An Accidental Discharge – and it was then an automatic 28 days inside. And of course he was late coming out, because those days were added on to his service. He was supposed to go to Manchester on October 1st and, of course, with the extra month added on, he missed out on his metallurgy.

From the word go, we were on operations – being the types they are; you know the Paras' reputation. When we first went out, I was on cordon-and-search in Nicosia. So there I was with this lot down Ledra Street – known at the time as Murder Mile. You're in two Land Rovers. Next thing, you screech to a halt. Four men would go in the front, four in the back, and we'd go through the block. Unfortunately, because of these types we had with us, they'd be in the shops and brothels and nightclubs, and of course they'd be pinching things, some of them. When I look back now, it was a hard battalion; it was an aggressive battalion – it was what they'd been trained for. You've got to have them, whether you like it or not, even in today's Regiment. Next thing now is you go back to camp, and the Military Police are there, and you have to be searched; of course, they're finding watches, and they're finding other things. So the next thing is, they say, 'Take them off Nicosia,' and they put us up in Troodos on more cordon-and-search. But that was good. To get out of the camp, that was what you were trained for; to be up in the Troodos mountains, for a week on end, two weeks on end, sleeping rough and living off the land and cooking for yourself. The food in the camp wasn't good. The way they were cooking when we first started was to get a petrol can, bury it in the ground, put sand in it, and tip in the old kerosene and light it; they were cooking like that. It was iron rations – corned beef, you know – and they'd mix it all together; it was as rough as that. You'd have a big dixie of tea with scum on the top; before you dipped your mug in, you'd go *whhhew* to blow the scum aside. The food was just terrible.

So what I liked was, when you were up in the Troodos, you had your own ration packs, and you did your own cooking, so at least you knew what you were eating; so I enjoyed being out in the mountains, because you were looking after yourself. We used to have tins of hardtack and tins of bully beef. There was one tin of hardtack we opened; it was from Weston's Biscuits in Cwmbran and it was stamped 1943 – there was the stamp on the side and there we were, eating it in *1956!* I've always vowed never to eat corned beef again, because you'd have your tin of corned beef, it would be all melted and you could almost drink it; you couldn't slice it. But up in the mountains you'd cook your own stuff, and then you'd have the grapes and the cherries and the watermelons. And again, the lot I was with, you'd be going along in a Land Rover and a lorry, and there'd be a Cypriot lorry coming along in the other direction and, of course, because you were the military lorry you'd have the right of way; they'd stop and, as you slowed down alongside, then you'd get the old bayonet out and stick a watermelon. It was just the type of men they were. In the battalion, there was only about five of us who were National Servicemen; in lots of other regiments you'd find – say, in the South Wales Borderers – that it would be sixty, seventy or eighty per cent would be National Service. In the Paras, because of the training, there was only four or five of us; there was one from Leicester, one from Canada and me and Owen. All the other fellows, they were the ones who'd been at Arnhem, ones who'd been out in Palestine; when I look back, some of them, they were tough, hard, ruthless, aggressive criminals. You had that type of men, and you have to say that even today's battalion is probably the same type of men; because of the actions they are going to take part in, that's the sort of men you need, you know. So it was up in the mountains, back to camp for two days, clean up, get new kit and new supplies.

In the mountains we wore lightweight jungle greens; you had your parachute smocks for the nighttime – because, of course, it got quite cold – and rubber boots and of course in those days, the Paras' equipment was far better than any other battalions, we didn't have blancoing, we didn't have polishing. Other regiments had these little square packs; we had Bergen rucksacks. The equipment we had then was marvellous, but I always remember – on the beach in Suez we were with the French Paras and

117

comparing our equipment with theirs and, although ours was the best in the British Army, we always said ours didn't compare with the French. All their equipment seemed to be far better; they had boots up to mid-calf and of course, our boots in the British Army had always been the problem — like we saw in the Falklands, the Argentinians had far better boots than us.

If I remember rightly, it was 5 November, 1956, that we went to Suez; unfortunately, because of the way the Army was, they decided that only the 3rd Battalion could go in by air. It was originally decided that the two battalions, 1st and 3rd, would be dropped at El Gamil airfield, which is at Port Said, and of course they then found they didn't have enough aeroplanes; and when they decided to invade, it took them — what? — three or four months to assemble the equipment and the ships, and bring them from Malta, and so on, and so on. So they didn't have enough aircraft then, and they decided — much to our disappointment after we'd had all the intelligence, after we'd all been briefed — that we would go by sea. In the camp in Cyprus in a tin shed they'd built a model of Port Said — the Intelligence Officer, a chap called Captain Elliot, who later left the Paras and became a Cistercian monk. They took us all in — and this is top security, now — none of the locals was allowed in; once Suez started, they were banned from coming into the camp. They briefed us; they told us where we were going, what we were doing — all hyped up, and then there weren't enough aeroplanes to drop the two battalions. In the meantime they'd brought us back to this country, we did two drops on Salisbury Plain; they brought us all the way back to Cyprus, and we did two drops on Nicosia Plain — so we did four drops, and then they didn't have enough planes.

The next thing, the 3rd Battalion went in by plane, much to our disappointment, and we were taken in by troopship — I can't remember the name of it now. We took a troopship for two days and two nights, and when we got to Suez we were transferred down rope ladders, which we hadn't practised before and, when you look back — I read all the books on the Falklands, and the one problem we had there was transferring the Paras down these rope ladders into these small Tank Landing Craft; you have seventy or eighty pounds of equipment in your rucksack, and if you fall....It was dark, the middle of the night, so we couldn't see what was happening on shore. You had to jump into these boats, and the whole of C Company — that was about seventy of us — was in one of these, full battle packs, black faces, the lot; the next thing, the order was given for a round up the spout. We went ashore; the old flap came down and you're half up your legs in water. We're on the beach and we start digging in — we weren't under fire, as far as I can remember. But you could certainly hear shelling and mortar fire. The next thing I can remember which sticks in my mind: there were a lot of beach chalets on the front, a long row of them; so this commando —

45 Royal Marine Commando, with a 3.5-inch rocket launcher − so he goes to the one end and sends the rocket launcher right through the lot of them; so there they were, a row of beach huts − and I'm talking now of a bloody great long row of them − and instead of searching each one, he goes to the one end and whoosh! − they're all flattened. Then we spent these several hours on the beach getting all the equipment ashore.

Of course, in any action there's rumours; there's counter-rumours; there's orders − you're told to do this; there's messing around; so you dig one hole and get down, like, and the next thing, you're moved five yards forward to dig another hole...and the next thing is, they've got no vehicles, so we commandeered some buses. It's funny looking back; I couldn't take watches off people like some did, but at the same time, because I was so disciplined, if I was told to shoot and kill, I would do it just like that. Anyway, we commandeered a bus, and I was sitting on top; there were about thirty or forty within the bus, heavily equipped, rucksacks; just imagine if we'd been ambushed and shot up − we'd never have got out. On reflection, no way should we have ever used the bus − one entrance at the front, one at the back. What a stupid thing to do.

I'd found a Lanchester sub-machine-gun which I had with me; I had all my equipment, plus my own weapon, plus the Lanchester. So I carried this for four or five days, brought it back to Aldershot, and someone in the MPs took it off me and I never saw it again.

The next thing, we were told to move down the Canal, to head for El Kantara. We set up roadblocks, and were stopping people and searching them. Again − unfortunately − certain Scottish soldiers were looting and taking things off people. We saw vehicles in the distance; there'd be big flaps on. There's always confusion − you know, what it must have been like in the Falklands − fighting in the dark. It's always like this in the Army; the poor soldier knows nothing of what's going on. They don't tell the private soldier anything. It would be nice if you had some idea of what you were doing, and where you were going, and why. Then the order came to move down to El Kantara, and the next rumour that came was that the Russians were joining in the war, and we began to say, 'Well, Gypos, OK, but if the Russians are joining in....'

Then it was down the Canal rather rapidly; we had a Land Rover by then. I don't know where that had come from. We never got to El Kantara, which was about half-way down the Canal, and the next thing was the stop and dig-in. This was late afternoon, and there was an oil refinery burning. I remember saying, 'Come on; I've got to have a pee in the Canal, to say I've peed in the Canal.' Of course, my father was there during the last war, spent seven years in Palestine and Egypt; and then David, my elder brother, was out in the Canal Zone with the Second Battalion, and then I was out there.

119

Well, we dug in, and I can remember being on guard duty at night, and the oil refinery burning, and it was like daylight. There I was on guard and, instead of being able to get into a shadow or a hole out of sight, there I was having to patrol silhouetted against the flames.

Then the order came that we had to go back to Cyprus, because the Egyptians, I gather, had dug in tanks at El Kantara – buried the tanks with just the turret showing, like these Iraqis might well have been doing in the Gulf War. We were going to drop the other side of El Kantara, so we were rushed back to Port Said; there was general chaos there. We were all rushed on to an aircraft carrier, HMS *Albion*; the sea was very, very rough, and the sailors on board tell you that, if you have a storm in the Med, it can be as bad as any ocean in the world. So it was back to Cyprus to practise the drop on El Kantara. But we didn't know the feeling of the people at home, that the country wasn't with us; we didn't know about the divided political scene and the fact that it was general chaos, and Eden was on the rocks; we didn't know any of this. Then it came to a cease-fire, so the four-and-a-half or five days came to a sudden end. We couldn't understand what the hell was happening; there we are, all psyched up and ready to go, and then the rumour came: 'Cease-fire.' 'Christ! What the hell's happening?' we thought.

We flew home on December 23rd by Libya and then Malta in a Shackleton; there were no seats, we were just sitting and lying amongst all our equipment – it was a hell of a journey, eighteen or twenty hours. I never talked about it to my family, never discussed it; just a job, I suppose, when you look at it – that's what soldiers are there for. I've never talked about this before, not even with Owen Parfitt. I've never even thought about it; and the more you go in depth now, the more it's coming back. I did not receive a medal; I just got a ribbon, which was sewn on. During Suez they called up the reservists and, oh yes, there was a lot of resentment, because the discipline was that tough. At the end of the day, mind, nothing materialized; it was typical barrack-room complaining and moaning. But – you just imagine – there you are; house, family, work, kids – and all of a sudden taken out from your well-paid job on to Army pay. No wonder there was resentment.

Some of these mountain villages in Cyprus were very primitive, very backward; life hadn't changed for hundreds of years. You go into this house; there they are, cooking outside – and this is what the whole operation is about; searching and finding, and if you don't search, you don't find. And again, I would like to think that our battalion was so professional that, if they went in, they found things. Other units may have gone in and looked around, and said, 'Nothing here', and out they went. But what did hurt me, you'd go into one of these houses, and you'd go in their best room, and they'd have one of these chests-of-drawers, and all their linen folded up, and all their lace folded up. What can you do? It's like Customs; they take it all out, and disturb what was neat and tidy, and you have to put it back. But you go in these houses, and it's only by being so thorough that you find things. I found posters, which at the time doesn't seem very important, but at least it gives you the lead for the Intelligence fellows. The only ammunition I found was in a well, and I was lowered down this well, and half-way down there were holes in the wall, and I found ammunition there – about six rounds of shotgun cartridges.

Another place that sticks in my mind is a village where they found weapons and arms, and the Royal Engineers came in and bulldozed it down...which again, you know, to all the others in the battalion, it didn't affect them; but being like I was – may I say it – an honest, good-living, innocent type of person, it worried me a bit; but then, that's what National Service is all about. Although, looking back, it's hurting me in a way, at the time it was the thing to do; it had to be done, you never questioned it. Because they found terrorist activity in this village, they said, 'Right: get the bulldozers in,' and it was a punitive thing, like you do in any military campaign, I suppose.

It was a tremendous two years, but I went in with the attitude that I had to make the best of it. When I look back, I had tremendous experiences; went to about seventeen or eighteen countries. I saw a bit of action and got around, whereas other people in National Service...friend of mine from the Blackwood area ended up as a typist in the RAF and came home every weekend. So, from their point of view, it was a waste of time, whereas I joined, like Owen, the best unit – may I say it – and you saw action; you saw life. So from our point of view it was tremendous; it changed us from being a boy one day into being a man the next. I remember Bill Hallaway (NCO at South Wales Borderers depot) saying, 'I've got twelve weeks to change you into men, because in fourteen weeks' time you'll be out in the jungles of Malaya.' And that was the reality of it.

Eddie Percival

Eddie Percival served in the Rifle Brigade in Malaya from 1955 to 1957. He now lives with his wife and family in South London and works for British Gas.

I had my medical and went along to Croydon, where you had to sign on. The actual place I went to was an RAF base. I was talking to the people there, and they said if I liked to sign on as a regular I could go abroad, and I was very interested in that. So they gave me a list of regiments' names, and I decided to join the Rifle Brigade, as a three-year man. But really I was a National Serviceman and called up as such. In fact, when I came back from Malaya, they wanted me to go on cadre to be a corporal, but I refused because I wasn't going to stay in the Army.

After I finished my basic training, I was posted to Malaya as part of the advance party for the battalion. We took off from Blackbushe and it took us roughly three days to get to Malaya by plane. I can't remember all the countries we stopped at, but we had to travel in civvies because of the trouble we'd recently had in India; we had to pretend to be civilians. We landed at Singapore and there was a base camp there and, of course, we were the advance party, so we had to go to a place called Johore Bahru, just at the beginning of Malaya across from Singapore, and wait for our battalion to arrive.

Then we had to do jungle training, and that took about six to eight weeks to complete. It was entirely different from what we'd done in England; you had jungle ranges. Where on a normal range you had to fire at a distance, out there you'd go along in the bush and someone pulls a string, and an 'enemy' cardboard cut-out springs up, and you've got to fire from the hip automatically. We were armed with the new FN rifle, which was an automatic really – no control with the bolt action; you just pulled the trigger and fired, and you were ready to fire again. We wore jungle green uniforms, with jungle boots that came up to the top of your shins, and the laces sort of went in and out, making it very tight. That was to protect you from all the different aspects of the jungle – snakes and what have you. Leeches were the terrible thing in Malaya.

Once we'd done our training, we moved further up in Malaya towards the capital, which is Kuala Lumpur. We had a camp there, and from there we started doing operations. When a particular operation came up, we used to be briefed: exactly what was going on, what we were going to do, how many days we were going in the jungle for — either a three-day or a five-day or even a ten-day spell, or more if it was necessary. With a three-day or a five-day, we managed to have the food and everything on our backs. With a ten-day, we'd have to have an air drop. You'd find a clearing and lay down white things — or anything different from green — so that they could see it. Then they'd drop these big cardboard containers by parachute. Our rations were quite good, but we liked the rations more from the air drop than the ones we were issued with. We had all the tinned food; you had rice and you had curry powder, biscuits, Rolos, condensed milk in tubes and the fuel to cook with. That was basically it, really. It was very, very good stuff. We never weighed our rucksacks, but all I know is that you could never stand up straight, because the weight would take you backwards. You'd got your bedding, your food and your ammunition, which was fifty rounds, and we used to help the Bren-gunner out; we used to carry spare magazines for him — his load was rather heavy, so we had to carry some of his as well.

In the jungle, you can't really sleep on the floor, because there are so many insects and things that crawl all over you. To protect ourselves in Malaya, we slept in hammocks, so we were all issued with one made of thick canvas. When we were in the jungle, we'd always stop for the night where the trees were very young, with trunks about four or five inches thick to tie the hammocks to. Then we had a two-minute time for cutting off branches and pieces of wood to stiffen the ends of the hammocks, so the amount of noise was kept low. We all had machetes for this. For the first three months I was in Malaya, I was the batman to the Platoon Officer, so I had to look after him. When it came to the two minutes' chopping time, I had to do his chopping as well, which made it difficult; I had a harder job than most of the others.

What we were there for was fighting the Communist Terrorists and the idea was to control them because they were sabotaging the rubber plantations out there, and our main aim was to protect the rubber plantations and to drive them away into the jungle. We had to do many ambushes; we got the information from somewhere, where I don't know. We had to be in a certain area, for instance by a river, because they had the information that these CTs were going to cross at this particular time. So we might be on an ambush for three days, just in one place, which is not very comfortable at all, and you had to be very quiet. I never had a 'contact' with the enemy, but I often wonder if they ever saw me. Once we were going along a river and we came across some baked beans, and they weren't very old at all, and we had an idea that they must have heard us and run; they must have been very, very quick. You had the feeling, though, when you were going through the jungle, that you were being watched from time to time. It would suddenly come to you: 'Hello; someone's there.' Fortunately, in one sense, I suppose I never came up against it.

I never saw the enemy at all, but after I'd been in Malaya about a year and I was quite an experienced person – and the officers get to know what sort of character you are – I was selected to go with a sergeant, a Malayan police fellow and what they call an SEP – Surrendered Enemy Personnel – one of the actual surrendered Communist Terrorists, and she was a woman. What she did was, she took the three of us to a hiding place in the jungle where they used to be. She took us right into the jungle, to this very big, high, steep hill, and when we got there it was full of rock formations. I was told to stand outside on guard, because it formed a sort of cave with the rocks. They went inside and then they came out, and they had big jars of salt; and we had to break them, because that's how they used to keep their food, in this salt. We got rid of all this salt, and then the sergeant said to me, 'Do you know what?' he said; 'I know you weren't in there with us, but it's unbelievable.' And I said, 'What's that?' And he said, 'They had a rope going down, all the way down under the hill, and they had a bucket, and that's how they get their water. It's unbelievable; how did they know it was there?' I listened to him in amazement. The woman was looking at me, because I was quite a young-looking chap, and she was going, 'Him *Chico*' (a young boy), and the sergant said, 'No, no, he's eighteen; he's a soldier.' She thought I was just a kid. I've always looked young, because I've got small features. But that cave was an amazing experience.

In my platoon, because of the situation we were in, the pressure of the jungle, we all became very friendly. We came from all different parts of England; you get country people, you get city people but, once you are all mixed together, you all become the same sort of people. It's very good, really, how you become very friendly. We also had some Iban trackers with us; they were what you call 'leading scouts' in the jungle. Where we would have to use a compass to find our way, they would use their heads. I often used to try and trick them when we were stopped for our little ten-minute breaks [*troops on the march rest for ten minutes every hour*]. I used to pick on one and go, 'Camp that way – to the west,' and they'd go, 'No, Johnnie, that way.' Completely the opposite way, and they were always right and I was always wrong. They had a perfect sense of direction, because they must have been brought up in the jungle. Amazing how they ever did it. They were very small people, covered in tattoos. When we had a few days off in the camp, I happened to be passing one of their tents, and I saw one of them doing a tattoo; and I went in there and I said: 'Think you could give me a tattoo?' And they all laughed in their little way, you know. I persuaded him to do a tattoo on me. What he used looked like mapping ink or something, and they got a piece of bamboo stick with a very sharp pin in it – a very sharp nail, really. They'd dip it in the ink, and they'd rest it on your arm. There was no drawing as such. If you wanted a tattoo in England, you'd have a transfer drawing put on your arm, but this was sort of guesswork. They lay it on your arm, and they get a hammer and they tap it in. It's quite painful; you think, 'Oh God!' I had the word LONDON put on my arm, being from the city and that, and then I had a little pattern put round the outside. A couple of days after I had it done came Pay Day, so I queued up for my pay, and the Captain looks at my arm and says, 'What have you got on your arm, Percival – is that a tattoo?' 'Yessir,' I said, and he said, 'I hope that's not going to go the other way, or I'll have you for self-inflicted injuries.' Anyway, I managed to hide it, because it did swell up quite a bit. They told me it would fade after ten years, but it hasn't.

Another funny thing happened to us as I was at the back of a patrol; I turned round, and there were about five or six of what they called pygmies with little spears standing behind us. That was the first time I ever saw them. They lived right in the middle of the jungle. The SAS used to drop into the jungle by parachute or helicopter and stay in there with these pygmies.

One of my best friends in the platoon came from Birmingham. I think I really liked him because of his accent. Coming from London, I thought it was really funny, the way he talked. He was quite a good character, quite a lot bigger than me, and you found that, once you got a friend, when you got into the jungle you generally 'base up' together, and put both your hammocks between the same two trees, like a bunk-bed. You'd do your cooking together, as well.

Our platoon sergeant was a good fellow. Unfortunately, he had a stutter, but we made allowances for that. Now he, funnily enough, was a National Serviceman, and he made the grade of sergeant; he was very good, we respected him for that. Anything he asked us to do, we were only too willing to do it for him. Our Platoon Officer – I think he was a National Serviceman, I'm not sure actually – his name was Mr John Roper. He respected me, I think. What it was, was that I was rather good at shooting on the jungle range, firing from the hip, what you call a 'natural', I suppose. He was one of these ambitious officers; he wanted to get a 'kill', but we never did.

As time went on and I must have been there about a year, they decided somewhere along the line in the battalion that they were going to do a new idea. Normally, you'd go out into the jungle as a platoon, and you'd split up into – say – six patrols of four men each. Then they came up with this new idea; they called it the Guinea-Pig Patrol, and it was one officer and two riflemen, and what we did was, you had a three-day pack, and you'd go out to the edge of the rubber plantations at first light, and you had a certain area to cover within the three days. This was the first time it had ever been done in Malaya, and I was one of the people chosen. The other man that was picked, he was a very hard person; he was one of my close friends. His name was Terry Herron, and he used to be a booth boxer before he came into the Army, because he never had no mother or father. He was a hard man. I was selected because I was a good shot, and I wasn't one of those people who panicked. Terry Herron was the leading scout, and I brought up the rear; the officer was in the middle of us the whole time. We slept on the ground and we didn't have a hammock, and made like a tent out of our ponchos, and our officer slept between us. When I think about that now, I think, 'How nerve-racking'; and yet I managed to fall asleep, and just wake up the next morning quite normally. The only time I ever got frightened, I was in the jungle and it was our turn to look after the base camp, the four of us. I was lying in my hammock – and you've got to remember that the base camp is made roughly in a circle with a perimeter wire – and you don't ever go to sleep, because you know the enemy is there. I was just lying in my hammock, because it wasn't my turn to be sentry, and suddenly I saw all the trees moving, and I thought: My God, we're being attacked; I can't believe it, and my heart was beating so fast it was unbelievable. I got my rifle and put one up the breech and I got it in my hand, and I was amazed to see all these bushes moving, and suddenly this big grey elephant came out. It just stopped, and it just sat down and looked at me. The thought went through my mind, What would I be really like if the enemy was there? Because you've been trained with a rifle, and you're taught to relax and take a breath, and all that. Now, when I was in that situation, I can remember my rifle waving about all over the place; it shows when the pressure is on, you become different. You might settle down after one shot, but the first time – God! That was terrible.

One particular time we were on operations, and the planes came over and they bombed the jungle; then we had to go in there to find the CTs, but there was no one there. The Royal Artillery was there, as well. Sometimes the Gurkhas used to come with us on operations. They were like a sister regiment to the Rifle Brigade. Gurkhas used to really like doing ambushes. They really thought the English soldier was the best soldier ever born; so they idolized us, the Gurkhas. I had a Gurkha next to me on an ambush; where, myself, I'd be very fidgety because the mosquitoes used to bite and you used to be slapping away at yourself...but them – they'd just get in a position and they wouldn't move, because they respected us, and they didn't want to let their own selves down. They were very good.

Each company out there used to have turns each for a fortnight or so on what they called 'gate checks'. The idea was that you had to check up on the civilians passing, and we had a list of the things they weren't allowed to carry, so they couldn't help the terrorists in the jungle. That was the contact I got with the civilians in Malaya, because you had to check them over; you used to get on the buses as well, and ask for their passes. Everyone had to have a pass and a photo. Batteries were one of the main things they weren't allowed to carry, and rice. We had to check bicycles, and look in the handlebars to see if there was any rice in there. Of course, then you start to pick up the lingo because you're on these gate checks, because you're not there on your own; you generally had a Malayan policeman with you. If you did a guard with them for two hours, you ended up talking to them and beginning to learn the language. I thought I picked it up quite well myself; it was interesting, that.

During my time in Malaya, I think I must have spent more time in the jungle on patrol than I did in camp, perhaps 300 days. Funnily enough, when you go abroad, you think you're going to get brown in the sun, but when you're actually in the jungle you go white; because you're so low and all the growing plants are so high, actually you come out looking ill, because you're drained — what with the heat — and when you come to an opening in the jungle where there's sun, it really hits you. It's so hot, you just want to get out of it; it's too much for you.

Some parts of the jungle were very picturesque. There were little tiny birds, and little pigs like wild boars. You'd never see them, you'd only hear them; they were too quick. You see their little footprints in the ground; they were everywhere, but you'd never see them. You'd see the occasional snake. Once I put my hand on this tree that had been split by lightning, and all these little scorpions came in and out of the tree. God! it frightened the life out of me. I'd never seen a scorpion before; I'd read about them. Oh, they were horrible, and what I did was, I ran, and what happened was, I had a big lizard in front of me, staring at me, and suddenly it was gone. They really put me off. Another time, we were on patrol, and the officer wanted to go to the toilet and, while we were waiting for him, we saw this snake and it was swallowing a frog. We were amazed at it; we were watching, wondering what would happen next. Anyway, it swallowed the frog and suddenly it came for us. God! we ran; we forgot about our officer, and he came running after us, pulling up his trousers. 'What's the matter? Is it elephants?' he said. Another particular time, the Iban tracker was leading us and we came to the edge of the jungle, and this Iban tracker went, 'Cobra, cobra,' and he ran, and we just followed him. We ran — oh, it must have been 500 yards before we stopped — and I was out of breath. I was the last one, and I couldn't understand what had happened. I said, 'What's up?' He said that if you see a cobra snake you have to run, because they attack you, you see.

We did have some 'kills' out there by my battalion; my company, actually. They killed the second in command of the terrorists. But they did a bad thing, apparently – I heard – because they actually hung the body out of the back of the truck and went through the town. We had one or two casualties in accidents on patrols, but we never lost anyone to the enemy – not in my battalion.

When I first went out there, I was very ignorant, when I was batman to the officer, he asked me if I knew why we were there, and I didn't really know; and then he explained to me what was going on: we were protecting the rubber plantations, and they (Communist guerrillas) were coming across from China all the time, weren't they? They had tin mines out there, as well.

I came home from Malaya on a ship; the *Dilwara*, I think it was called. It took nearly a month. I had a long disembarkation leave, because I'd done the full stretch in Malaya. It's a funny thing; you don't see your mother for a long time, you feel you're a big man, you're so with it because of what you've done. When I got on the bus from Waterloo Station, it was all hustle and bustle. I wasn't used to this now, and I thought: 'God! This is England.' It's only eighteen months away, and yet it's so different – amazing. I was pleased that I'd done my service in Malaya; quite proud, actually.

Peter Robinson

Peter Robinson served with the Royal Army Service Corps in Malaya, 1948-49. He is retired and lives in South London.

I had a slight problem initially on the troopship going to Malaya. We'd had a long journey by train from Thetford, where we were in a transit camp, down to Southampton. My memory says that it was overnight, and I'd won a lot of money at pontoon and brag – which persuaded me that the one thing I didn't want to do on the troopship was to play cards; I might lose the money. My position on the troopship was a little different, because I was in the Orderly Room on the ship, with a colleague. We were both Royal Army Service Corps clerks, and we ran the ship's Orderly Room. We had civilians on the ship – military-related civilians – and, after several days at sea, a dear old lady came into the Orderly Room and asked which of us young men played the bugle so beautifully at Lights Out and Reveille, and with a straight face we told her we took it in turns. The reality was that we took it in turns to put the gramophone record on. A slightly disturbing experience on the boat was that, since I worked in the Orderly Room, part of my duties were to distribute daily orders around the ship, and we had on the ship a lot of QUAIMNS *[Queen Alexandra's Imperial Military Nursing Service]* who, of course, were officers. One of my tasks was to deliver the daily orders to the cabin of the lady in charge of the QUAIMNS, and I remember being very disturbed, as an Other Rank, one day in the quarters of these nurses being faced by a lady stark naked, dressing in her cabin with the door open. I fled as though the fear of God was in me – mainly because I was very conscious of the fact that to have any kind of sexual contact with an officer was a very serious offence.

We lived on the mess deck of the ship. We had tables that folded up at night and I had a hammock, but the reality is that I didn't like the hammock, and I spent most of my time on the troopship sleeping either on the floor of the mess deck or, when the weather was good, on the (upper) deck of the boat. We went ashore at Aden, and we went ashore at Colombo. At Aden, we spent most of our time at the main NAAFI, which had a cordoned-off section of the beach for swimming in — cordoned off to keep the sharks out. I was very impressed by the NAAFI because, I can remember, it was full of birds flying all over the place and settling on the tables, eating crumbs.

I suffered a lot from seasickness, first in the Bay of Biscay and going through the Straits of Gibraltar, and then for a week in the Indian Ocean catching the fag-end of a typhoon. That's something that's stuck in my memory.

We arrived at Singapore and spent several weeks in a transit camp there. I was a Motor Transport Clerk, so I was posted to an RASC Motor Transport (MT) unit in Kuala Lumpur to be in charge of the MT stores. About eighty per cent of the unit, I think, were LEPs — Locally Employed Personnel — Malays; Chinese; Indians. For the first few weeks we were in hut accommodation, but then the unit was moved to a different site, where we had tented accommodation. It was strictly segregated; we did not live with the locally-enlisted personnel, most of whom lived at home.

Our unit supplied the infantry. We were part, originally, of a Gurkha brigade and, when we left camp to go to distant places, we were always armed; we were always supposed to travel in convoy, but some drivers didn't like to travel in convoy, and faked temporary breakdowns in order to travel independently. One of the joys of my life in Malaya was that I actually had a six-gun — a Smith & Wesson .44 — which I used to carry in my pocket or in my belt. It made me feel like John Wayne. But our normal small arm was a version of the .303 rifle. It wasn't like the old Lee Enfield; it had an exposed metal barrel with a flash eliminator. But going round the camp we weren't normally armed, except for parades and guard duties, because we were not in a guerrilla area. When we went to Kuala Lumpur in the evenings, we were never armed. We had the free run of Kuala Lumpur, apart from the red-light areas, where we weren't supposed to go.

As an MT unit, the unit's lorries spent a lot of time on the road, so there was always the risk of an ambush. In fact, one of our captains in a jeep did get ambushed, although it was rumoured that those who were ambushing him thought he was the vanguard of a convoy of Devons infantry, who were, by chance, a little bit behind him on the road. But by and large our particular unit was not very often caught up in the violence. I can't remember whether we had any casualties apart from this captain and his driver — one of whom was killed and one wounded — but I don't think so.

Someone took a potshot at me once. It was possibly an accident. I was actually in the workshop one Sunday morning, doing some work, and somebody took a shot at me from a distance. My first reaction was to hit the ground as fast as I could; my second feeling was one of rage — a sense of outrage — somebody shooting at me, and my not being able to do anything about it. But if I'd ever used my Smith & Wesson in anger, I'd have probably shot my own foot off.

But in Malaya there was a 'sharp end'. A lot of the war was fought by ambush; on the road or in the jungle. Large parts of the country were no-go areas — dangerous areas. Other parts were safe; we could happily go into Kuala Lumpur without being at risk, but away from the larger towns there were certain areas which were 'black' areas. That's where the sharp end was; where the infantry operated.

I more or less enjoyed my time in Malaya, I suppose — apart from the fact that I hated the Army and wanted to get out as soon as possible. For me, in a safe area, every day was in a sense a normal day. One did a parade; one did one's job; one went out in the evening for a meal and a drink as long as one had the money.

The politics of the situation couldn't be ignored. I suppose I felt there was a job to be done out there. I was conscious of the fact that the Communists were mainly Chinese, whereas the Chinese only accounted for forty per cent of the population of Malaya. I rather liked the Chinese — we had Chinese civilians working in our workshops — but the fact is that there was a revolt going on, and it seemed to me at the time, I think, that this was an attempt by a minority to dominate a majority; so that, although I then had pinkish beliefs, I certainly had no feeling that I was involved in an unjust war. I still feel that there was a rightness about it. In all those wars — like Korea, Malaya and Cyprus — the issues were not necessarily clear-cut; it was difficult to see which side was right, and there were a lot of cock-ups. But, as for my particular little war, I didn't have any political objections to it while I was there — which was from June or July '48 to the end of November '49 — I could not see any alternative.

I can't remember the exact size of my unit, but my guess would be about 250 people, the majority of whom were locally-enlisted personnel. As far as I'm aware, we (the British soldiers) all lost touch straight away once we left the Army. I was very friendly with a handful, and the ones that I was friendly with were all ex boy-soldiers who, I learned then (and later in relation to ex boy-airmen), were a highly intelligent bunch of men with considerable strength of character.

The food in the Army was *horrible*. I was earning, probably, more money then — actual cash in hand — than I'd earn for the next twenty years; I think I had £5 a week clear. I was a First Class tradesman; a corporal with an overseas allowance and an active service allowance. But a lot of it I spent on food. My evening meal was usually eaten in some local Chinese, Malayan or Indian café.

I still think that the best thing I've read about National Servicemen in Malaya is — despite certain exaggerations — Leslie Thomas's *The Virgin*

Soldiers. That fact that I was in a unit where, among the British troops, there was quite a high percentage of regulars who had stayed on after the war also coloured the situation. And it's worth mentioning, I think – and this must have been true throughout Malaya – the obsession with sex among these youngish chaps in an environment where, for all practical purposes, there were no women except for prostitutes.

There were all sorts of funny experiences. I remember that I and one or two of my friends started going to a local Evangelical Protestant church in Kuala Lumpur when we discovered that you got a free meal at the home of one of the congregation after attending the service. We didn't go for very long, mainly because the company was largely white middle-class expatriates and, no doubt inadvertently, condescending; so, despite the free food – and it was good – we didn't find it easy to mix with them, since we were Other Ranks.

During my service, there was one occasion when I was just a bit frightened. We had been on a Sunday trip to swim at a place called Port Dickson, which must have been about sixty to eighty miles from our camp through the jungle. Coming back, the lorry broke down because, as we discovered, the second tank was full of water and not petrol – presumably because the vehicle's normal driver had been engaged in some fiddle with the petrol. So we had to strip the engine down, and my recollection is that some of our party had to walk a few miles through the jungle as dusk was about to fall to get some petrol in jerrycans. I remember being a little disconcerted when I discovered that, of the handful of rifles we possessed, one was being held by a Christian chap who was effectively a pacifist. I remember grabbing his rifle fast.

I was a bit apprehensive then, but the real fear I remember was in the middle of 1949, when the Chinese Communists were sweeping through China and approaching Hong Kong. I think all of us suddenly had a horrible fear that we would be sent to Hong Kong to fight the Chinese Communists, and spend the next ten years of our lives in the Far East. I think most of us conscripts were probably very worried by that possibility, particularly since it must have been about that time that the eighteen-month period of National Service was extended. I ended up serving about twenty-one months. In a sense, perhaps, that's probably the time when I had the greatest anxiety, but the actual risk of physical danger didn't bother me much; I was far more frightened by the authority of the Army and of Army prisons, where several of my colleagues did time. Army prisons, at least in Malaya – or particularly in Malaya – were not very nice places. One lost a lot of weight in the Army prison, because you 'doubled' everywhere, so you were liable to lose the odd couple of stone.

We were not a fighting unit, but I don't think the fighting troops that we mixed with from time to time shared the attitude of the chaps you just mentioned in Cyprus, who would fire a shot 'accidentally' in order to get twenty-eight days in the regimental prison. My impression was that their morale was pretty high. That might have been because they were on jungle patrols a lot, which might have been helpful in producing high morale. Also, they did get rest periods. In my day, there were rest centres at Penang and in the Central Highlands. It was also possible to spend time in Kuala Lumpur and in Singapore, so in the larger urban areas when I was there you could relax. It's perhaps interesting that in Malaya in 1948-49 — and, as far as I know, right throughout the troubles — the urban centres were relatively safe for British servicemen.

The rather bizarre nature of the defence forces early in 1948 is something else I remember. You had the Malay police; you had local rubber-planters and the like, who were sort of part-time soldiers; you had whatever there was of the British Army. I've got a feeling that there might have been the odd Australian unit in Malaya when I arrived there. Sometimes they were all mixed up together. Then there were some native trackers; it was said that they were Dyaks from Borneo who, in the not-so-distant past, had been a head-hunting people. When I first saw these native trackers, I looked at them with some respect. But, of course, all that was in the early days, the very beginning of the emergency. Within a few months, the whole of the defence forces were much more orthodox, and organized on conventional lines. By 1949, things seemed to have straightened out, and were much better organized. In my own unit, the majority of our Locally Enlisted Personnel were Malays, while the majority of our civilian workshop people were Chinese.

At the end of my service, I came back as I went out: by boat. It was much the same as the voyage out, apart from the fact that, with demobilization ahead, our emotions were completely different. We were at sea on Christmas Day, 1949. It wasn't a very good Christmas. We were in the Mediterranean by that time; as I remember, it was only after a protest by some of the troops that we were actually allowed one bottle of beer apiece.

We arrived at Liverpool, and we were shipped straight back to Aldershot, where we were demobilized at the speed of light. My recollection is that we travelled overnight from Liverpool to Aldershot, and I was in a train on my way home by that afternoon. When I came home, I didn't talk to my parents about it at all; but I certainly spoke to my friends who had been doing their National Service elsewhere.

I don't really have any desire to go back to Malaya on a visit, mainly because I suspect it's changed so much. Occasionally I've thought to myself: Well, what about it? — but no, not really. I thought it was a marvellous climate, though. Being in the Army I think was, for me, a bad experience, but the experience of going to Malaya – in retrospect – was a good one. I did not like being in the Army but, despite that, I don't think I would have missed going to Malaya. I had a lot of experiences I wouldn't otherwise have had: I saw the world, and I matured a bit faster.

Geoffrey Saunders

Geoffrey Saunders served with the Royal Greenjackets in Cyprus, 1958-59. He lives in Cardiff and is a banker.

In March, 1958, having been trained by the SLI (Somerset Light Infantry), we were re-badged to go to the Oxford & Bucks, later to form part of the Royal Greenjackets, because they were short of men in Cyprus. I was given 'salt water stripes' to take the whole platoon across, there being no officer or NCO going with the platoon at all. This had the added advantage that I was able to give someone else the duty of mucking out the toilets downstairs (on the troopship). We were, of course, not allowed to roam the whole ship, as it was very much regimented between officers and non-commissioned officers. I was actually allowed into the non-commissioned ranks, as I was holding a pair of stripes – which gave me some little elevated status. The main time on board ship was spent playing cards, mainly for cigarettes, because cigarettes were so cheap; if I remember rightly, about a shilling (5 pence) a packet, and you would find four, five, eight people sitting below the bunks, having packets and packets of cigarettes around them, playing various card games – none of which got too serious, because the troops virtually had no money; they were not well paid in those days.

It was quite an interesting trip, with three days to get to Gib, three days to get to Malta and then, finally, three days to get to Limassol, Cyprus. As soon as we got to Limassol, we were taken up to the tented barracks just outside the town, just away from Berengaria Village. The tents were square, four-man, 160-pounders, sandbagged and trenched, and I slept under canvas for the whole of the fourteen months I was there. In the summer, of course, it was baking hot – even with the sides rolled up; and in fact, the only winter I spent there–1958 – was the first time in fifty years that Limassol actually had snow, and we were absolutely battened down as much as we could go. The food we were given was excellent, but the method of cooking was not as good as it is now, not by a long chalk. The Army could in those days – when it was still nearly all National Servicemen – basically ruin

135

anything it cooked. The main thing was that, being in Cyprus, we had a tremendous amount of fruit, and the fruit was the absolute saviour. Of course, the British Army on active service is always looking for anything it can pinch. In the season, there were the grapes and the oranges and the lemons and the grapefruits; out on patrol, we would go through the orchard, just pick what we wanted and walk out the other side and nobody had any argument – especially as you've got nine people with sub-machine-guns, semi-automatic weapons and a Bren gun. One time we went out, found a beautiful vineyard of grapes, ate them, and three of us ended up with very serious dysentery, which means that I always wash fruit from that day until this.

Having disembarked and gone up to the camp, the first thing we did was to go into some extra basic training for the sort of work we were going to do, which was anti-terrorist. Because we, of course, were all looking for Uncle George (Colonel George Grivas, leader of the EOKA guerrillas), his number two and their little team. Having done our extra seven days of basic training – which was learning all about ambushes and various bits and pieces – we then were put straight out on a major operation. There was a village called, I believe, Mutiarka, which is a little bit north of Limassol, into the bottom of the south Troodos Mountains. Our Intelligence Corps people had been told that Uncle George was in the village with his men, so they immediately threw out about 2,000 troops. The whole of our battalion was set out around the village, in a circle completely enclosing it.

There was another village a little way away, and another battalion – which may well have been the 3rd Parachute, because they were operating a little to the north of us into Troodos itself, not that they were much good – encircled that and then, I believe, the Gunners were entrenched in a complete circle around *both* these circles. So basically, the first night out, we were sat in pairs twenty yards apart, right around the village. I have never been so scared in my life, waiting for a terrorist with a knife to come and stick me in the back. The greatest protection I had was my rifle with twenty rounds of ammunition; we had the FN. We were the first to have the FN; we had this magnificent little rifle with twenty rounds of automatic to keep you going. We sat there for about seven to eight days. We learnt later – and this is rumour – that Uncle George got out the first night. There was a little gully, and there were people sitting either side; he flicked some stones towards them. 'Who's there?' No response. So he knew exactly where they were, and went up the gully and got out. A little later the Engineers came and, any hole they could find, they stuck dynamite in it and blew it.

So that was our first bit of active service, and back we went to barracks. Now, for the rest of our time in Cyprus, we spent the whole of the time on duty: a fortnight in camp guarding, two hours on, four hours off; then we spent a fortnight on town patrol, and this was basically doing snatches of suspected terrorists, doing street blockages and searching every house, putting up road-blocks. As far as I know, there was no looting in the houses; if it was out in the fields, yes, fair game. If a lorry went through a road-block carrying watermelons, then obviously a couple went off the back, but there was no looting from inside the houses at all. We were nearly all National Servicemen. Nothing was ever taken from a house; if you were found with something, then I am sure that the corporal in charge would have had you inside.

But the thieving within the Company was atrocious, and on occasion I joined them. One day, the magazine of my rifle was pinched. There was no problem; I knew where the next person's rifle was, and went and pinched *his* magazine. There was no compunction about that at all. It was pure survival; if I hadn't done that, I'd have been inside for six months, and you'd do *anything* to avoid that. When you were out on patrol for three or four nights at a time, you slept with your rifle absolutely strapped to you. I know when we were on duty once down along the beaches, one of the boys had his Bren gun pinched. He was in serious trouble; but what happened I don't know.

The real problem in Cyprus was that you didn't know who your enemy was; whereas they would very often offer you drink, olives, fruit or something, but you were shot in the back when you left. I don't think there was hardly a soldier ever shot in his front. The whole of the time the Oxford & Bucks or the Greenjackets were there, they didn't lose one soldier to EOKA terrorists; they really were on the ball. They did have a couple of accidents with rifles going off in tents when being cleaned, or rifles in the backs of the lorries going off; and of course the Sten gun was notorious – bang it on the deck, off would go the whole magazine. I did hear of one instance, which was not our Regiment. A whole patrol was out – nine people in the patrol; Number Seven dropped out to have a pee, Number Nine was Tailend Charlie with a sub-machine-gun and heard Number Seven coming back, didn't know who he was and put twenty-eight rounds straight into him – end of story.

The other thing was, we then did fortnight guards on various places, like the asbestos mines, like ammunition places. The best one we did, in fact, was the one we were allowed to do in Limassol, which was the Keo beer and wine factory, and they put up a barrel of beer every single day for the troops, which was absolutely stupendous. The other fortnight we did was waiting for problems in town, so if there was any riot or anything, we were on twenty-four-hour call-out. In the whole of my fourteen months I was out there, I only went swimming twice, although we were living next to the sea; it was quite incredible. We actually guarded the other people who were swimming but, because we were on duty, we couldn't.

137

There is, of course, one Limassol street, where the brothels were, which was out of bounds to all ranks at all times. The only time you could go in was if you were actually on patrol. It was known as Zigzag Street. I do remember very well taking my patrol of nine down through Limassol, and it had already been agreed between the people in the patrol who was going to drop off. So I walked into Zigzag Street with a patrol of nine; I walked out with a patrol of eight. I then came back fifteen minutes later with a patrol of eight, and walked out with a patrol of nine. That was quite a regular going-on. It wasn't expensive; five shillings – that's all.

The men I was with were very country; mainly farming people. Something I discovered when I went back after Cyprus to go and train the new recruits coming in on their ten weeks' basic training – and also when I was doing my basic with the Somersets – was the number of people who could not actually read and write, who were in the Army; I had to read Part I orders to people on patrols, because they couldn't read it.

I was in the Army when the corporals were absolute God; there was no one who had more authority, who could crush a man if they wished to. But the calibre of the officers coming out was not of the highest. One of the new officers came out, and he'd obviously been doing all this training, and his map-reading, and everything else, and the boys wanted a bit of a lark and, on a map-reading exercise, we actually took him through one village three times and he didn't realize he'd been in the same village; quite incredible. His map-reading was that poor, now; he was leading – what? thirty men–a platoon on active service. You get your basic Army sergeant, and he probably knows more than the rest put together.

I was never under fire, and never fired a shot. Of course, we were not allowed to move without our little red book, which you had to take out of your pocket and read to see if conditions were right to put a bullet up the spout and pull the trigger. Only once was I involved with a riot – a small one–and must admit that I did have my rifle lined up on the smallest boy right at the front; the girls and their mothers were behind and, of course, the trouble-makers were right at the back, protected by the children. The Army stated that you *never fired a warning shot*; your weapon was given to you to kill the enemy, and that is what was in the little red book, and that is what you did. If you did fire a shot, you had to account for it. If you lost a round of ammunition, it was automatically twenty-eight days inside, and so – you can imagine – in all the tents there were spare rounds of ammunition in all our kitbags somewhere, so that you never, ever handed back a magazine with less than the required amounts of ammunition.

There were two accidental shootings in the battalion; one when someone was cleaning an SLR, which we had just towards the end–it must have been around February/March, 1959, when it replaced the FN. The muzzle velocity of both the FN and the SLR was very much greater than that of the old No. 4. Two things to prove this: once, on a road-block, one of the boys fired off a round at the back of a bus; it went through the back of the bus, right through the seats, hit the driver in the side, just grazed his hip, went through his hand and out of the front, in a straight line. When we had target practice, we had something called 'falling plate', which was firing at one-foot squares of iron plate from one hundred yards. We found that we weren't knocking the plates down – not because we had missed them, but because the muzzle velocity was so great that it had gone straight through the plate without knocking it over. They had to put an extra one on the back to stop it happening.

In the Army, of course – especially in the Infantry–you did exactly what you were told; you did not argue. You were not allowed to think; you were told exactly what to do, when to do it, and there was no reason why. So the politics of it never came into the argument at all on any occasion. Looking back, I think basically: What a waste of time – because the whole thing was given back anyway, and it was just fourteen months with a tremendous amount of loss of sleep. A few lives were, obviously, lost; but not as many as Northern Ireland at present, because it wasn't quite as dirty as that.

Apart from that first night at Mutiarka, I wasn't ever frightened. Even when we went out on ambushes, we got so ingrained in the routine, we knew what was going on, we were always well prepared and, as I say, as far as I am aware, the Royal Greenjackets – as we were by then – didn't lose any men to EOKA at all. We drove round the mountains without lights on. We used to do long patrols at night to be in positions where the enemy didn't know where we were. Most of the corporals could read maps well; we did special exercises, route marches, being dropped out by trucks to get to somewhere else fifteen to eighteen miles away by six o'clock the following morning, and they would have spotter aircraft out to see if we could get there without them seeing us. The Greenjackets were very, very good at their job.

I was in Limassol when the manager of Barclays Bank was shot. Now the Company that was on duty to do town patrols literally took the town apart; every car was stopped; people were pulled out, legs apart on the thing, spreadeagled, and the town of Limassol was very much under Army control. Because they had been so tough, they decided for a while to take the Greenjackets away, out of Limassol, and in their place they put in the 3rd Paras. We had the place absolutely under control, and nothing ever went on at Limassol apart from that one shooting. We were always based at one camp; we knew the area backwards; the drivers knew the roads backwards. There's nothing more hair-raising than driving about at night in a 3-tonner lorry, going round the hairpin bends, having to drive up and back round the corners at night with no lights on – that made you scared! It wasn't the terrorists who made you scared; it was these drivers who did incredible things with these 3-tonner trucks.

We wondered what the hell we were doing out there and why; nothing was ever explained to us as to why we were there – we were just sent and told what to do. There was no lecturing as to what the EOKA terrorist was all about, and why he wanted union with Greece, or why the Turks were just in the north of the island, and why they wanted their section of the island. Nothing was actually explained to us, so there was no political side to it at all; it was just that you were paid X amount a week for doing a job for the British Army. This is what you're doing with your National Service.

I came back when the Battalion was sent back to the UK. I was a full corporal by then, earning £5 a week. But I had one or two beefs with the Army. I was nearly court-martialled for persuading somebody not to sign on for nine years. The other beef I had was that when I was in Cyprus, my mother was seriously ill and I was not allowed home, because I had a brother left in England. Had I been an officer, I would have been home the following day. There was that distinction; it – the Army – was very class-biased.

My family and friends showed no interest in my experiences; the only thing was that my parents were obviously glad that I was home. It was as though you'd just been away to college or somewhere for fourteen months. The only thing was, I had a medal, which came through while I was still in the Army so I could wear it on parade. It's still shining brightly on the dressing-table now. I was supposed to wear it on Armistice Day, but I went to play golf instead.

Philip Shepheard

Philip Shepheard served with the Royal Navy off Cyprus and at Suez in 1956-57. He is a stockbroker, married with one son and lives in Sutton Coldfield.

I started to get interested in the Navy when I was at school, with the possible idea of a career in the Navy. I was persuaded to put that to one side, because my teachers thought I ought to go to university and, in compensation for that in a way, I joined the RNVR. I was still at school; I was about seventeen when I joined that. I did the pre-military training; that was three weeks at HMS *Flying Fox*, which was a ship very firmly attached to the land in Bristol. It wasn't quite a 'stone frigate' (the name given to Naval shore establishments). A stone frigate isn't a ship at all; this *was* a ship. I can't actually remember; it might even have been in dry dock. If it wasn't in dry dock, it was floating in Bristol Dock. Then the actual basic training took place at Portsmouth on a ship of the Reserve Fleet, so the main armament was all in mothballs, and the accommodation was used for training. It was small-boat skills, knots, drill and slinging a hammock and all those general essential things. I knew I would be going in the Navy for my National Service because I had done all this RNVR training.

I was called up in August, 1955. I went to Victoria Barracks in Portsmouth for initial training, injections and all that kind of thing, and then it was hanging around there for a while to wait for a Commission Board – to become a midshipman. The training I did was very short; it was possibly three weeks at that stage. The next stop was to go to one of the aircraft carriers that was devoted to training. I went before the Commission Board and I failed – or rather, they politely said I was deferred, which meant I had to come back three months later, or whatever. So I then departed for training as an ordinary seaman, which took place on HMS *Ocean*, an aircraft carrier. I joined *Ocean* in Devonport and, rather excitingly, the ship was loading with lorries and all sorts of military equipment, and was bound for Cyprus. That was part of the gearing up of the back-up for the emergency. So we sailed, within twenty-four hours of my joining the ship, for the

Mediterranean. Not that I really took part in it. You just had to get used to doing drills on a deck that was rolling slightly, and things of that kind. But quite a large part of the hangars of the ship was full of lorries and other military equipment, so we unloaded that at Famagusta Harbour. We had to put it on to lighters — Famagusta was not a deep water harbour — to be taken ashore. That was in fact my first experience of the Mediterranean and, although it was late November/December, the climate — compared with the frosty English one — was very attractive.

Our training cruise was a bit like a tour, in that whenever we passed close to a Greek island the Navigating Officer announced on the tannoy where it was, and a few essential facts and so on. That training, which I think was six weeks, took place with calls at Malta and also a sort of Christmas treat of two days in Tangier, and then home again for Christmas leave.

Then, after Christmas leave, I went to Devonport Barracks, again awaiting a Commission Board. While I was waiting there, I had duties as a roadsweeper and, rather than sweep the same roads — which were already immaculate — morning and afternoon, I went to the Education Officer and used the excuse that the interview board had said I didn't know much about Naval History to persuade him to allow me to sit in the education office in the afternoons and read Naval history books. This was much more pleasant, and the roads were quite adequately cleaned by one trip round in the morning, anyway.

After a few weeks there, I went back for the second Commission Board. It was quite interesting that about ten of us had been together at that stage, and we'd first been to a Commission Board and failed; we didn't know each other then. We were very co-operative the second time around, and our leadership was very impressive because everybody was helping. I think nine out of the ten men passed and went forward to training as midshipmen.

That meant going back to HMS *Ocean*. We weren't midshipmen; we were called upper yardsmen. We wore a uniform that was only distinguishable from that of an ordinary seaman by the fact that under the cap ribbon there was a white band which could be seen on the top and bottom. We wore white shoulder tabs as well. The upper yardsmen's course was sixteen weeks — and a fairly extensive sixteen weeks, including our classroom studies on navigation, various types of Navy lore, and all the things that needed to be known if you were going to be Correspondence Officer, or having to keep accounts, or re-victual ships, and so on. It was a very, very potted version of the training Regular officers received, plus drill and boat work. The bookwork on navigation and navigational calculations, which some people found very difficult, was fairly easy and straightforward for me, because I was going to read mathematics at university and had done a bit of spherical astronomy.

I was then commissioned as a midshipman and assigned to 'Flag Officer Malta for disposal into small ships'. That was July, 1956, and Suez was very much looming. I think it was almost within days before – or days after – that I arrived on Malta that the Canal was nationalized by Colonel Nasser. I remember that there was actually an Egyptian frigate in Malta Dockyard at the time. We did notice that, immediately after the announcement of the nationalization, there were two sentries with tin hats and fixed bayonets on the gangplank, taking it very seriously. I was assigned to a minesweeper, which at that time happened to be in dry dock doing its annual refit, which meant that as a newly-joined, totally green midshipman, I had very little actual duties at that stage. The ship I was assigned to was in fact the Senior Officer's ship. We had a full Commander as Captain, and he did his Senior Officer duties by inspecting the other ships for a day at sea, and he took me along.

On that type of minesweeper, we're talking about a crew of thirty, including a complement of four or five officers. The ship was about – I think – a hundred and twenty-eight feet long and twenty-eight feet in beam. It was armed with one light ack-ack (anti-aircraft) Oerlikon gun, one Bofors (anti-aircraft) gun and one heavy machine gun amidships, and all the sweeping gear on the stern. For reasons of being of low magnetic attraction, it was largely made either of wood or of phosphor-bronze. There was very little iron or steel on it, so it wouldn't attract magnetic things. It was called the *Sefton*.

Because of the Suez crisis the normal pattern – which was to do a six- to eight-week tour in Cyprus, and then come back and have three weeks off – was all interrupted. Once our refit was over, we were retained for duties in connection with Suez. This meant one or two night exercises with the entire Fleet, cruising around Malta practising landing and then, when the Fleet was assembled – rather than going immediately to Cyprus – we went off on the Suez Expedition itself.

When we went to Port Said we had, for our own defence, a machine-gun detachment of the Grenadier Guards on board, who had their machine guns mounted on the sides of the vessel. One of the interesting things was that we knew we were going on the operation, but the Grenadiers didn't; they thought they were coming on an exercise. When the Grenadier officer came down, he said to the Captain of my ship, 'As this is an exercise, I'm just proposing to bring ammunition boxes filled with sand.' My Captain said, 'Don't do that; from the point of view of the magnetic field of the vessel, it's very important that you bring exactly what you would need in time of war.' So he brought his bullets, and then was aghast when we sailed and said, 'We're not going back.'

The role of minesweepers was largely hypothetical, because I don't think there was any serious expectation that the Egyptians were going to lay mines, and in fact that proved not to be the case. But we took our duties very seriously in terms of practising minesweeping in formation, and we went with the Fleet to the actual landing at Suez. We led the Fleet in, and our role was then to go into the harbour and sweep that area; but our activities were somewhat curtailed by the fact that large ships had been sunk by the Egyptians across the harbour to blockade it, and in trying to thread our way through we touched the wrecks with our propellers, and were therefore not very manoeuvreable or serviceable.

We had a very vivid sight of the planes, which were firing rockets as part of the street-clearing ahead of the Infantry. The landing itself was not quite in view from where we were; it was on the beach further across. The British landing was, I think, on the west side of Port Said, and the French to the east.

The hostilities didn't last very long, but the Fleet had brought in an enormous amount of equipment, including a French dry-dock ship. So we were dry-docked in this, and our propellers were replaced, and we then did a sort of notional foray up the Suez Canal as far as the Front. We didn't see any opposition, but we saw Israeli tanks on the hills on their side of the Canal. In fact, the hostilities were over very quickly – within twenty-four hours, from what we could see in one dock area. The population was not at all hostile. They were a fairly friendly, sight-seeing crowd that was gathered to see the Fleet in harbour. We were there for another week or two, and then it was our turn to go to Cyprus. Apparently, I was entitled to a Naval General Service Medal for Suez, but I never collected it. Although the hostilities were brief, they were serious. A friend of mine from school was a Royal Marine officer, and I think two of his contemporaries were killed which actually – although it seems cold-blooded to say so – seemed less shocking to us at the time than it would to any eighteen- or twenty-year-old now, in the sense that National Servicemen did actually die on active service, and that was it.

After Suez we headed off to Cyprus to do a tour. It was normally six weeks and then back to Malta, and I think I did three tours. The routine was that we worked out of Famagusta as home port; there were five minesweepers, I think, on station at any one time. The sea around Cyprus was split into patrol areas. The Army and Army Intelligence thought they had a pretty tight hold on the arms that were available to EOKA within the island of Cyprus; our job was to prevent gun-running. I'm not aware of any occasion – at least when I was involved – where any guns were found being smuggled into the island, or any ship stopped from that point of view. Though we were never involved in a search of a large ship, we did stop fishing-boats, and once apprehended a man who bore a striking resemblance to Grivas in the book of photographs we carried. He protested at first, but came along quietly. We found out later that he had been pulled in many times because of his face, but was harmless. Our patrol area would be, typically, that you would start in Famagusta and go up to the Panhandle on the eastern end of the island. That would be one night; then you would move on, rotate round the island and do however many it was — five or six — and then have twenty-four hours in harbour, and then start off again.

A minesweeper is a very small ship, and a very uncomfortable ship in the sense that it would roll on a duckpond, and it took even seasoned sailors a long time to get used to it. I'd been going to sea regularly for three or four months before I stopped being sick; having joined a ship where the crew had already been in commission for twelve months or so, I thought I was a very inferior being because I was being sick and they weren't. But then the crew changed over, and I was one of the 'old guard', and I found that even the able seamen of seven or eight years' Naval service were finding it a little bit difficult, at least in the initial weeks or months. The normal accommodation in a minesweeper was that there was a captain's cabin and two officers' cabins with double bunks, and normally one of the midshipmen would have been in one of those two cabins. The cabin would have been seven feet square, I suppose, with one wall taken up by the two bunks and a small chest-of-drawers with a desk-lid that folded down. It was a bit like being in a small caravan. There were no other National Servicemen on my ship. In home waters, one or two of my friends who didn't get commissions ended up in minesweepers, but not in the Mediterranean that I was aware of. The ration was one National Serviceman per ship. Regarding my fellow officers, I came to understand that, in their eyes, a midshipman was the lowest form of life, a dogsbody. To begin with, I felt that was exactly how I was treated. The complement as far as officers were concerned: there was our Commander who was Senior Officer of the Squadron; the First Lieutenant, who was a Lieutenant-Commander; the Navigating Officer, who was also a Lieutenant-Commander and two Lieutenants — or rather, a Lieutenant and a Sub-Lieutenant — and then me. It was because we were the senior ship that we had this excessive complement of officers including, in effect, one of those officers who was a reserve captain, if a captain was needed for any reason in any of the other ships.

The other ranks knew I was a National Serviceman and, to begin with, they were much kinder to me than my fellow officers were. I was Correspondence Officer, and the Chief Engineer — who was a petty officer — befriended me at a very early stage and was able to put me in the picture as to how things worked; and the other petty officers and leading hands were quite helpful. I was asked to join the ship's football team — which was not a great distinction because, when we played the Argyll & Sutherland

Highlanders in Cyprus, they gave us four of their team and we gave them four of ours, and they still beat us fifteen to nil. That battalion had an almost professional standard of team, because so many of their National Servicemen were apprentice football professionals.

A typical day would be that we would actually be on patrol during the hours of darkness. There would be watchkeeping − a fairly high level of vigilance, both radar and visual. It was fairly testing from the point of view of navigational ability, because we went in quite close to the land and the winds were quite variable, although fortunately there wasn't much tide or current in the Mediterranean, so from that point of view it wasn't too difficult.

On some minesweepers there would have been two National Servicemen midshipmen and two Regular officers and they − the midshipmen − were full-blown officers with all responsibilities. I was supervised until quite a late stage, until I was given freedom to stand and watch along overnight for four hours. It was quite a responsibility, but because I hadn't been pitched in at the deep end, as some of the others were, I felt I'd grown into the job. Midshipmen alone on watch were not officially competent and therefore, if anything went wrong, could not be proceeded against. One of our minesweepers went aground off the north-west corner of the island when a National Serviceman was on watch. His Captain was court-martialled and reprimanded. Two or three years later, he was promoted Commander; the midshipman was punished by being made a real dogsbody on our mother ship in Sliema Harbour in Malta.

I don't remember ever being frightened. As far as action was concerned, I never saw the consequences; I never saw people with bits of them blown off, or anything of that kind, and I was never under fire. We used to carry revolvers when we went ashore in Cyprus. We stopped from time to time to pick up fresh supplies, if we could get them, around the island in a fair number of places. During the day when we weren't patrolling − and particularly during the summer − we would anchor where we could have a good swim. We had very little sense of there being a dangerous situation on shore; it was theoretical. If you went ashore, you took someone else with you to act as an escort and keep a lookout. We had contact with Army units − which gave us more tales of what was going on − such as the Argyll & Sutherland Highlanders on the north of the island, north-east of Kyrenia.

The only Greek person I had contact with was a Mr Papadopoulos, who was our provisioner in Famagusta, who stepped on the ship when we came in for our twenty-four hours in. He would provide anything we required − fresh vegetables, meat, football shirts − anything. Cyprus was a sort of paradise island from the point of view of food for somebody who'd grown up in wartime and austerity Britain. It was the first time I saw oranges and lemons and grapefruit growing on trees. We had the fall-back, if we needed it, of tinned food and so on, but we bought fresh fruit, vegetables and meat. The diet was very good indeed; I think the economics worked out that we were allowed more money per head than a large ship, so we lived fairly well. The cox'n under one of the professional officers was in charge of that.

After my tour of duty in Cyprus, I came back to Britain. I was still available for three weeks, or something like that, and I was drafted into Cowes Week to be officer of the watch on one of the guard ships, and that was quite an interesting holiday-type final engagement.

I was shocked when I got back to realize the extent to which the country had been divided over Suez, certainly when I got to university. I had been wholly in favour of what we were doing at the time, on the basis of that being what we were there for. The idea that the security of the Suez Canal was essential to safeguard oil supplies and so on from the Middle East was something I accepted entirely. The view I always had was that we'd been stabbed in the back by the Americans.

Cyprus was much more complicated, and I felt that the nature of the difference between the two communities – the Greek and the Turkish communities – was never fully appreciated, certainly by outside commentators, and the task of giving Cyprus any stable form of government which would be accepted by the whole community had not been fully understood. So we were in a situation very much like Northern Ireland today, where you can't please all the people within a particular piece of territory.

Overall, I felt that my National Service had been a worthwhile experience, because I had an education in a school of selected individuals. It was the only time, apart from primary school, when I spent life in a complete cross-section of the population, and got to know boys from Newcastle or Glasgow or whatever who'd had pretty hard upbringings, and got to know them quite well. I thought that was a very valuable part of the experience. We came to laugh and be very cynical about the spit-and-polish element of it; but I must say, as I grow older I do think that a little bit of spit-and-polish and discipline in the late teens is something that does people good.

National Service is something I wouldn't have been without in my life. It was a positive experience.

Walter Smith

Walter Smith served with the Royal Inniskilling Dragoon Guards/Royal Tank Regiment in Korea, 1952-53. He is married with two children, works as an electronics engineer and lives in Essex.

I did my basic training at Catterick. At that particular time, the resident regiment happened to be the 8th Royal Tank Regiment; in those days you weren't attached to any particular unit for your basic training, you just did the training, the marching-up-and-down bit, and after that they sorted you out. Because I had a background in wireless, they immediately said, 'Right: wireless training.' I did my training on the famous 19 set – which I've got in the garage, by the way, and it's in working order. From Catterick, I went to Salisbury Plain, to a place called Tilshead, where I did my driving. At the time, they used Cromwells and Comets, although I did my wireless training in a Centurion. From there, I went to Lulworth Cove and did my gunnery course. It's not a 100 per cent course, but it gives you an idea; if any one of the four crew is hit, you can carry on doing the other man's job. You have the commander, the gunner, the driver and the wireless operator, who also did the loading of the gun. This is the Centurion, of course; it might be different today. You were all in the turret except the driver, who was down in the hull. The Centurion we had in Korea – the Mark IV – was about fifty tons all-up weight. It had a 20-pounder gun, very accurate, and it was also fitted with a ranging machine gun alongside the gun barrel. You fired the machine gun, which had a tracer every fifth bullet; you ranged with that and, when the tracer hit the target, you pressed the button and the big shell went off. It was the only tank at that time that had the stabilizer; it was a very good system. It would keep the gun right on target while the tank moved up and down and round and round – if I remember rightly, to within ten yards in a thousand.

When you first go in the Army, you think a tank is a monster; it's twenty-five feet long, twelve feet high and eleven feet wide. You were probably only used to a push-bike, and it was a little frightening at first. But remember, you're only eighteen or nineteen, and you soon get into the swing of it. It was a big tank, but slow; the maximum speed was about twenty miles per hour on concrete, and something slower on hard or soft ground.

The shells we had — unlike today, so I'm told — the projectile was part of the case, so it looked like an enormous bullet. We carried sixty-three shells in the tank. They were heavy; I suppose they weighed about forty pounds and, after firing about forty shells, they seemed heavier still. They were stored around the turret. You picked it up by the top, put your hand under the cartridge, pushed it into the breech with your fist and away it went. One problem was that, when a shell had been fired, the cartridge came out and went into a cradle at the bottom, which could only hold about twelve, so we had to put them out through little portholes at the side. But I still think I would sooner have been in a tank than in the Infantry or the Artillery — mainly because, being a wireless operator, I had other jobs as well.

I was actually in Germany when I was posted to Korea. I can remember going to Germany, but for the life of me, I can't remember coming back to the UK. I left from Liverpool on the *Halladale*; it was an old German First World War ship. It was very slow; it managed to do about five knots, and broke down outside Aden, and we had to get another one. The whole trip took six weeks and two days, and we finally got to a port called Kure, about twenty miles from Hiroshima. This was the main port for all the services; British, American and Australian, they all arrived there. We got sorted out; our revolvers were changed from Webleys to Smith & Wessons — I don't know why.

From Kure, we went across to Korea. It was only about four or five days later that we got inoculated, and we were issued with new kit. Because we went over in normal battledress, we were given this green stuff and the big parka — because, remember, when we got there it was February, and it was jolly cold. Off we went on this ship — not a big ship — to Pusan. From there, we met up with other personnel — Americans and Australians — and we went on a train...if you can call it that. It was an experience I shall never forget; it managed to go twenty miles an hour if you were lucky, and this thing chugged along. We went past Seoul; it was a long journey, Pusan to Seoul. Our tanks were already in the area of fighting. There were only about fifteen or so British tanks, plus a couple of recovery and breakdown tanks; but there were only fifteen Centurions that I can remember, and only five in the front line at any one time. But I didn't know that then.

One has to remember, people talked of Korea in 1950, and you said, 'Where?' I'd never been further than twenty miles from home — until I went to Catterick, of course — so when I got there, to Korea, it was a little frightening, because it was so different. It was a funny sort of place. There were hills and flatlands; there were no sort of towns or cities as we'd know them — just shacks here and there, even in Seoul. When I see Seoul today

149

on television and know it as it was, it's unbelievable. But the people seemed happy; they'd come up to you and speak to you in their own language, asking for food and cigarettes. We had plenty, so we did give them cigarettes and chocolate. But the thing that struck me: we got off the train in a sort of military area and got on a 3-tonner, and that's when I felt frightened, because something happened to me there that hadn't happened since the Battle of Britain and the bombing of London — because I was right in the middle of that as a child. When we got out of that train and we were going on the truck, you could hear the guns in the distance, and that really frightened me, because it brought back all those childhood memories. When I heard all those guns, that really turned my stomach over.

We went, I suppose, thirty or forty miles in this 3-tonner. When we arrived, various people went to various jobs. I was sent to a Major — or perhaps it was Colonel — Monkton. He was a very tall man, and I would say he was about forty-five — remember, I was only nineteen at the time, so he was an elderly man. He carried two white pearl-handled revolvers; I'll never forget that. He was a very interesting character, slow-speaking, and I was his wireless operator. There was this four-wheeled caravan, full of dozens of radio sets, and he said, 'Your job first of all is to net our tanks in before we go up to the front.' So I did the wireless netting for the squadron, or at least for the four or five on the front line. Then up to the front line with a tank called Buccaneer. The weather in Korea — God! it was cold in the winter, and I remember this, because I wrote it down for the Colonel — *forty-two degrees below*; and in the summer it was well over the hundred, right the other end of the scale, and you had that lovely time in the spring.

I was up in the front line within about two weeks of getting there and, no sooner had I arrived than we had this mortar attack. It was this white phosphorus stuff. It didn't look explosive; it didn't appear to blow things apart. That was the funny thing; it would hit anything, and you'd hear this hissing noise, unless it got on you, when it would burn. We had two hits on the tank, which did no more than damage the paintwork. They were two-and-a-half- or three-inch mortars; they weren't the big ones. Another time, one of our chaps was killed — the only one — when a mortar went straight down the open turret hatch: a miracle shot.

When we were in the front line, we lived in the tank or in what they called *bashas*; these things were foxholes, actually, but they were known as *bashas*. We were there for six weeks at a time. You didn't have a bath, or anything like that, because you didn't dare to take your clothing off when the temperature was twenty or thirty below. The clothing was so designed that the back was split, so you could sort of wriggle around and open this out to have a crap, and the same with having a wee, so that wasn't too difficult.

Talking of baths, an Army bath unit turned up in Korea. It was two bell tents with a long tent between them. The idea was – I could never believe this, and I only wish it was photographed – you'd go in there, and you'd take your new clothing and give it to one of the other chaps, who'd run up to the other end of this other bell tent. There'd be someone outside pumping water, and down the centre of this long stretch there was this pipe with holes in it. You had duckboards on the floor. You had to take all your clothes off quickly, because it was very cold; you'd run – you daren't stay still – to the other end. They'd have your towel there and you'd wipe yourself as best you could, and put all your new clothes on. That was the Army bath unit, and I've never seen anything like it.

But the food was excellent. There was just one thing that was very difficult to get hold of, and when you did it was like gold dust, and no one ever believes this: it was bread. Mostly, it was tinned stuff; you could have chicken, you could have turkey. But on the front line you had to get what you'd got in the tank – K rations. Back in the reserve place, they had the Army cook unit, which had great big fifty-gallon drums cut open, with water and cooking things; you got a fair choice then of food. But you did tend to stack the tank with all sorts of food; you had plenty of everything, and everything was free issue. You got free-issue soap, free-issue razor-blades. I don't know whether many people know this, but at Christmas Phillips Razors sent each tank an electric razor between four people. It was nice to use in the summer, but nigh on impossible to use in the winter because you had to have hot water. It worked off the tank's 12-volt system.

Even when you were in reserve, you were on standby all the time; you had to run the engines every few hours to make sure they were all right, because if any of the tanks up front got knocked out you had to motor up sharpish. The distance you're talking about is, I suppose, about five miles – within artillery and mortar range.

When you think of artillery, the Americans had a gun called a Long Tom, and this thing would be twenty miles back. A particular case I remember: I was in the front line in the tank, and we had a message over the radio to say there was an enemy movement on the side of the hill, and we called this Long Tom thing. I gave them the map reference, and they gave me the time they were going to fire. You could see these things in the air, an unbelievable sight. They would be literally thirty or forty feet above your head to clear you and to get to the hill the other side. You'd see the smoke in the distance for miles, and you'd hear this choo, choo, choo and you could literally see it coming towards you. A frightening sight. When it hit the ground, it seemed as though half the mountain disappeared. They kept that up for about an hour. We were told to keep our heads down in case one fell short because, if it hit a tank, even without the explosion it would knock it over; it was so heavy.

151

On one occasion we saw coming out of the mountain, like out of a hole, some enemy infantry. They went for a hundred yards and back into another hole. That's what it looked like from where we were; I suppose the distance was about 2,500 yards. They kept coming out of this thing, doing something and then going back in this other thing. Then the Major said, 'We'll open up when we're ready.' We only had two tanks at that particular time, at that particular spot. We fired; out of the sixty-three shells, I think we put forty shells into that mountainside, and no one ever came out of that, because you could put these shells down that hole — again ranging with the Besa. I didn't think about what was happening to these blokes; it never occurred to me. As far as I was concerned it was a target; it was up to them to keep out of the way, just as it was up to me to keep out of the way.

I personally came under fire another time when I took the Colonel, this Monkton chap, to see the Colonel of the Black Watch. I took him in this jeep. It wasn't our jeep; it was an American one we'd just borrowed. We went for some distance and we finally arrived at this sort of a road — there's no roads; just tracks. I drove him up to there, and he said, 'Stay here and let me know if anything else comes on the wireless. I'm going to see Colonel Whatever-his-name-was of the Black Watch.' He disappeared. I had the earphones on — and this is so clear in my memory — listening to various things, and all this mush (static) going on and all of a sudden I saw all these little red things bouncing round in front of me, and it was a few seconds before I realized they were tracers. It was bouncing on the bonnet; it hit the wheels. They'd spotted me, you see; I was sort of in the open, not totally in the open but far enough for them to see me. Alongside this track there was a ditch, and there was a Signals bloke in there laying cables — telephone lines — and he shouted at me, and I'm still sitting in this jeep watching these things, and all of a sudden it occurred to me what they were. I threw my headphones off and I dived out of the jeep into the ditch, and there we stayed for what seemed a long time, until they stopped firing. They knocked out the jeep; it wouldn't go after that. I said, 'God! The Colonel *will* be pleased.' We made our way back, and I said to the Colonel, 'I'm afraid our jeep...' and he said, 'It's not our jeep.' I remember him saying it; he had that sort of voice. The Black Watch gave us a lift back in one of their vehicles.

I remember once we'd come back from the front line, and we were doing nothing in particular, and I thought I'd go for a walk. I went for a walk up this hill and, provided I could keep the tanks in sight, I felt safe. I walked up this winding track and, as I was going up, I could see all these bones — skeletons and bits. I couldn't believe this; they were dead people — soldiers, presumably. There were no uniforms, they were just skeletons; a skull here, a hand there — they were all over the place. Funny thing was, as I was bending down to pick up one of these things just to have a closer look, my foot got caught in a piece of wire and I tried to get this off. I sat down and I pulled this wire, and I pulled a mine out of the ground — an AP (anti-personnel) mine. It was one of ours; a green box-looking thing, about the size of a cocoa tin only square, a little bit sticking up with three prongs. I pulled this wire, not knowing what it was, and I pulled this mine towards me. It wasn't until I got it right by my foot that I knew what it was. I picked it up in my hand and I threw it, and it went off! All I saw was a blinding flash. I don't know how long I was out; maybe only seconds. I came to, and I lit twenty cigarettes, and the only thing that worried me was, did they hear it down there? Because you're not supposed to wander off by yourself. I came to and realized what I'd done; I was lucky. I carried on to the top of the hill and it was, in fact, where the Gloucesters made their last stand. I'm assuming the skeletons were all Chinese because obviously we'd have picked all our own dead up. At the time it didn't frighten me. Why didn't it frighten me? I've often thought about that. The only time was right at the start, when I heard those guns; other than that, it was nothing to me at all. You'd get in the tank; you'd get out of the tank; you'd load up; you'd carry on. It just went on; there was no particular fear of anything.

We did get attacked on one occasion by Mustangs. We had to put out these different-coloured strips of material — on the wireless you'd be told which colour to use — so the aircraft would recognize you. We put out a particular colour — red, I think it was — with bricks on it so it would stay down. I remember these Mustangs coming over, and they opened up on us. We just got in the *sangar* out of the way; it was only bullets. They realized fairly quickly, and they were off.

We saw a lot of the Americans; they were eighty per cent of the UN forces. There were Canadian troops, South Africans and Australians. The Americans weren't allowed to drink, and we had an issue of two pints a day. I don't drink, so I stuck these in the tank. Well, of course, I met some Americans, and they wanted to know where they could get some beer. If they saw our NAAFI, they would make for it because their own PX was dry. But the NAAFI people wouldn't sell it to them. I had this crate of, I suppose, about twenty bottles and I swapped all this, including some other bits and pieces, for a .45 Colt automatic. I carried it all through Korea. Not only that; I also had a Sten gun — we had two of those in the turret. But it would have been risky to have brought the Colt back.

On the American side of it: I met some Americans when it was quiet, and they said to come back and have something to eat. We arrived at this place, and it was a massive area, all built up. It was an ice-cream parlour, in the middle of Korea. The funniest thing of all was that on one side of this hill there was a big screen, and on the other side of the valley there was a projector, and they were showing films across the valley. It was *Making*

Whoopee with Eddie Cantor, and you could hear these speakers for miles — and we were only a few miles from the Chinese front line. They were probably sitting in their tanks, watching. I liked the Yanks; they were very good people. Sometimes they were difficult to understand, they could very rarely understand us; but they were fair people. They'd give you anything, more or less. Mind you, they had everything to give; we had to account for *everything*.

I remember, we were bivouacked on the side of a hill and, for the first time in ages, I took my gun belt off. I put it on the road wheel of the tank. At four in the morning there was a bit of action, so I got up and put my parka on, by which time the driver had started the tank's engine and motored off. My Smith & Wesson had gone round the road wheel, round the sprocket and been chewed into a thousand pieces. I reported it the next day. In the middle of nowhere, the CO gets a card table out, green baize on the top, and sits down. 'Bloody daft thing to do, isn't it? It's a very serious offence.' Just then the Sergeant put this heap of rubbish on the table. The CO looks at it and says, 'Is this it?' 'Yessir.' 'It's a waste of time, isn't it?' And he folded up his card table and walked off.

Anyway, when my time was up I came home on a ship called the *Dunera*. We came back with the first lot of released prisoners, British prisoners. There was mayhem; there were four suicides. Someone said that it was because they paid them too much money, which had piled up while they were prisoners. They were just spending it, getting drunk and doing all sorts of things. In fact, one port we called in, forty of these prisoners didn't come back, and the Captain said, 'Right: we're sailing,' and we went on and left them. They were transported by helicopter to the next port of call and we picked them up there. I think it was a mistake to let them ashore.

I've been a musician since I was sixteen, and I played in a band all the way home. There was an RSM who played the piano; there was a trumpet player, a corporal; there was a lieutenant who played the guitar; someone else played another guitar and I played the drums and was a bass player. We played for other ranks one night, naval personnel another night, officers and their wives another night on the promenade deck — we played all the way back until just coming past the Bay of Biscay. The weather got a bit naughty then, coming up for November, getting a bit cold, so we packed up. This is something that struck me: you got to know these people, know them by their first names; and you left the Army, went somewhere else and forgot all about them.

When I got back to Bovington where you got the leave arranged, I think I had about six weeks. I remember coming back home, and they'd put the bunting out, and the flags. It just didn't seem to have the impact that it now appears it should have had; I think it's because you're so young. Then I was posted to a secret gunnery place up in Scotland to finish off.

154

My service certainly widened my horizons on places, and it showed me lots of different people. I had a wonderful holiday in Japan, and I saw Nagasaki and Hiroshima. With my service in Germany, it showed me, I suppose, what the last war was all about. The travel was marvellous. When you think: If I had to do that today as a holiday, to go to all those places I'd have to be a millionaire. It was certainly all worth while. I would never have missed it; not in a thousand years.

Mike Webb

Mike Webb served with the Royal Signals in Cyprus from 1958 to 1959. He is a butcher and lives in Bletchley.

I served in the Royal Signals and, after finishing my training, I was posted to Cyprus. We went from Catterick to Chester, to Woolwich, to Southend Airport. Then we went to Cyprus in one hop in an old Dakota, a twin-engined aircraft. It wasn't like flying today; it was so cold, there was ice inside the fuselage. You had to take your Army boots off before you got on the plane and put your plimsolls on, because of wearing out the floor of the plane – it must have been very fragile.

I must say, I quite liked Cyprus when I first arrived. Mind you, we all had sunstroke the second day we were there. We sunbathed, and we used Brylcreem for this, because we didn't have any suntan lotion, and we got burnt to a cinder. But I quite liked it, because we didn't do a hell of a lot for the first few days; we just lazed about the beaches. Because of the troubles, we couldn't go outside the camp, which was GHQ at Episkopi, unless we were on escort duty, but we didn't do that for a while.

I was a teleprinter operator and we worked a three-shift system; mornings, afternoons and nights. They stopped doing the nights after a time, which we were glad of; it was pretty boring. Occasionally we'd have to go out and do escort duties; someone would just come in and pick a couple of us up, and we'd go out in an armoured car or a Land Rover to take messages up to Famagusta or somewhere. For this, we were armed with the old Mk II Sten gun.

I can't remember exactly when, but we were out on one of the escorts, and we were involved in a crash. We thought a taxi-load of EOKA men were after us. What happened was this – it looked very sinister: we were in the back of the vehicle, four of us acting as escort and, of course, the driver up front. We were driving along this narrow, winding road, when this taxi seemed to tag on to us; there were four or five Greeks in it. It looked very sinister, so one of the guys in the back with me said to the driver, 'There's a car following us.' We picked up speed, but it kept following us, all the while getting closer and closer. Of course, this made us go faster and faster. It ended when we came to a turn in the road, and we didn't make it and hit a telegraph pole. We jumped out with our guns in a great cloud of dust, expecting all kinds of trouble. The taxi just carried on as though nothing had happened; as we jumped out, pointing our weapons at him, he just carried on to wherever he was going. Our driver was panicking; he was just sitting there transfixed – he was so scared, he was stuck to the wheel. We had two or three of these escort duties.

Even if you went out just to visit somebody, you had to go out in uniform – and armed, of course. Also, you used to have to be in a group of at least four. Once on the way back from wherever we'd been, one of the guys I was with left the magazine of his Sten in the taxi. Of course, it was panic stations; luckily, the taxi driver came straight back with it. The guy who lost it was a corporal as well, and he was panicking; he'd have lost his stripes, at least. It was a chargeable offence, of course.

I was in Cyprus at a time when there were bombs going off everywhere. They had to change all the NAAFI staff, because an EOKA guy had been working in a NAAFI and blew it up; so they got all new staff and it was wonderful. When they brought these girls out, Greeks weren't allowed to work in the NAAFI any more.

Because of these bombings, sometimes we'd have to do these twenty-four-hour guard duties. That was the only sort of action we saw, really, but it could have been nasty, because you'd hear the bang of a bomb going off occasionally. One time, the corporal of our guard came near to shooting this RAF guy. When you were on these guards, it was up to the guard commander whether you loaded your rifle or not. This time I'm talking about, he – the corporal – picked a rifle up as a joke and pointed it straight at this RAF guard. I said, 'It's loaded!' He didn't check or anything, and he was about to pull the trigger...and that was a corporal, would you believe.

Another time, I was on a guard again. It was when Lita Rosa, the singer, was over doing a show for the troops – remember her? I was walking down the hill and there was a Greek walking up the hill towards me. As he got near, his hand went inside his coat and I thought: He's got a gun, and my rifle came up, and he turned about and ran away. That could have been a very near thing there, and I was actually inside the compound at the time. You never saw the enemy as such. I suppose it was the same as it is now with the IRA; just so many faces. As well as guard duties, we used to do road blocks and things like that. We would take civilians into the tent and keep guard on them, checking their identity cards and stuff like that and, of course, you had to keep a rifle trained on them at the same time – and naturally they'd be scared stiff. They would be sitting there, petrified. We'd

157

keep a rifle on them the whole time they were in there, and of course they were probably completely harmless. Once when we were in a road block, there was a little old guy who, for some reason, didn't have his pass on him, and I was told to take him into the tent and keep an eye on him, I was just sitting there looking at him, and I kept flicking the bolt of the rifle back and forth as though I was thinking about shooting him. The poor old guy was scared stiff. A stupid prank, really; you look back on it now, and realize how stupid it was to do something like that to a harmless old guy. I don't know why I did it, really.

After the troubles were over and the barbed wire started coming down, things got a bit easier. For instance, you could go out without being armed. The last six months of my service − that would be in 1959 − after the EOKA campaign was over, we used to go looking for trouble, really. We used to go to Nicosia and to Famagusta and places like that. Each troop would go out, and come back with a souvenir; it was a sort of competition. In fact, I think I was the one that started it. What you would do would be to get tanked up a little bit, and grab one of these Greek flags, which was on a massive pole fixed to the wall, and you'd pull it off and all these Greeks would come round, thumping you about, and you'd walk off with the flag. Once, we'd done something like this and we were walking away, when we saw this whole crowd of Greeks charging along behind us. We thought they were after us, so we hid in a mosque. When they'd disappeared, we came out and started walking back. Then we met one of our drivers, a guy called Tony Harris, coming down the road holding his head, which was split open and bleeding all over the place. He was staggering down the road, and there was this great crowd of Greeks coming after him, so I walked up beside Tony and said to them, 'No, no: keep away,' and they let him go, and we carried on to where we were going.

While the troubles were on − or even afterwards − we never really thought about why we were there in political terms. As far as I can remember, the Greeks were trying to chuck the British out, and trying to chuck the Turks out as well. Of course, because of this we were friendly with the Turks and not the Greeks; and that's all we thought about that situation, really. There was one of our officers who I was quite friendly with, actually; when the troubles were still on, he used to say things like: 'I'd like to take a squad and just bump Makarios off.' He was a bit of a head case, I suppose, but a decent enough bloke.

We lived in this barracks block. There were tents in the compound behind us, and we used to have running battles with the Devon & Dorset Regiment, who lived in them. They were like a garrison guard. When we'd come off shift, they'd be doing all sorts of manoeuvres. This meant that we'd be sitting there, sunbathing and that, while they came crawling past us with their rifles and all their kit on. We'd jeer at them, shouting out things like: 'There's another of them, whey hey!' Mind you, they got their revenge; when we got off the late shift, they'd bring their band out, and march up right next to our barrack block, and have a band practice.

The blokes I was with were a pretty mixed crowd. When I first got there, I had quite a lot of friends, but then some were posted or got demobbed, and two or three went off to be officers. A dozen or so of us were selected for Para training. We went up to Famagusta — or it might have been Nicosia; I can't remember. When we arrived, there was this Para sergeant, and he said, 'Right, lads: get into your PT kit; we're going for a little run.' I'd eaten this big bunch of grapes on the way there. Anyway, we started off just walking along, then: 'Right: pick it up, pick it up,' and we had to run faster and faster. We ran down this great long hill and back up. I got half-way up and I thought: I've had it. I don't know how old this sergeant was; he looked old to us — probably in his thirties. Running rings around us, he was. Anyway, I had a good rest at the top of the hill and, when I got back to where the others were, he said, 'Where did you get to?' And I said, 'I didn't quite make it.' But they still wanted about eight or ten of us, including me, to go back to the UK — to Bovington, I think it was — for this Para training, but none of us went. It was all cancelled; I don't know why. That was a pity, because it was a chance to get back to England and see a few people.

Being in Cyprus during the troubles didn't worry me at all, actually. I remember when I first told my family I was going out, they all said, 'Oh, you'll be killed!' I didn't worry about it at the time; it's not until you get older and more mature that you worry about these things. In my case, I'm fairly easy going. I'm just that sort of character. I didn't see terrorists everywhere. I don't ever remember being scared, and some of our security was really lax. When we were on escort duties, we used to stop off at this place; it was like a half-way house, and we used to leave our rifles piled up just inside the door, I remember seeing a great stack left there by Paras and some Scottish guys. Anyone could have come in and got hold of them.

Sometimes we used to go out with working-parties of Greeks and Turks, and they used to have fights amongst themselves. We used to wander off into the foothills, and sometimes we got lost up there. We could easily have got ourselves shot at that time, but we never thought about that.

I was in the unit's shooting team, and that was fun; this was just before we got the SLR (self-loading rifle). The Infantry had them, but we still had the No. 4 Lee Enfield. I only ever got to fire my Sten on the range, and then I'd left it on full automatic, and the recoil made it come up and hit me in the mouth.

When it was time for me to come home, it was quite touching, really. As my troop got into the truck to go to Famagusta to get on a troopship, all the others lined up on their balconies and were cheering us. In tears I was, then. I was one of the last of the old group to go.

We went from Famagusta on the *Devonshire*. It was a terrible trip home. I had a busted tooth, so I had this toothache all the time. I was on the RP (Regimental Police) staff. When we got to Malta, the Devon & Dorsets appeared again, and they took over all duties *except* RP, so I couldn't go ashore. Because I was an RP, I used to talk to the MPs who were coming back. They used to talk about interrogating suspects. They told me about lobbing suspects out of the back of a moving Landrover and then taking them back to their home village, chucking them out and leaving them there. They also told me that if they were driving out somewhere and there happened to be a Greek wandering along at the side of the road, then he'd get side-swiped. They told me a lot of nasty things like that.

Of course, we all had a slap-up meal and a drink when we got back. We hadn't seen women for ages, except for NAAFI girls, so that was nice, too. A lot of my mates wanted me to go home with them for weekends, but I said no; I wanted to get home to my family. I didn't bore them with any of the political stuff, but I did talk a bit to my brother, who is five years older than me. He'd been in Hong Kong, so I had some good chats with him.

I've got one souvenir: this tattoo on my arm. It's pretty faded now, but it was done by a guy who'd done about six months in the pokey. When he came back, he said, 'Anyone fancy a tattoo?' He did it with a needle wrapped in cotton wool with just the point showing, and dipped in plenty of ink. It says 'Cyprus 1958-59'. There was no infection or anything.

Out of that whole time, my most hairy moment was probably when I'd come out of the Army and was back in England. I went to have my hair cut. I was chatting to the barber, and I said I'd been in the Army in Cyprus, and it turned out he was a Greek Cypriot, standing over me with a razor in his hand, ready to give me a razor-cut at the back.

I think that doing National Service made me much fitter physically, and a lot more self-reliant and confident. Before I went into the Army, I was at my parents' beck and call, and they did everything for me. My Army service also taught me a trade (telephone operator) and, in fact, when I came out I applied for a job with the GPO, but unfortunately there were a lot of other ex-service guys who did the same thing, and I didn't get in. So I became a butcher instead. Actually, I think National Service was a good thing, and I'm glad I went to Cyprus; but I wouldn't be able to do it again.

POSTSCRIPT

This book is neither a military history nor a sociological tract; it is simply an attempt to recapture the events of a generation or more ago by drawing on the memories of those men who served as conscripts in the confusing and frightening circumstances of these almost forgotten campaigns. Their recollection, after such a long interval, is inevitably sometimes patchy or inconsistent but, just as a dog-eared and faded snapshot may summon up the essence of another time and place, so the fragmentary memories of these ex-National Servicemen can give a very real feeling of what it was like to be on active service all those years ago. While these reminiscences speak for themselves, it may be of value if I make some general observations based on what these men have said.

The journey out was itself often an interesting experience, particularly as most conscripts had never been abroad before. This usually involved a sea voyage on a troopship — which was 'a very leisurely trip' according to King, who went to Kenya on the *Empire Ken*. For others, it meant travelling by air, still something of a novelty in those days. Hartley recalls flying to Cyprus in the tail-gunner's position of a Shackleton bomber, while Webb went to the same destination in a Dakota so decrepit that ice formed inside the fuselage during the flight, and the troops were made to wear plimsolls for fear of damaging the floor of the aircraft.

On arrival, after a brief period of acclimatization and training, the young conscript found himself at the 'sharp end'. It is remarkable that these men, who were mainly townspeople with no experience of communities other than their own, adjusted with surprising speed to the strange environments in which they found themselves. They also seem to have encountered no difficulty in working alongside men from backgrounds as unlike theirs as it is possible to envisage, such as the Ibans in Malaya and the Masai in Kenya. All seemed to like or, at least, to tolerate the civilian population among whom they were living, while the usual feelings towards the enemy seem to have been indifference — perhaps because they were so rarely seen — although occasionally a kind of grudging admiration is expressed: Hawkes says of the Mau Mau, 'To look at them, they were only wiry little people, but they were certainly tough.'

Most of those interviewed experienced action in the sense of having some sort of 'contact' with the enemy. The nature of these campaigns is such — with the possible exception of Korea — that these contacts were very fleeting; for example, Flowers was in Malaya for about a year, and was involved in two brief actions involving 'kills', and King and Hawkes in Kenya also had one or two contacts with similar results. In Cyprus, Hartley was ambushed once — an action lasting a matter of minutes — but saw nothing further of the enemy. Because guerrillas tend to attack soft targets Davies, who was part of an unarmed RAF detachment building an airstrip in Malaya, came under fire, as did Robinson in his RASC workshop during the same campaign; conversely Percival, who was a member of a crack infantry battalion—the Rifle Brigade — hunting the same enemy, had no contact at all.

All this seems to confirm what has been said many times before: that soldiering consists of long periods of boredom, illuminated with flashes of frenzied activity. If someone were to make a feature film of the individual experience of active service in the literal, flat style of Andy Warhol then, of the film's hour-and-a-half running time, only a few seconds would be needed to represent each burst of action.

As one would expect, because they were near the bottom of the service hierarchy most conscripts had very little idea of why the campaign they were involved in was being fought or, indeed, what their role in it was. Pask says of his time at Suez: 'They don't tell the private soldier anything; it would be nice if you had some idea of where you were going, and why.' And Brown said, 'I never really understood what we were doing in Korea.'

Many contributors mention accidental deaths among the men of their units. These were caused mostly by firearms, although some resulted from road accidents or other causes. Three men recall the experience of almost becoming victims of what is nowadays known as 'friendly fire'; Hughes in Malaya and Hawkes in Kenya both came under small-arms fire from their own comrades during a brush with the enemy, while Smith's tank in Korea was attacked by two American Mustang fighter-bombers in what seems uncannily like a preview of that notorious incident in the Gulf War almost forty years later, when nine British soldiers in armoured vehicles were wiped out by American aircraft.

It has proved difficult to quantify the number of accidental fatalities occurring in each of the six campaigns in addition to those inflicted by the enemy. Hartley who, as Medical Officer of 1 Para in Cyprus, would have had access to the official records, says that they lost four men in accidents, of whom two were shot, and that 'there were about thirty "accidental discharges" of firearms while I was there so, in fact, the chance of being shot by one's own side was far higher than [of] actually being shot by

EOKA.' Similarly Harper, who served in a rifle company of the Royal West Kents in Malaya, remembers a friend of his being shot and killed while returning from patrol, and of an officer of the battalion being mown down by his own Bren-gunners. If I may be permitted a moment of personal reminiscence, the nearest I came to death in Cyprus was when my tent-mate inadvertently fired his service revolver point-blank at me.

These, of course, are the sort of events that have occurred in every war that was ever fought. As is well documented, tens of thousands of men in each of the armies who took part in the First World War were massacred by their own artillery, and the highest-ranking American officer to die in the Second World War, Lieutenant-General McNair, was killed in Normandy by his own bombers.

Nonetheless, there do seem to be particular risks attached to placing sketchily-trained conscripts, armed with powerful modern weapons – some, like the Sten gun, notoriously temperamental – in strange and hostile environments such as Cyprus or Malaya, where the enemy is either not readily identifiable, or is elusive to the point of invisibility. This highly stressful sort of situation seems to be tailor-made for accidents of the type described above.

Overall, the level of casualties varies widely from campaign to campaign, with Korea being by far the most dangerous – the Royal Fusiliers, in their tour of duty lasting about one year, had thirty men killed out of a ration strength of something under six hundred. If we assume that the chance of being wounded or injured, or of suffering a serious illness would run at about six or seven times this figure, then a man serving in that particular unit would have not much better a chance than evens of coming through his year in Korea unscathed. At the other end of the scale, only twenty-two British personnel were killed at the Suez landings; considerably fewer than the losses suffered by one battalion of the Duke of Wellington's Regiment in the two-day Battle of the Hook. Between these two extremes, Harper recalls that his battalion lost twenty-four men during their three years in Malaya, 'some in action and some in tragic accidents.' Out of the twenty-three men contributing to this book, two were wounded in action – Butt and Brown – and two – Hawkes and Smith – were slightly injured in accidents involving explosives; all these incidents occurred in Korea. Campbell was seriously ill with scrub typhus during his service in Malaya, and Flowers ascribes his subsequent ill health to service in the same campaign. Thus, if we had to construct some kind of league table of these campaigns in order of danger and discomfort, then Korea was undoubtedly the toughest, both in terms of casualties suffered and the conditions under which the war was fought; Suez was probably the easiest, not least because it lasted only a matter of hours against an already defeated foe. The remainder seem, with benefit of hindsight, to be much the same in terms of the hardships endured by the men who fought in them, but with some significant differences dictated by the terrain and the nature of the enemy. 'Jungle bashing' in Johore was probably physically much tougher than searching Greek Cypriot villages in the Troodos Mountains. In the former case, however, it was possible to enjoy periods of rest and relaxation safe from enemy activities, whereas in Cyprus – as in Northern Ireland today – one was, in effect, always on duty, as there was nowhere on the island where the British soldier could feel completely safe; for example, Baker tells of a pipe bomb exploding in his unit's latrine, which was in the middle of a camp occupied by hundreds of British troops. Also, the environments in which the campaigns took place varied tremendously. It is difficult to imagine two sets of experiences more widely at variance than being in the front-line trenches during a Korean winter, as were Brown and Butt, and serving in a minesweeper in the eastern Mediterranean during the summer, as did Shepheard.

We cannot ignore the fact that in all these campaigns British troops, albeit on a relatively minor scale, were sometimes guilty of offences against the enemy and the civilian population which, under the terms of the various Geneva Conventions, would be categorized as war crimes. These range from casual assaults on civilians – Brown describes Korean labourers being beaten with a rope's end – through the destruction of an Egyptian school's equipment and fittings in which Gretton took part, to the taking of heads for identification purposes from dead CTs witnessed by Flowers and mentioned by Edwards. Also, as Saunders and others have emphasized, stealing was a way of life, as in all armies in the field. Such incidents seem to have been quite prevalent, but no more so than would be expected. It seems to be a lamentable fact that, if armed men are gathered together in large numbers and exposed to the attentions of ferocious and ruthless enemies such as the CTs or EOKA, not all of them will behave with the forbearance of Mother Teresa. Recent revelations regarding the behaviour of British troops in the Falklands in 1982 and in Malaya in 1948 serve only to confirm this.

It is also apparent that not only did individual British soldiers act in ways that run counter to the traditional image of the good-natured Tommy Atkins but, it seems, the higher authorities were often responsible for actions that do them little credit. The taking of heads in Malaya was part of a deliberate policy, and the destruction of the school in Port Said was ordered by senior officers. There were also persistent contemporary rumours among the troops that Mau Mau food supplies were systematically poisoned, presumably as a result of orders from above.

These actions are not readily defensible, even given the circumstances in which they took place. However, before adopting too high-minded an attitude, perhaps we should ask ourselves two questions. The first is: how would we have reacted if confronted by that particular moral choice? and second: how would, for instance, the American Army of the Vietnam years have responded to the activities of an enemy like EOKA or the Mau Mau? In any case, why should we be shocked when young men who have been enrolled as State Registered Assassins go out and actually kill someone?

While all the respondents were very willing to be interviewed, several mentioned that they had not talked to anyone about their active service or indeed, in some cases, thought about it for years, and the level of interest shown by friends and family appears to have been very low. Hughes says, 'I didn't talk much about my experiences; this sort of information is normally best swapped from soldier to soldier, because they know what you're talking about,' and, similarly from Billings, 'You begin to realize, after the first war story, that nobody believes you.' Hartley says, 'The average acquaintance was supremely bored by it all − totally uninterested − that's amazing, really.' Others remember talking to people about their experiences overseas; Robinson recalls, 'I certainly spoke to my friends, who had been on active service elsewhere,' and Ascherson: 'I did tell my mother some of the more horrific things that weighed on my conscience.'

As well as encountering indifference on a personal level, some returning servicemen seem to have been treated quite shabbily on an official one. Both Butt and Hawkes complain of having their kit pulled apart by Customs officers and of having their small souvenirs confiscated, and Brown, despite being a stretcher case at the time, also had his carefully-wrapped gifts torn open. Others were treated less than hospitably at the units to which they returned; Harper spent his last week in the Army delivering coal to the married quarters: 'The depot staff treated us like outcasts − rather like *janker-wallahs*, and Billings mentions '...the resentment shown by the pasty-faced regulars around the camp, who had never been anywhere or done anything, and hated us.' Sometimes even the most minimal official recognition of their service was withheld; Parfitt, Pask, Shepheard and Baker never received their campaign medals. Furthermore, little or nothing was done by the authorities to smooth the transition of men returning from overseas to civilian life, although, because of the speed of air transport, this transition could be very abrupt, taking only a matter of days. Strange as it may seem to a generation where counselling is available to sufferers from dandruff, the returned soldier was left to get on with his life as best he could. This could and did lead to tragedy; Smith remembers, 'We came back on the troopship from Korea with the first lot of released prisoners...there were four suicides,' and both Billings and Gretton speak of encountering problems of readjustment. All this seems a poor reward for men who had served their country well in difficult circumstances. We should also remember that, with one or two exceptions, none of these men was old enough to vote, and thus they bore the duties of citizenship without having any of its rights.

The contributors' current feelings about active service vary enormously. Gretton, as a reservist who had already served his time in the Canal Zone, is deeply resentful of being called up again, and remembers hating almost every moment of his service at Suez and in Cyprus. Others have mixed emotions: for Campbell, it was '...a worthwhile experience...but it was good to get it behind me and get back to living a normal life in Civvy Street,' and similarly, for Ascherson: 'It's difficult for me to say I would do it all again...[but] I wouldn't have missed it for worlds.' Many others see it as a positive and important part of their lives; Parfitt says, 'Certainly it's something I wouldn't have missed,' and Shepheard feels that 'National Service is something I wouldn't have been without in my life. It was a positive experience.'

To place the experiences of these men in their proper context, it is important to remember that the fifteen years spanned by National Service witnessed immense changes in the economic, social and cultural life of this country. When the first National Servicemen were called to the colours in 1948, the Second World War had been over for only three years, and Britain was in the grip of a regime enforcing the most rigorous austerity. By the time the last National Serviceman was demobilized in mid-1963, the '60s were in full swing, there was unprecedented affluence and the very idea of austerity was a fast-fading memory. National Service was abandoned for sound military reasons: the Empire had virtually gone and conscripts were no longer required to defend its outposts; the need was for highly-trained professionals to be ready to meet the Red Army on equal terms in Western Europe. Even were this not the case, it is extremely difficult to see how peacetime conscription – in itself, a very un-British concept – could have been enforced in the libertarian, freewheeling atmosphere of the middle and late 1960s.

Perhaps it was being brought up in the austerity years of the '40s and '50s, coupled with an immense esprit de corps, that enabled these men, with the minimum of training, to perform so well in the six campaigns, displaying those soldierly virtues of courage, stoicism, humour and loyalty which seem to remain with them to this day. I hope that this book will go some way towards setting the record straight and, albeit belatedly, provide a monument to the achievements of these 'Virgin Soldiers'.

GLOSSARY

AK47:	Kalashnikov assault rifle
basha:	small hut made of sticks and leaves
Besa:	medium machine gun
boma:	mud hut with thatched roof
Bren gun:	standard .303 calibre light machine gun of British forces 1930s-1960s
compo rations:	composition rations to provide a balanced diet for troops in the field, similar to K rations
CT:	Communist Terrorist
cushy:	comfortable, easy (Anglo-Indian)
DCM:	Distinguished Conduct Medal; gallantry award for other ranks up to warrant officer
dhobi:	laundry (Hindi), hence *dhobi-wallah* (laundryman)
draft:	contingent of troops travelling to join their unit(s)
EOKA:	national organization of Greek Cypriot freedom fighters
FN:	Fabrique Nationale, Belgian armaments manufacturer; applied to 7.62mm semi-automatic rifle made by them
GHQ:	general headquarters

Hermes:	four-engined propeller-driven cargo/passenger aircraft
janker-wallahs:	defaulters; origin of *janker* unknown, *wallah* derives from Hindi and in current usage means a person
jock:	Scottish soldier
kubu:	a little tin fort
Lanchester:	9mm sub-machine-gun, a forerunner of the Sterling, made exclusively for the Royal Navy
Lee Enfield:	in its different versions, the standard .303 service of the British Army from the Boer War to c.1960
Mau Mau:	Kikuyu secret society dedicated to driving the British out of Kenya
MM:	Military Medal; gallantry award for junior other ranks
Mustang:	piston-engined fighter bomber
NAAFI:	Navy, Army and Air Force Institute
OR:	other rank
Owen gun:	9mm Australian sub-machine-gun
Patchett:	9mm sub-machine-gun; an intermediate stage between the Sten and the Sterling
pipe bomb:	a home-made bomb constructed from a piece of piping
PTI:	physical training instructor
RP:	regimental police
sangar:	a small stone fortification, which replaced dug-outs where the ground was too hard to dig
squaddy:	British soldier

SLR:	self-loading rifle
Sten gun:	9mm sub-machine-gun, perhaps the most temperamental and unreliable firearm ever issued to British troops
Tamil:	people of south-east India and Sri Lanka, some of whom migrated to Malaya
TCV:	troop-carrying vehicle
tiffy:	Naval sick-berth attendant
Valetta:	two-engined propeller-driven transport aircraft
Vampire:	jet-propelled fighter-bomber of 1940s and 1950s
Viscount:	four-engined turbo-prop passenger aircraft
wadi:	dried-up water course (Arabic)